FREYA STARK
Letters

FREYA STARK
Letters

EDITED BY CAROLINE MOOREHEAD

VOLUME EIGHT
TRAVELLER'S EPILOGUE
1960–80

MICHAEL RUSSELL

© Freya Stark 1982

First published in Great Britain 1982 by
Michael Russell (Publishing) Ltd
The Chantry, Wilton, Salisbury, Wiltshire
and printed in Great Britain by
Western Printing Services Ltd
Chittening Estate, Avonmouth, Bristol

Set in Linotype Granjon

ISBN 0 85955 089 3

Dedication

This collection of letters was chosen by Lucy Moorehead and completed by her daughter Caroline and is dedicated to these good friends.

Asolo 1982   FREYA STARK

Asolo

14 January 1960

Dearest Jock,

By the skin of our teeth – Desirée's[2] and mine – and with 'flu and all to
hinder, we are getting the ms. into shape. You will see it isn't final. I do want
this to be a good book: it is the small climax of my life so I must do the best
I can with it and don't mind how many times I go at it if I can get it right.
So you may look forward to being pretty tired of it too before the end.

The two young ones[3] are off in Verona to see Mardersteig.[4] I am so sad
that this flash of time has fled so quickly and they leave tomorrow. They are
great dears. Joanna I knew but John I had seen so little of and I love him:
he is so thoughtful and *limpid*, a lovely honesty about him. The house will
seem very empty.

Well, this is only love and thanks, and all blessing for the year to all at
Cannon Lodge.[5]

                                                                    FREYA

LADY CHOLMONDELEY   Asolo

19 February 1960

Dearest Sybil,

I can manage June quite easily, the later in the month the better, but it
doesn't really matter; at the end I would drop off at Istanbul and spend
a few weeks over my Turkish there. If you don't know Greece, nothing could
be better than to hire a car and go about from Athens, either south round the
Peloponnese – Olympia, Bassae, Pylos etc. or north through Delphi to
Janina (which I know very little and would love); and one could then make
another little expedition by sea in those small steamers that go from Piraeus
and are very comfortable and perhaps stop off at one of the Sporades and wait
there for the next steamer – or find a way of getting off on Thrace and going
by Troy to Istanbul and separate there? Persia is getting dusty by June, and
the coasts of Anatolia, all the good places in the south, are sizzling: one must,
for *enjoyment*, keep near to the places where one can bathe – and Greece is
wonderfully full of bays.

[1] F.S.'s publisher and friend of long standing.
[2] Desirée Granville was helping with the typing of the fourth volume of F.S.'s
autobiography, *Dust in the Lion's Paw*.
[3] Joanna and John Murray, who were staying with F.S.
[4] The celebrated Italian printer.
[5] The Murrays' house in Hampstead.

It is very good of you to ask me as your guest, dear Sybil, and I accept with gratitude. (I plan Peking for October and that takes a lot of saving up for!) What would be perfect is if you would start from Venice and so come and look at Asolo on your way? Greece and the islands are very easy and need no visa; but a permit is necessary for Troy and takes quite a time, though Nuri might put it through easily.[6]

I have just had Harold and Vita[7] for three days on their way home (awful weather: they never saw the mountains). It was a pleasure: we sat and talked by the fire in a civilised mellow way – they are dears. Otherwise my life is *book* from day to day: I hope to get it done before I leave. It gives me the feeling of a double life, as if I were in 1940 and 1960 simultaneously.

I would love a book to take me right away – either the Armada, or Queen Mary's Life (which I should like to have from you and your name inside it). I do read, though little: but I read Thesiger and liked it, and have just reviewed a rather promising Persian travel book by Michael Carroll.[8]

Much love to you both,

FREYA

JOHN GREY MURRAY   Asolo
                                                19 February 1960
Dearest Jock,

How wonderfully good you are to go so carefully over and over this typescript. I have taken all your deletions except I think two. With all this docility, however, I have one uneasiness and that is that I hope you are remembering that our ideas on *modesty* differ slightly (or perhaps even a lot). It seems to me that the suppression of the nice things that people say to one is a mere passing fashion (just as when I was a child no one admitted going to the loo, and a little earlier one had to hide the legs of pianos): it isn't basic because it isn't truthful. The truth is that I was liked and encouraged in the Middle East, that I was continually told so, and that it gave me immense pleasure. If I now keep on suppressing this, it is like taking all the sunshine out of a picture. I don't think it shows a want of modesty to recognise the fact; it was, and always remains, a delightful surprise and a thing for which I am ever so grateful – and what I think I would do is to say this more or less, in the foreword or somewhere else, and that might make it all right?

[6] Nuri Birgi, a Turkish friend, then at the Turkish embassy in London.
[7] Nicolson.
[8] *Seen from a Persian Tea House.*

2

What prompts me to write this is what you say about the putting in of letters as illustrations being 'pretentious'. The point is that they are interesting in themselves and in fifty years' time people will like to see Lord Wavell's handwriting when that of Mr. Snooks would leave them cold: it seems to me all wrong to suppress it merely because someone might think I do it for reasons that are quite foreign to me (Harold incidentally says he always likes to put in handwriting if he can).

What do you say to John Sparrow[9] to read it over? And to MacMichael[10] for the foreword?

Apart from the book, and the garden, there are labyrinths of plans for summer and autumn – the autumn trying to unravel the complication of getting from Bokhara to Peking. Bokhara is quite near (as Asiatic things go) to Tabriz where I hope still to go once or twice, so it may be simpler to make it a separate journey another year. (I talk as if I had eternity before me, but I hope for a *few* seasons yet.) Peking I think of definitely for October.

Lots of love dear Jock,

FREYA

CHARLES HARDING   Asolo
                                                              20 February 1960

Dearest Charles,

It must have been telepathy: all last week I was thinking that I must write, it seemed so long since I heard from you. Yes, I too have a nostalgia for my nice London interlude – but *next* winter will be along in no time (alas) and then I will make up for all omissions, and hope to be able to give you descriptions of Peking and all its sights. I am saving up for this journey and hope to go in autumn when I shall be part way already, in Turkey: the Michael Stewarts[11] are in China now and asked me out for a few weeks and it seems too wonderful a chance to miss. I thought – as the route goes slap above them – that one might step off and look at Samarkand and Bokhara, but that seems to involve a detour round most of Asia so it will have to be left.

The great event here is that I have a Consulting Gardener. He is the best

---

[9] Warden of All Souls.

[10] Sir Harold MacMichael, High Commissioner and C.-in-C. Palestine and High Commissioner for Transjordan 1938–44.

[11] Michael and Damaris Stewart. He was then Chargé d'Affaires in Peking; later Ambassador in Athens.

in Italy and spent years directing the Villa Taranto gardens and now has retired with his Italian wife to a village near Treviso and I have got him to come once a month to give advice. Already new plants with unknown names are ordered and I hope they may not all die as they were apt to do in Checchi's hands. A white drooping wistaria is to be planted as a tree: there will be marvellous things to show you, if ever you can come – at a time when I am here.

Affectionately,

FREYA

JOHN GREY MURRAY

Asolo
6 March 1960

Dearest Jock,

I think you overdo the taking out of personal bits and are in danger of turning it into a Report rather than an Autobiography? I was not happy about this and then Pam and Derek[12] read it (especially Egypt and Baghdad for Pam's references) and were both begging me to leave more in (the Wavell dinner in Cairo, for instance, and the personal touches to my mother etc.). Well, I agree with this, but at the same time felt that there is probably something wrong with the paragraphs you dislike and especially with those on Egypt where you seem to think I have a servant-hall taste for grandeur. One can't just *eliminate* a year with the Eighth Army in Cairo in 1940–42! So I have recast that whole chapter and tried to convey more clearly the extraordinary 'Napoleonic' war atmosphere, leaving in the vignettes of people who will be remembered, but shortening and tightening. I hope it may be better now, and carry across to the reader. Otherwise I have kept a few of the more personal things – like the remembrance of Adrian Bishop[13] who became one of the *deepest* friends I have ever had and can't be left out – it is *my* story after all.

You need not worry about people's reactions to their own references as I shall send extracts to all. Isaiah Berlin for instance will most probably insist on deleting. The only one I think perhaps one ought to soften, as I don't think of sending it to be vetted, is the bit about Eden – though I should like it in. As for B.B.'s[14] letters, their whole interest is in the fact that they *are* his

[12] sc. Cooper. Pamela (then Hore-Ruthven) had worked with F.S. in Cairo in the war.
[13] Adrian Bishop, Assistant Public Relations Officer in Baghdad, had been killed in September 1942.
[14] Bernard Berenson, the art historian and critic, who had died the previous year.

letters, so they should either be left or not put in at all. I think they bring an atmosphere of gentleness and affection at the end?

Daffodils are bursting out at last, and soon the riot will begin. Little plants come in from all directions, and two tiny trees arrived in Pam's super Land Rover (which has built-in wardrobe, cooker, water and flattens to a bed: all this furniture puts it in a *caravan* category and takes away the purchase tax). They spent five days here, not good weather, but it was agreeable all the same to all; and I am joining them in September for a jaunt up the Middle Euphrates and back by my Lycian shore.

What a spate of friends and even acquaintances *dying*: Len Woolley,[15] Ernest Barker,[16] George Trevelyan[17] someone said today.

Love,

FREYA

P.S. My poor little car got an awful bang because, in the dark, I pushed the accelerator instead of the brake and crumpled up its front on the garage wall.

JOHN GREY MURRAY   Djerba[18]
                                                    31 March 1960

Dearest Jock,

Two days already have gone by in this hard strong sunlight; it was wonderful to feel so at home in it, waking in Tripoli to see a man in a white toga riding on a Vespa down the road. I had the usual accidental start from there, as it was the first day of Bairam and the police who register one's passport were all asleep. Luckily the taxi man, pleased with my Arabic, knew where the chief of police lived, went into his house to wake him and came out with all the formalities in order!

This island is flat with two imperceptible rises, about twenty miles square, filled with thin crops and the shells of old contorted olives that still produce surprising crowns of green. It has a strangely pleasant feeling of nothing ever happening or mattering – the seas so shallow all around that even Events can't come sailing up. Angus Malcolm had to dash back to Tunis to salute the

---

[15] Sir Leonard Woolley, the archaeologist who supervised the excavations at Ur 1922–34.

[16] Sometime Professor of Political Science at Cambridge.

[17] The distinguished historian. He had commanded the unit in which F.S. had served as a V.A.D. in the First World War.

[18] The island on which F.S. was meeting Angus and Jacqueline Malcolm. He was at the British Embassy in Tunis.

ruler on the feast-day but came back in time for a picnic yesterday, the children bathing, Angus and I drawing, nothing about but sand and green peacock-sea and little salty plants and palms. There are four girls but the baby left in Tunis: the three here are all gay, different and pretty and it is nice to be with them.

Love,

FREYA

JOHN GREY MURRAY

Tozeur,
Southern Tunisia
3 April 1960

Dearest Jock,

This is a very sort of Beau Geste desert edge, with the rather welcome extras of a good hotel, a clean deserty air that flaps the red and white Tunisian flag against the sunset and above the palms, and the brightest of municipal flower gardens blossoming under arc lights in a low-walled square below my window. A charabanc from Hamburg has arrived with fifty-two people and all the old dragomen have turned out with their red skull-caps and blue gowns. The proper desert men come in and out with a long thin walk and necks and mouths wrapped in white like all the rest of them against the dry wind; while the women flutter about with flowing draperies, dark blue and maroon and embroidered; but it is all rather hard put to it to look genuine against the squalid but successful European inserted by the French. How successful they have been in *really* Frenchifying their districts: our places revert to the Oriental as soon as we leave, but here nothing will go back except possibly to a Western tinge of squalor.

I have seen nothing Roman yet except a rough provincial ruin, inland now but then it must have had a small estuary of its own on to a shallow sea. There is still a life about these places – the lintels of shops or houses showing along the wadi front (as they do still in the places that survive); and a paved way from the lost harbour; a floor of rough but beautiful mosaic, brown-black, and coral and white; and the archway that led by the curia to a little capitol with three temples across a colonnaded square. All this is still clear enough. I am glad to have come here to see the provincial and Roman places, where the Greek refinement is all thickened and the barbarian pierces through.

The rest has been Berber I should say: old rows of houses of rubble piled to three storeys with no level spaces, like children's mud with crazy steps and no windows; and even stranger at a place called Matmata in the hills (near where the Eighth Army skirted the Mareth Line). There they let circular pits into the soft sandstone, with a tunnelled way out onto the hillside, and opened their rooms out from them as if they were courtyards. Very safe, they said, during the bombing.

We are now quite south and the Sahara beyond. Angus has gone to the last oasis but I thought I would take a quiet day (one palm oasis very like another). There is nothing beautiful except the wonderful vitality of the desert air and the fashion they have in this region only of pattern-building with brick – it must have come from Iraq perhaps in early Muslim time. It would be a splendid quiet place to bring one's work to do in the winter sun. Tomorrow we have a long day, by two Roman cities, to Kairouan.

Love,

FREYA

JOHN GREY MURRAY
Tunis
11 April 1960

Dearest Jock,

Got to Tunis just as the weather broke and now there is far too much to write to you in one letter – the drive to Kairouan across three Roman cities at various states of ruin, one just stone teeth of ex-doors or windows sticking from the ground; Kasserine with an arch of yellow sandstone carved about the plain against the pass where the U.S.A. were routed by Rommel; and Sbeitla where three temples still stand side by side above their forum and the columns of a theatre have been dug out from the wadi bed. The feel of the life comes out of these ruins and the *oneness* of that Graeco-Roman world is apparent. It is this which makes it so topical: Lollobrigida now advertised all over the Mediterranean would have been no surprise to the citizens of Sbeitla or anyone of those provincial towns, prosperous and enjoying the general civilisation of their day.

Kairouan too has the universal feeling but in a severer form and bound by Islam. It is a noble affair, its minaret like a pharos seen far away, its court porticoed with ancient columns very roughly put together, and the forest of inside columns, the Mihrab with tenth-century lustre tiles and lovely dome above – all severe and serene and very *manly*. A charming librarian has charge of a small room filled with priceless Cufic. Apart from the mosque and its blue doors looking out between Corinthian columns on to quiet white-washed streets, there isn't much in Kairouan and we reached the coast next

7

day and spent two days between Sousse, Mahdia, El Djem, and Monastir – with Roman (rather Greek Hellenistic) mosaics in the museums, and Byzantine walls remodelled by Arab and Turk, and the monastery forts the early invaders lived in. Then up across the foothills of the only Tunisian mountain with *sheets* of flowers, by another Roman city where the fine mosaic pavements were covered with blocks of barbarian masonry in the fourth century; then to the ruins of the Carthage aqueduct striding across wide slopes of corn; and now to Tunis, which I haven't yet looked at, as I came with a tummy which only *just* held out so far. (Luckily every local doctor knows what to do for *that* complaint.)

Love. So *glad* you are resting.

FREYA

JOHN GREY MURRAY   British Embassy,
                                                              Vienna
                                                          6 May 1960

Dearest Jock,

I am finishing the season's travel here with a weekend with Jim and Elsa Bowker, who are always a delight and a refreshment. I took Sandro (who drove the party to Cortina) as I felt my driving powers insufficient and we had a twelve-hour drive and anything more lovely than Carinthia under its pear trees in blossom you can't imagine. There is something tight and bourgeois about Austria that would get me down after a while: they seem to like and glory in the bourgeois quality, unlike us who rebel against it in our hearts. But just for a visit there is something very pleasant in the tidy country with its woods clipped into shape and so many fences and no one in sight any less ordinary than anybody else.

When I get back I will see what I can do with the first chapters of the typescript (how I hate it) and leave the rest till probably 1961 when I get back from China. How little you know me after so many years to think I do not suffer. When one fails at sixty-seven it is the veiled figure that appears, at the end of a vista that alas! may still be rather long. It is in fact that spot that Keats saw on his pillow and is never pleasant, whenever it shows itself. And surely you should know by now that I make a lot of fuss over small things but not so much over big. Anyway I will do what I can in the month that I have.

Turkey seems tricky, but may settle down. I get tired of people who put down everything everywhere to Communism. The Turks get tired of one government always, like everyone else everywhere, and anyone who now and then wants a *new hat* can understand that feeling!

Love,
FREYA

MRS. T. DEUCHAR[19]

Asolo
16 May 1960

Dearest Dulcie,

I am so relieved to get your letter and alas! not at all surprised at the slow progress. It is like a transplanted tree, you sit still for ever so long, but the day comes when suddenly you feel that your roots have taken on again and all is well. Perhaps you will come in November when Asolo is usually lovely, with sunsets on the mountains and the house cosy and warm? Anyway, you have the summer to lie *fallow*.

I wish I could waft a sight of those African ruins into your bedroom! I was so lucky in having a day at Leptis with only two nice quiet Englishmen in the houseparty. Our hostess[20] took us fifty miles or so over olive lands the sands are slowly re-conquering, to walk for two hours along the Roman streets, with side walks, and stone seats here and there for the weary, and a phallus with one eye (so very inappropriate) set up in relief at most corners, to make the street lucky. The theatre is there with a seated Ceres presiding and many of its columns restored, and a marble foyer with alcoves for the actors, and the sea beyond against the yellow stone. Columns were *everywhere*, of red onyx or green *cipollino*. An old forum with the sharp carving of Greek workmen and a newer one with strange Medusa heads along a portico, no doubt carved by some Syrian compatriot of the Empress of Severus, who built the basilica and harbour, etc. for his African home. The harbour is filled with tamarisk and swamp, but its contour shows with great quays and stone bulkheads to tie the ships, and stone-built warehouses below a temple where an almost Roman lunch was waiting for us (two nice Italian servants *kneeling* to serve us with hot macaroni, as we sat rather low). Then siesta on rugs under an awning against the temple wall and three more hours of slow meandering among basilicas and baths. It almost makes one regret the Italian loss of Tripoli, as this glorious excavation is now trickling along very slowly. It gives one more of the feeling of Rome and what she meant than anything I have seen, certainly more so than Rome itself.

[19] Dulcie Deuchar was recovering from an operation. She and her husband had a house at Ockley in Surrey where F.S. often stayed when she was in England.
[20] Contessa Cicogna, with whom F.S. stayed for a week in Tripoli after Tunis.

A very lovely thing has happened to me: Berenson dedicated his last book to me (*The Passionate Sightseer*). I didn't know and it has touched me so much. And it is a lovely book, as if he were talking of this and that. But the library is open and working. Must work too now.

With love, dear Dulcie, and to Tom too.

Your

FREYA

27 May 1960

Dearest Jock,

How sorry I am to have caused uneasiness by my paragraph. It was not you, but things in general that caused the depression: it is such a year. I have been writing my tenth letter of condolence: first Kinahan,[21] then Leonard Woolley, Whiffy Bramly,[22] Ernest Barker, Lord Halifax – all old but one doesn't think of that when people go whom one has known for thirty years; B.B. and Owen Tweedy;[23] now Aly who was younger than me and though I never saw him again because of friendship to Joan, I was fond of him.[24] Even Edwina Mountbatten, though I scarce knew her – but *Perseus* was her bedside book and she was always good to me. Sandy Reid Scott, one of the dearest human beings – cancer and dead at forty-seven; Tom Boase an eye, two female friends serious operations; Momo's[25] recovery they tell me an illusion; Charles Lambe in danger of his life and out of work for good. Add to this the two old bedridden campaigners – Alix and Amy Hollitcher whom one visits in hospital, and all except themselves expect to die; and then this incapacity to write – can you wonder that I feel the shadows creeping up?

On re-reading I agree the book is all wrong as it is now – being neither one thing nor the other. I am putting it into the present, shortening and speeding it – and will send you what I can do before I leave. Then if you will read it, not stopping at detail but for the general effect, and tell me where it drags, I shall feel hopeful or depressed according, but anyway it is better to know. It is just possible the letters may some day be preferred, but not till I am dead!

I picked up a Meredith after years of neglect and, far from sharing the

[21] Sir Kinahan Cornwallis, Ambassador in Baghdad when F.S. was there in the war.

[22] Colonel Wilfrid Jennings Bramly, who had lived in Egypt at Burg el Arab.

[23] Another wartime friend; he had been Assistant Director of Publicity for all the Middle East.

[24] Aly Khan had been killed in a car crash in France.

[25] Lady Marriott.

verdict of oblivion he seems to suffer under, thought it excellent in all but style, which does perhaps make more demand than is legitimate on the reader's agility. But what a *living* thread; and a wonderful understanding of the nuances of a situation; and what a public that could take it and do its own thinking itself.

Well dear Jock, cross your fingers: I feel so at sea about this book. Never have I so little known what is good or bad!

Thank you, and love,

FREYA

JOHN GREY MURRAY

S.S. *San Giorgio*
18 June 1960

Dearest Jock,

Off I am – alas not carefree but *clogged* with that beastly book. Have been re-reading the first six chapters and it does seem to me to run more easily. I long to hear what you think.

I am travelling in luxury and must say it makes everything wonderfully easy to have a cabin and *bathroom* to oneself. Meals lavish, waiters charming, passengers, apart from a few unobtrusive gentry, quite monstrous – a fat blonde with pale mauve shorts and a mauve *boater* has just walked by in gilt sandals: what a result for 5,000 years of the classic world! Sybil paying for all this: can't believe it!

The garden was a dream of lilies and hollyhocks, Venice, lunch with Martyn,[26] tea with Victor,[27] very pleasant; sailing out, past the sunset and evening lights on the Grand Canal and Doge's Palace, had all its now familiar magic; and already those evening-before-departure regrets have gone and the wonderful effervescence of being loose and headed for the Aegean has taken hold.

Love dear Jock,

FREYA

P.S. Snapshots to amuse you. I look like Sarah Bernhardt with one leg?

JOHN GREY MURRAY

Nauplia
1 July 1960

Dearest Jock,

This is being begun in the fortress-islet-hotel off Nauplia but who knows when it will be finished, as I spend all the spare time we have – and that isn't

26 sc. Coleman.   27 sc. Cunard.

II

much – in falling instantly into one of those delicious sleeps made up of sun and sea. We have had five days now in Athens, going off once to Eretria, across the ferry into Euboea, and back by Chalcis where the tide turns backwards and forwards and boats are released only in the favourable direction of the moment (except the Duke of Windsor years ago who insisted on going contrary and broke his yacht). In the museum we found an exquisite archaic statue of Theseus carrying off a (very willing) Antiope – and in Athens too the Acropolis museum is open and those lovely girls are all alive again around its walls.

We travel in luxury, with a car, so nothing much happens, but it is all agreeable and lovely to see the familiar places – and Sybil is finding it as good as she thought and was as happy as I am on the walls of Tiryns. They are better, I think, than Mycenae – and it is twenty-two years since I saw them and the enchantment has not faded.

We drove yesterday to Sunium. Building cropping up but no serious damage yet except one hideous box hotel. Lord Byron's name accentuated on the marble with green ink, but we looked in vain for the J. M. beneath it – was it so modest that it has *vanished*?

Yesterday morning we left and deviated before Corinth to Perichora – an enchanted sea-lagoon landlocked in empty hills of orange precipice and pine and olive, with – on its outer ledge out of sight – a tiny deserted harbour, a pool of green water under rocks and fifth century B.C. jetty.

In a few years this land will be crawling with tourists, but as yet there are still many places and few roads.

Love,
FREYA

JOHN GREY MURRAY   Delphi
                                                    9 July 1960
Dearest Jock,
    I was looking at that little path up the cliff and thinking how active we were twenty-two years ago![28] Otherwise the Sacred Way and the view of that noble valley is the same, and I drank a good tumblerful of the Castalian spring for the sake of my book.

We have had a splendid tour and Sybil such good company – a very good companion and mostly wishing to see the same. Great joy too to revisit the old familiar places – Mycenae and Epidaurus, with Paxinou acting Jocasta.

---

[28] F.S. had visited Delphi with Jock Murray in 1938.

How rarely now one sees *real* tragedy, not just a domestic mess coming to the boil!

There is a wonderful statue here supposed by Lysippus: surely that was not here before, was it? *Very* beautiful. What fragments and crumbs are all that we have left – and enough to bring us from the ends of the earth. The glades of Olympia were filled by a party from Pakistan.

The only new sight I saw was the castle (Venetian going back through Turk to Byzantine and Greek, all still in bits in its walls) of Naupactos-Lepanto: a quiet pleasant little town with *tiny* walled harbour – one can't imagine how it held the Turkish fleet; but then Carthage is equally minute – the galleys must have been quite small.

It has been a serious responsibility to take Sybil as she thinks this is to be the only visit to Greece in her life. I didn't do the itinerary – and it was all good except Mistra which she found too Byzantine. I do think it would be improved by eliminating practically all the ugly and badly built ruins and leaving only the churches and castle up above.

Love,

FREYA

JOHN GREY MURRAY

c/o Lord Kinross,
Istanbul
13 July 1960

Dearest Jock,

It is particularly good to get letters dropping into places like these: Patrick gave me yours when I lunched with him before we went on to bathe with some charming people – aristocratic Turks of the vanished age who live on the seashore of Marmara. So civilised, international and delightful – and the brother, who looked like the nicest sort of English retired colonel, is an enthusiast for *Alexander's Path!* As my books are practically unknown here, this was very pleasant.

I am up for two days chasing permits in Ankara. They are tricky this year (with the 460 M.P.s shut up on that island whose faint sad outline just shows from Stambul on the western horizon).[29] All seems very orderly and quiet however though the country is hard up for some time. They are a wonderfully decent and dignified people, and when they have to endure, they just tighten their belts and do so.

Stambul keeps its enchantment – no city in the world so magically sited;

[29] Since the army-led revolution in May 1960 most of the members of the Grand National Assembly had been imprisoned.

I don't believe it *can* be spoilt. The gaiety of the Bosphorus is incomparable: the ferry boats like beetles about it, the caiques still with their legendary outlines, the great ships drawing long furrows and the rowers rowing in and out; the houses piled steeply, the line of mosques and minarets against the sky compensating for anything that may have been lost by the loss of Byzantium. I wonder if I can show those youngsters enough to give them the magic of Stambul in a few days? It is not like Greece which is at once unmistakable – it's a subtle charm that might escape one. I have a teacher and spend an afternoon with his family in their summer *yayla* on the Asiatic side, with Anadolu castle showing its old walls and the Sweet Waters of Asia behind it, and the Bosphorus illuminated by the sunset light as if all history, all that had ever mattered to mankind, were mellowed there into an evening brightness. We sat on the wooden terrace and lifted our feet when motor boats sped by to avoid the splashing through the boards of the Bosphorus, and ate little fishes just caught by our host on a nylon line baited with little white feathers that look like fish; and I came back at night in a taxi with four strangers.

Simon[30] writes and all seems O.K.: they arrive 17th a.m.: boat for Skiros 18th; hotel rooms postponed I hope. I am not too well – the old machine begins to creak I suppose. Wish you and Diana were coming.

Love,
FREYA

JOHN GREY MURRAY

Rainbow Hotel,
Istanbul
30 July 1960

Dearest Jock,

I register a little wail that my books don't *exist* in Turkey so that I am quite unknown and therefore unlikely to get permits or anything else. Can nothing be done? It is really adding a lot to my obstacles.

Patrick suggested this ultra-Levantine hotel where I get quite a lot of Turkish practice in the usual disorder – two widows running it with incompetence and refinement. Whenever the taps don't work or the bed hasn't been made, they say: 'C'est ici la vie de famille.' It is a wonderful contrast to my glimpse of luxury travel with Sybil, and one might too be thousands of miles from Anatolia and the real Turkey. It is a suffocating atmosphere, this minority Levant: perhaps the harm comes from being always on the

[30] sc. Lennox-Boyd, F.S.'s godson. The holiday party, nine with F.S., was to consist of Elizabeth Loxley, Teresa Onslow, Joanna Murray, Simon Lennox-Boyd, Mark Lennox-Boyd, Henry Berens, John Moorehead and Mark Amory.

defensive? The defence of gentility is pathetic but also extraordinarily sterile – holding a castle which has nothing left worth holding inside it, for there is no real *beauty* of any sort, nor even any cleanliness or order, merely dilapidated curtains once lace, dead flowers, stained linen, and the two widows with gently embittered faces and well-kept little hands, who never once go round to see what happens to their bedrooms. But the lodgers, who come for a month's summer bathing, are all friendly together and we sit with each other at breakfast at little tables carried across the road to the opposite pavement which overlooks the sea and the islands.

I have got my teacher for two hours a day and hope even the short time may do something. On the 11th I leave in the *S. Marco*, touch at Smyrna, and am back in Athens to meet the horde – four days too soon as it turns out. They will have three nights before the next boat to Skiros (as they miss the 16th one) – so we might go off to Delphi or Olympia; anyway Joanna will be able to do some of her sightseeing. The Stambul end of the rest seems fairly easy and I hope to find a good and cheap hotel near all the mosques. The only dark point is how to get to Troy: it looks as if the easiest might be across from Mytilene by caique.

The charm of my hotel (its only charm) is that one sits out and sees the coming and going of this old pathway of Marmara – the steamers farther out and the caiques near in where the current is easy, and dozens of little yachts, motor or rowing boats like insects here and there. The caiques keep their lovely ancient shape, low-waisted on the water (which often laps over into their holds) and high at poop and stern, and painted with gay bands of various colours. They too have an air of gentility, but very aristocrat and triumphant, carrying several thousand years of history in their beautiful shape.

Patrick is hard at work in a flat nearby and belongs to a club whence one can bathe not too crowded, looking at a sort of anthill of brown bathing bodies, like those medieval frescoes of Inferno, on the piers of the public beach opposite.

Love dear Jock and do please write.

FREYA

P.S. An elderly Turk shows every sign of proposing!

JOHN GREY MURRAY   Istanbul
                                                11 August 1960
Dearest Jock,

This is the quaintest relic-suburb of a bygone age – a sort of 1900 watering resort or even a decade or so earlier. One expects little feminine boaters on the girls' heads – and some do have something of the sort, swathed in tulle. I was taken to a hammam and it was agreeable and like something painted by Delacroix – females shapeless and soft as puppies with water slushing over us all the time out of scooped-out marble from the Byzantine world. It is curious how easy one feels at being naked: largely perhaps because there is no mirror in which one sees oneself, so any preoccupation is done away with – and there one is, just as the Lord and Time have made one.

I have met a whole bevy of new people and wonderfully mixed. Patrick took me to some charming cultured Egyptian Turks – the two wives sisters, nieces of Muhammed Ali (Momo's friend),[31] all living in pleasant houses, but reduced, on the Marmara shore. We were talking of slavery and they told me the story of a slave they had known in their grandmother's house. She had been bought as a baby by poor people as a speculation and kept happily in their family till she was fourteen when they thought to sell her – but to avoid the pain of parting told her she was to be married. Two women came and took her away and brought her to a room where two girls sat weeping, and it was only slowly that she realised this was no marriage but her slavery. The three girls were smuggled out of the country on faked passports to Egypt, and this one was bought for my friends' grandmother and became happy in the household; and when the old lady travelled to Stambul would come with her and wait outside the Sultan's reception room while her mistress was inside. Here the Chief Eunuch, a very important person, saw and came to know and eventually married her – and they lived in affluence and content till he was hung, on Galata bridge; and she married his successor! I wonder how many people we know have met and talked with eunuchs? Few, as time goes on. The only one I remember was huge and bad-tempered and guarded the harem of King Ali in Iraq when the poor Regent was a child.

The other character met here is a Miss MacCallum who was head of Middle Eastern affairs in Ottawa when I went there – daughter of an American missionary in Marash. She has now retired and wants to go back to those hard landscapes of her childhood and 'plant trees on the Taurus'. It is like seeing a clear flame to find single-minded eccentricities of this sort. I hope there is not some miserable disillusion at the end: it is a lot to expect of life, to be able happily to revisit the places of one's childhood.

Love dear Jock,

FREYA

P.S. About English books: I have given your note to the Head of Education but not much can be done as Turkey is bankrupt. If our Government made

31 Faisal's heir apparent.

even quite a small grant – at least for books about Turkey! – it would help and perhaps some mutual agreement could be come to. It would pay us more dividends in the long run than half the things we spend far greater sums on. The Americans do something of the sort, so why not we? We are such idiots at underestimating the influence of these things – far greater when it is books *they buy for themselves.*

JOHN GREY MURRAY   Skiathos
                                                              28 August 1960

Dearest Jock,

We have reached the third and last island. We put into one scarcely mentioned, Halonnesos, and saw a fine pine slope for camping and on the spur of instinct got off and spent five days there of perfect bathing – such gem-like clearness of the sea and the nightly star-procession spread out as if on a stage with us in the best seats. We are too large a group, but otherwise a cheerful friendly and nice one – and it is sad that Joanna and Teresa leave for Athens in three days' time while we go on to Stambul. What happens then after they all go on the 9th, I don't yet know as all my plans are dished by want of permits. Pam and Derek unable even to cross the Syrian border.

Much love dear Jock and thank you and Diana for sending Joanna. She is taking the ms.; the notes you sent me I will go into as soon as I get home.

                                                                    Love,
                                                                    FREYA

JOHN GREY MURRAY   Boat from Chanakkale
                                                              4 September 1960

Dearest Jock,

Yesterday we were lunching in the luxury of the Park Hotel when an Oxford invasion, 320 Hellenic tourists with Culture written all over them, burst upon us, and there among them (but not like them) was David Cecil and his son Hugh (growing exactly like him). We inveigled them to our table and had a gay and hurried lunch as they were going to the Blue Mosque and we off to Troy. He asked me about my book and I asked him if he would read it and he said he gladly would; so either in type or proof I feel happy to send it as it has not yet been read from a literary standpoint – I mean details of style as apart from the matter. I feel it can be done now that the general shape is fixed; but leave you to decide. I myself would prefer it to be read in proof, hoping that the changes are slight. It was so pleasant to have this accidental meeting.

We flew to Chanakkale, saw the police, hotel, etc., and were in time to find a taxi and see Troy in the sunset – about three-quarters of an hour's drive away. Who can have said the site was unrewarding? There it all is – the ramparts above the Scaean gate where Helen walked, and Simois and Scamander meeting in the plain below. The oak tree has gone but the country has the Vallonia oak still scattered with its dark leaves all about it; and there far south in sight are the crests of Ida, and north is the shore with a crumbled outline of some hamlet where the ships and the wall showed clearly as they still would do; and Tenedos vague in the evening light (but lost in the morning), and most dramatic now the outline of Gallipoli comes down parallel to the Trojan shore with the columns of the Anzac monument upon it as if the streams of history were meeting. The walls of the first Troy are there, wrapped like a moth in a cocoon, in the road and gate of the second, the temple-site of the third and so on – later and later. Helen's Troy was the second, as far as I vaguely remember, but the *site* is always the same, and the view. On a western low ridge are the two tumuli – one said to be Hector and the other Achilles; and on the city height are bits of a later temple but still on the site of the Palladium and still dedicated to Athene. If one knew nothing the place would still have a breadth and beauty of its own; but the pleasure of it is in a recent reading of *Iliad* and *Aeneid* and then the whole panorama breaks into life. All the young were very excited and pleased – and we all got up at four this morning and went again to see the sun roll over the ridge like a ball, and went over it again and breakfasted in the small museum garden. A nice old Bekchi told us about Schliemann who came in 1871 and began just below the northern gateway where the treasures of gold were found. No one is there now, but visitors come in spite of the trouble with permits. We got back at 8.20 only to find that the nine o'clock boat now goes half an hour earlier, and we caught it by the skin of our teeth and are now chugging along the rather dull Thracian shore on a dark sapphire Marmara sea with the heights of Gallipoli, the valley where we climbed with so great losses, and Sidi Al Bahr with a tall medieval fort all very clear in the morning.

I am sad, for I found news of Victor Cunard's death and also of Charles Lambe. All friends seem to be dying this last year. Victor had a sad old age ahead, but he could have lived happily a few years longer, and Charles is a grievous loss – to his friends, his country and himself. It has made me very sad. And Momo I fear will be fading away too very soon.

Much love dear Jock,

FREYA

18

S.S. *San Giorgio*
15 September 1960

Dearest Sybil,

I saw the last of my horde off five days ago – and they all want to come back to Turkey, and all got on together and never complained of anything though the train from Salonica took thirty hours! I did enjoy it and like to think that one or the other will think of me as they trot across the Bosphorus when I'm dead. An unknown and unexpected addition to the party arrived in Athens – young Mark Amory, a relation of the ex-Chancellor (whom I thought one of the nicest people ever met: is he a friend of yours?).[32] Then there was Mark Lennox-Boyd only seventeen and a dear; and John Moore-head who managed the only accident of the trip by running a kebab skewer into the back of his leg (such a difficult thing to do one would think) in the middle of the Stambul bazaar and was very efficiently medicated by the police.

I kept very well – walked down and donkeyed up the island ridges, and the bathing was heaven. There is nothing anywhere I believe to touch the Aegean and we found an uncontaminated little island and camped. But these last days my trouble returned; I think the liver is just tired of Turkish food.

I have a few days in Athens, and shall always think of you there now dear Sybil with those good summer days about us.

Love,
FREYA

JOHN GREY MURRAY   Leaving Stambul
15 September 1960

Dearest Jock,

All the effervescence has gone out of the revolution and there is a great atmosphere of despondency. I have a deep suspicion of intelligentsia govern-ment anyway and there are very few in this country who have the mere *technique* of governing, and most of them – however corrupt they may be – are shut up on that island. The students for instance thought out a bright new law to make everyone speak Turkish. The older heads have now rescinded it, but in a country full of minority feelings it has an unsettling flavour – and how silly a *time* to do this when one needs all the smoothness there is. Already it caused a clash between a non-Turkish student tourist and

[32] Viscount Amory, as Sir Derick Heathcoat-Amory, Chancellor of the Exchequer 1958–60.

police. I hope they may win through: they are such a *decent* people and all their decency unfits them for our world.

I am sad these days. I feel as if I were in an emptying room and hope not to be among the last to leave. All my truly intimate men friends except yourself are dead. If I didn't write a book now and then, would you ever write to me? And if I didn't reach England and No. 50[33] now and then, would you ever travel to see me? It is a bleak world, its happiness cluttered up with too many small unnecessary things.

Must go now – with love dear Jock.

FREYA

LADY CHOLMONDELEY   Rome
28 September 1960

Dearest Sybil,

I am coming home this way because of my fortnight's 'cure' at Chianciano and must send you another 'thank you' for the luxurious voyage: I thought of you as I lay in my cabin and wished you were there – though perhaps the pleasure of the luxury is enhanced by the preliminary 'tourist' from Stambul (it was quite comfortable too as a matter of fact – and gave a day in Smyrna to see the wonderful new excavations). I landed in Naples and went for the first time to Pompeii, almost as crowded as before the earthquake; and having found my way into the Dionysian mysteries and been impressed by the atmosphere of them that comes through those painted walls, I was surprised to find two *nuns* coming in to look just as I was leaving. What would they be thinking? One can speculate quite a lot.

Naples is still Greek. It has decayed but inside its own traditions; and, with nothing left worth their intelligence to care for, the Neapolitans amuse themselves by being clever and despising their slower visitors, and make the same sort of Hellenistic toys as once upon a time – cameos, corals, gay little terracottas – whose meaning was already lessening 2,000 years ago. I still love it and Naples and Stambul are my two Mediterranean cities – the one still imperial in spite of all and the other like some profligate old tart who recollects the glamour of her youth.

Love, dear Sybil.

Affectionately,
FREYA

[33] sc. Albemarle Street, address of the publishing house of John Murray.

Hotel Principe,
                                                            Chianciano
                                                        8 October 1960

Dearest Jock,

Of all dreary things to be alone at, a 'cure' is one of the dreariest – like a
hen at end of a string, always being given a tug to drink those waters whenever it wants to stray. But it is of course a very good place to work in and the
last (I do hope) look over the typescript should be done by tomorrow.
It would be most beautiful country, too, if left to itself and yesterday I
wandered away from it all and found natural little paths in a tangle of limestone, oak, juniper and chestnut, and ended with two tough old women
looking for mushrooms who, far from knowing a path, led straight down
the roughest of hillsides saying that all ways were alike to them. One was a
white-haired old toothless crone of sixty-one, so I was rather pleased to tell
her I was six years older when we got safe to the bottom.

I have just been reading *Prospero's Cell* which the *New York Times* want
reviewed, and see how very poor mine is by comparison, but I don't think
I can do much more to it and shall just go on feeling dispirited about it till
it is out and can be forgotten.

Why should one envy the young? You say one should try not to – but I
can't imagine doing so. It would be so *awful* to go back when one is so much
nearer to the goal. I think you have got it wrong, Jock: one is old in this
world, but young oneself for the next step. I feel about it as about the first
ball, or the first meet of hounds, anxious as to whether one will get it right,
and timid and inexperienced – all the feelings of youth; and for that one
needs the comfort and companionship of one's own generation.

                                                              Love,
                                                            FREYA

Asolo
                                                        16 October 1960

Dearest Pam,

I got back yesterday, bored stiff with my cure though it couldn't be less
exacting: an hour's walking about drinking delicious radio-active water in
the morning and then no diet and the day to drive about (if one had a car) to
Perugia, Orvieto, Siena, etc., all the best of Italy. I did none of that but
finished my loathed autobiography and read Turkish while it rained on and
off. But if only someone I liked would have a liver at the same time, it would

be quite enjoyable. They say you can't tell if it does you good for *five years.* Pretty clever.

There is here a mountain of paper to deal with and a new lodger next door with an Italian secretary, which foreshadows trouble with Emma.[34] I am preparing the oil even before the waters get troubled.

Love to you both, dear Pam.

Your

FREYA

LADY CHOLMONDELEY

Asolo

14 November 1960

Dearest Sybil,

I have been waiting to write till the photographs came, and here they are, *dreadfully* disappointing, because you are hardly there – either dim in shadow, or non-existent because two films were blanks! I shall take the new camera for a heart-to-heart talk with the shop, but meanwhile it is sad. I will bring the lot over to show you. May I come to Houghton 14–16th January? I am longing to be back in England and to see my friends.

The book is off at last and David Cecil has kindly offered to give it a look-over: it left me so harassed that I have no idea of it any longer. There is Diana Cooper, whose life work isn't writing, doing just what I would have liked to do, weaving the public and private events with a beautiful natural spontaneity which all one's literary labour can't attain. I am going to spend a few days with her while in and out of Paris for a little suit and hat or two (three years since the last!) – and then hope to be at Jock Murray's from 20th to 28th December.

Love, dear Sybil,

FREYA

MRS. DAVID PAWSON

London

4 March 1961

Dearest Pam,

I am still here and enjoying my 'season' after a bad start, three weeks in bed with bronchitis, but all well now and I am slimming, which is good for one I feel sure. Only now I am so broken in to fatless foods that Turkey is

[34] Maid at Asolo.

bound to *kill* me! On the 20th I fly to Angkor from Rome, to Hong Kong at end of month and trust to luck and Michael Stewart to let me find a visa there for China. My only real preparation is a super summer suit woven in a mixture of linen-silk-wool which seems to be as creaseless and resilient as one would like to be oneself.

Lots of love, dear Pam, to you both. Hope to have lots to tell you in June.

FREYA

JOHN GREY MURRAY

Asolo
15 March 1961

Dearest Jock,

I hope for news of you today or tomorrow – for after that I shall not hear till Peking. The splendid news is a telegram from Michael to say the visa is waiting in Hong Kong. Otherwise, 'my boat is on the shore and my barque is on the sea'. I feel as if I were on the tip of the world and it tilting to the East though Asolo is so ravishing just now it seems silly ever to leave it at all: blossom tumbling over itself not to miss a day of the spring and the Afghan tulips all out and daffodils waving. The Michael dress is ravishing and my luggage only overweight by a kilo!

The London kaleidoscope slid quite suddenly as these things always do into its pleasant background of past. So many past years now – it is good to think of the number of them in which you come to Victoria Station to welcome or wave goodbye: long may it continue – not *too* long – not up to ninety, but another dozen years or so if all goes well!

Love dear Jock,

FREYA

JOHN GREY MURRAY

Angkor
24 March 1961

Dearest Jock,

I have been meaning to write these three days, but sleep comes over me all the time, and yesterday as I was groping in the half dark I luckily saw a movement five inches from my bare foot and it was a snake: sitting on its coils like a peeress with her Coronation robes, with a narrow head, looking lost and angry. With no delay at all I leaped on to my bed, put one foot reluctantly down to reach the bell, and tucked it up again while a little Cambodian tackled the snake with a broom. It made the most disquieting curves and leaps and was carried out dead – just because we were Incompatible. No doubt it felt rather lost on a bedroom floor and, if we could have communicated, would gladly have gone back by the drain through which it came.

Everything else, except the heat which is sticky, is beautiful beyond dreams. It *is* dreams, the place doesn't belong to the waking world. Not the great quadrangle across the river, the long bridge and the yellow-robed monks, the two elephants wading in the morning and the children bringing their buffaloes back at sunset – riding them across; and the five towers flaked and shaped like pineapples in grey stone, and the secret courts and long grey cloisters – not only all this but about twenty other temples covering five centuries are hereabout in clearings of the forest. Some still left with the huge white roots of trees twisting and destroying them, others opening alone to quiet clearings. Expense and distance and heat keep the visitors at bay, and long may they remain so with a few lucky exceptions like ourselves. I have seen about twenty of these holy shrines: beginning with simple towers to house their gods, they ended like mountains of tiered masonry now lost amid the high forest trees, but once at the busiest crossroads of cities. I wonder why one is proud of one's country's *past*. Surely one should feel sadness at having lost whatever it was in every citizen that made the greatness; but one settles down to enjoy (and profit by) the vanished virtue as if it were not something lost and betrayed – by oneself? And what makes the watershed? That is the historical question above all others I would like to find an answer to.

I shall try to get to Hong Kong a little earlier – 31st perhaps – as Bangkok looks very unattractive. All their best roofs end in wavy arms like stags' horns, very mingy and poor after this Cambodian splendour of solid brick and stone. There is here a strange Oxford atmosphere about the quads and courts and long galleries – as if New College were just round a corner.

Must send this: with love,

FREYA

MRS. T. DEUCHAR   Angkor
27 March 1961

Dearest Dulcie,

I wonder if I can keep this letter dry enough to be legible – water runs off as if one were a fountain and alas! there is no slimming about it. One drinks all the time. But I shall have been here a week tomorrow and feel that the things I have seen are with me forever. No Gothic cathedral, none of our monuments, was ever more noble than this central creation; in its broad basin of water, brown-gold, whose steps have crumbled, with the forest (immense trees) beyond; and the building itself rising from enclosure to enclosure, the outer wall with splendid gates, the balustrade and causeway, and the temple itself from terrace to terrace enclosed in cloisters carved and mellowed with grey lichen or dark with time. The last terrace is a bit of mountaineering up steep steps, and there you are with the five towers and the serene Buddha at the centre, and the roofs graded below. Not a wall or step is left undecorated, but it is done with great restraint.

One can never forget that it is *great* architecture, as great I almost think as the Parthenon. The whole base is carved with a tumult of battle scenes and I was thinking, as I was walking along, of the Elgin marbles and the difference. The *adventurousness* of the Greek makes him supreme, every movement, every flexibility of muscle in horse or man is experimented with. Here the liveliness is the same but it seems as if, when the right formula was found, the sculptors were satisfied and continued to repeat it. But in architecture, which gains by symmetry and repetition, they seem to me to be on a par. The serene, mounting to a climax, was never better felt in any place of worship. It is already there in the early temples which I have been visiting (in one of the bright little motor-cycle-rickshaws that run about these flat forest roads). But the greatest later temple, carved with elusive faces in all its towers, is the decadence; and then the forest came gradually and ate the cities, and nothing but the stone-built temples are left. How mysterious it is. The people are the same, one can recognise the faces. But *something* – what? – has gone.

One has to have something very worth looking at to linger in this heat and today the clouds are massing as if the rain were to begin. What I have enjoyed most were three quiet mornings with my sewing in a court of Angkor and in one of the forest temples where the roots sprawl among the ruins, and only a few birds far away in sunlit tops were talking to each other. Sudden crowds of butterflies appeared, flying with slow heavy wings dark-brown or black, or flickering gay and light yellow, as if the souls of the old city were about.

I wish you could see it all, dear Dulcie, but I didn't wish for you for I believe you would pass out in the heat. I am just beginning to feel normal in it, and get up with the sunrise when the forests are delicious.

Dear love,

FREYA

Angkor
                                                        29 March 1961

Dearest Jock,

I feel rather trapped in Cambodia at the moment as the Bangkok people put a permanent instead of temporary stamp on my visa; and as there is no authority here to put it right and no aeroplane will risk a $14,000 fine to take me back, here I would be, except that a kind Scotsman at the airport talked to the B.O.A.C. in Bangkok, who arranged with Lufthansa to take me three days earlier to Hong Kong – and so I hope to be back in the transit-visa category and able to leave this afternoon. You are allowed twenty-four hours in Bangkok without a visa, and as I have taken rather a dislike to it, I won't mind. I will, I hope, have an evening to see Siamese dancing, a morning to see the rather hideous temple, and be in Hong Kong with a whole week of shopping before me the day after tomorrow. All this may sound complicated in writing, but it was much more so (and so *hot*) in doing. This world bureaucracy is a monster: poor people who are not good at it get lost in their forms yet cling to them as if they were Arks. It might be better if the art of writing were lost. It has however stood me in good stead, as the Scotsman asked me if I was the Saudi Arabia Freya, told me in the few hectic moments that what he knew and liked were the steppes of Mongolia, and saw me through after I promised to do the same by him in Arabia if ever necessary. There is a Brotherhood of Deserts.

A question that has been teasing me is whether one *feels* in one's dreams? One does, of course, but what does one feel *with*? I dreamed that a small child was hurt and I lifted it up and it snuggled up to me comforted and – in my dream – I felt a wonderful warmth of love that could not have been greater waking. Now what was I loving *with*? It opens up a very big field.

The weather is breaking – clouds heavy both yesterday and today and a shower as if a bath had been turned on. The leaves don't drink it in a sprightly way as ours do, but droop deadened and happy, as if after too much ardour, and only recover by degrees.

                                                        Love,
                                                        FREYA

Hong Kong
                                                        2 April 1961

Darling Dulcie,

I sailed in a Comet to this most exciting city, where the climate is normal and delicious after the equatorial heat. It is so beautiful, the curving shallow beaches and retreating bays, the blue distances of peninsulas and islands, the domestic look of the smooth waters with crowds of sampans or junks dusky and slow, built out of the vast planks of the forest trees.

Michael Stewart is due down tomorrow and he and a secretary and I all go up together, D.V., on Thursday. I am now being transferred to Government House, and the Pink, beautifully pressed and not yet *froissé* by a camel, will be inaugurated for the occasion. ·

Meanwhile you will perhaps not be surprised to hear that I have gone quite mad, sables and pearls: years to recover, but how well worth it. How I wish you were here to enjoy it all. To shop in these streets full of colour, crowded with their lovely Chinese letters on strips of red or blue or yellow, where you never see anything ugly except some European advertisement intruding (and very few of them), and to find people all eager to *make things*, enjoying the use of their craft. If you admire anything, they say 'Thank you'. I believe it is all very different as one goes north, but here one can see the old fashion of China and I can't understand how people can find Hong Kong uninspiring or insipid. For one thing, it gives me a feeling of terrific danger, as if on the edge of a volcano that at any moment might pour down. Long jerry-built houses are built for the refugees in rows and the whole thing has a pre-Deluge flavour.

Love to you both, dearest Dulcie. I will write from Peking.

FREYA

JOHN GREY MURRAY
Peking
14 April 1961

Dearest Jock,

The most remote place I have ever been to: it makes one realise how much the Middle East is still our own Hellenistic world. I wonder where the division begins? Certainly *this* side of India. Here it is like a window opening on to something as rich and strange as the *Tempest* poem. The beauty is everywhere and brought by such individual unexpected touches: the blue of every tone of the people's clothes in their pale landscape, treading the water up on to their shallow terraces of rice in the south and moving along the narrow edges as if in a land of old mirrors whose visibility is dimmed but not destroyed by the yellow mud and the fragile green that shoots up now in innumerable furrows. The water buffaloes have ploughed them, their feet and the ploughman's and the plough itself submerged; and the buffalo head with flattened horns is, I feel sure, the original of the marble animals that push out from the temple steps and balustrades.

Michael came down to Hong Kong to fetch me – otherwise there were so many visa hitches I don't believe I should be here. He, and his First Secretary and the Dutch Ambassador all shared a compartment from Canton – two days and two nights. We woke up after a beautiful winding along the North River to a landscape this side far more like the Asia I knew – dry and cultivated in pale spring colours and with few trees. So beautiful when you drive to the plain's edge, and the walnuts and oaks and orchards begin where the Ming tombs stand in a great semicircle, each in a landscape and solitude of its own but in sight of one another. Each has a double roof of shining yellow tiles on green and yellow slabs, majolica clouds, and a marble stele, on the back of a marble tortoise, in an open vault below, with their names engraven 'their days their joys their all they have'. The most lovely are those half ruined and not yet repaired, with their altars darkened with lichens and the stone vessels overturned. And always some flat-topped pine to soften the outline and lovely roofs of temples and pagodas.

The people are nice. As soon as you smile they smile back, and even their poorest clothes, the girls' sloping jackets and double pigtails, the old men's black padded trousers tied in at the ankle over white socks and black shoes – they have a natural elegance as like the Parisian in an Oriental way as is their delicious food.

Love,

FREYA

JOHN GREY MURRAY

Peking
30 April 1961

Dearest Jock,

A letter has at last penetrated this remoteness – the first so far and sent by you on April 18th. A mailbag however is due, delayed by floods south of Nanking, so I hope to get the two letters you mention, though only on the day of my departure.

I spent a week in the South-East – Nanking, Hanchow and Shanghai – and got back two days ago in time for the May Day celebrations (with fireworks) tomorrow. Nanking was charming chiefly for its trees – miles of avenue of planes pruned with love and skill to meet (not yet but soon) in an open-work of carefully planned branches. The tomb of the first Ming Emperor, fourteenth century, is here in its park which is left natural, with rare trees round the tomb, all beautiful and pleasant; and the town itself still has its wall of stone cut small like brick, and moat full of water lilies below it.

The Japs sacked this city with unspeakable horrors – a man in Hong Kong was there at the time and told me appalling things he saw – but now it looks prosperous in an easy countryside with waterways. The landscape in all this region reminds one of a Canton plate with sheets of yellow mustard flowers and pink clover, the slow rivers winding – Yangtse at Nanking, Chankiang at Hanchow – with mountain rims behind them and many square-sailed boats or shallow sampans or clusters of logs floating down – all looking so absolutely *Chinese*.

Hanchow is the centre of the silk industry and is on three lakes linked by causeways lined with flowering fruit trees and small pavilions and strange goggle-eyed goldfish in bowls. I was lodged in the hotel for 'overseas' and became popular with the cook as I insisted on eating the delicious food (with chopsticks). It was all very friendly and comfortable; though each bedroom has another bedroom looking into it through opaque glass and opaque glass too on the corridor. They give you a tall thermos with very hot water everywhere and always, and make 'flower' tea, green tea, in a slapdash way at any moment with no chi-chi about boiling water.

I was happy to get back to Peking and this sheltered home (as I have been having another of these horrid near-bronchitis colds), and this morning went walking into a charming valley by the Ming tombs with Michael – where the mountains come down filled with blue and barren shadows to the plain. I have now seen all the places I could get leave to see. The Great Wall most stupendous. The direct route to Burma is not authorised, so next Wednesday I start back – two nights and days – to Canton for Hong Kong and then fly. The distances are very great: five degrees latitude south for my weekend in Nanking.

Love always,

FREYA

JOHN GREY MURRAY

B.O.A.C.

8 May 1961

Dearest Jock,

China is behind me: with a certain relief. Loaded with Sung Ming and Ching pottery and jade and a few little bits of the Ming tombs collected on the road, I stepped across the frontier posts and found a nice A.D.C. waiting under an umbrella with everything lush and green around me as if it were England (as this is the rainy season in Hong Kong). He gave me a cold lunch in an easy country house where the Governor stays with not a fence or sentinel about him – white paint, green lawns, chintzes and roses; and then raced down to catch the boat for Macao. I spent a night there and am glad to have seen the easy Mediterranean life of the Portuguese: their brightly colour-washed porticoes and the houses and the atmosphere which is neither Portugal nor China but a sort of easygoing marriage of the two. The fishing junks flock like soft brown butterflies with their dark brown sails in the Macao island fjords, and everything is leisurely about it.

Late last night I got back to Hong Kong, had a rushed morning designing John's cuff-links, lunch with the Governor – and now here in the Comet 35,000 feet above Vietnam. It has been a wonderful month, and I feel that something essential to a knowledge of the modern world has added itself to my store. But I never want to live for long behind an iron curtain. To have to speak low because of dictaphones, to be always conscious of the machine in which the human lives run down their grooves (quite smooth so long as it *is* the groove and not a little sidepath of one's own) – no benefit makes that worthwhile except perhaps the freedom from actual torture, which of course it has meant to a good many in China.

Love,
FREYA

JOHN GREY MURRAY · Delhi

20 May 1961

Dearest Jock,

I leave Delhi tonight for Teheran – very glad to have the tropics behind me and to have survived them with no disorder. Mandalay was hotter (damp too) than I can take for any length of time, and we had two days of eight hours in a jeep and a day in between of pagodas gone mad – a Salvador Dali landscape of pagodas of every size and shape, mostly that Burmese fancy which looks like the apotheosis of a turnip. Many other designs were there however, all built along the flat Irrawaddy shore by a dynasty of tenth to thirteenth century before the Chinese under Kubla Khan marched down and stopped it all. Some are whitewashed, some are gold with gold-leaf renewed every two years like the great Shwe Da-Gon in Rangoon; some are left to ruin and their stucco is peeling off the dark red brick. The temples climb in pyramids round their Buddhas with griffins barking at the edge of terraces but without the strange mountain feeling of Angkor and indeed without the imagination. But strange intrusions are there, like the Gothic arch – from where? – and the Baroque fancies of doors and windows. Two works I should like to see: a study of the Hellenistic fashions in Asia and a study of the Baroque there – with comparisons. I wonder if that has been done? Burma – the inland parts of Mandalay – gives a feeling of immobility: the wooden houses unchanged through the centuries, the 'lungi' or sarong the same surely as worn in the first pagoda days; enough to eat; a garland of flowers round the tight knot of hair at the back; the thin Burma tea which is given gratis everywhere in thin celadon bowls; the ox-carts with fine wheels of many spokes from large centres; the pretty little ponies and elegant bright closed carriages with coats of arms painted on the door; no one with money except some Chinese or Italian trader; but a feast every night, or two or three, with dancing girls and comedians (the dancing rather ugly I thought, jerking through angular poses, too clothed – in a long tight skirt – to make the energetic movement alluring). The students, my host told me, nearly all fail their exams, as the feasting by night and heat by day make study difficult. Those South-East Asian countries seem pretty precarious. The bandits in Burma have just killed twenty-two people officially (but a good many more really) in a hold-up of the Mandalay-Rangoon train. The general feeling is one of decay, as if roads, bridges, everything were slowly going downhill; and of course Laos, Vietnam, Korea, etc., all make a surrounding concert of troubles. The priest-ridden life of the land goes on, and everywhere the monks walk about in their marigold-yellow togas, their black begging bowls or a red sunshade in their hands: thousands of them – while the police are too few for the bandits.

Delhi is like coming home – I wandered over the Mogul palace, and the old minaret and its tombs, and Humayun's tomb built by his Persian widow, and felt back in my parish. Went up to the mosque, the court so hot that I was glad of a drugget laid down for bare feet. It was Thursday evening and the country had brought its goats to sell for the Friday meal – white goats with henna spots for rejoicing (not theirs of course but their *eaters*); and all the booths round the mosque carrying on their tiny trades. Tomorrow I hope to find letters in Teheran.

Love,
FREYA

MRS. T. DEUCHAR   Porto Ercole
                                                  31 May 1961
Dearest Dulcie,

It seems as if I had done a Rip Van Winkle tour and come back after ages, and I can't get over the feeling of surprise at finding the spring here still on its way. A little mountain of letters was waiting and yours among them.

Lucy and Celia[35] were in Rome to meet me and watched me trying to carry twelve lbs. of Ming tomb fragments and jade with a *degagé* air through the customs in my handbag. We then drove here through the high lush meadows and it felt very good to find Europe where it was. I find I just want to sleep and sleep: the last week in Burma rather knocked me out with the heat.

The pink dress has been *wonderful*. It seems right for every occasion and a setting for all my wild oats in Hong Kong in the way of pearls and sable stoles. I wear it for Embassies, dinners, and in the aeroplane where the air is cooled and it does instead of a light wool. The only impossibility was in the heat of Burma which is unimaginable until one experiences it.

Dearest love, darling Dulcie. I have a little jade nonsense for you.

Your

FREYA

AUSTEN HARRISON[36]

Dolomites
15 August 1961

My dear Austen,

I am now up about 3,000 feet under a very flamelike Dolomite peak, with a godson and brother, both supposed to be reading hard for the university; a very pleasant sort of company, though I get worn now and then with strenuous argument. The place is near Bolzano and talks pure German and looks it.

In a month, I leave Asolo for Smyrna with more godchildren. If, later, I get no permits, you may see me on your doorstep; but my plan is to go from Diyarbakir back by Beirut and Egypt and that cuts Greece out this year. But next, I hope certainly to land off that little ferry. I think you have done so well to find a place filled with cicada noises and few roads. Italy is getting too crowded. All the same, do look in on Asolo if you come west. I hope to be writing there from end of December.

Love,

FREYA

35 sc. Fleming (the actress Celia Johnson), who was staying with the Mooreheads at Porto Ercole.

36 An architect friend, now living near Athens. F.S. was writing from Siusi in the Dolomites, where she had gone with her godson Skimper Hore-Ruthven and his brother, Lord Gowrie.

Siusi
15 August 1961

Dearest Jock,

The reading party is going along nice and quiet and harmonious. Brought face to face with nineteen and twenty-one years, one is staggered to realise what an immense number of things one had to make up one's own mind about: how did we do it? Skimper is a very nice godson and, slowly gathering his tools, will be a good life-builder; Grey may take *any* turn. It will so much depend on whom he follows, and he follows only by opposing if you know what I mean. What distresses me is how this generation has to get along with no steady belief to help it. I have been reading *Le Milieu Divin* by Chardin and leaving it around in their hands hoping that one of its many sparks may light a candle. Have you got it? It is I think the most helpful book I have found since meeting Socrates in my youth. I am enjoying the revival of things long forgotten, talks about *Beowulf* and Middle English Sagas, and Pope and Dryden: not so much the New World – Graham Greenes and Joyces and a welter of present poets mostly it seems to me extremely fourth-rate.

I am walking and can (just) do four hours but something is still wrong and I can't quite think what. Hope it is not the poor old brain which Polizzi says needs a rest. So I am doing no work at all though I would dearly love to write my first chapter of 'Rome on the Euphrates'. (Do you like the title?)

We had a snowfall and next day took the little car for a tour of passes – up Val Gardena between Sella and Sassolungo like huge white bastions; down to Canassi with Marmolada glacier on our left; by Karersee under Latemar and the Vaiolet towers (both once climbed *so* long ago!) – and back down very green and narrow valleys. This is lovely country though too smothered in conifers.

Love,
FREYA

S.S. *Izmir*[37]
18 September 1961

Dearest Jock,

The *Lion's Paw* arrived just as I was leaving and Simon is now on deck beside me reading it. It was good of you to get it to me just in time. It looks very well and the jacket colour very good. It is tantalising to wait till I reach Istanbul to know what the reviews say.

[37] The party consisted of F.S., Simon and Mark Lennox-Boyd, Henry Berens, Ann Blaber, Caroline Moorehead.

We ended Asolo with two good days in Venice; I drove down with John Sparrow who arrived in Asolo to find me surrounded by about a dozen undergraduates and graduettes (if such a word is permissible) and was the life and soul of the party. Henry and Ann Blaber had arrived in the minibus, which is a traveller's dream, white and red, with fans inside to cool it, and a torch like a searchlight to throw its beams in any direction. A day at Torcello, and a bit of shopping for food chiefly, and here we are very comfortable third class with chairs and deck which no Italian boat gives for its thirds, clean cabin and quite good food. The sea getting bluer and bluer. We should get news tomorrow of what has happened in Turkey: no one on board very communicative.

Love – from Athens when this will be posted tomorrow,

FREYA

JOHN GREY MURRAY   Side,
                                                            Pamphylia
                                                        1 October 1961
Dearest Jock,

I found your good letter in Antalya, very consoling for I behaved badly and got acute sciatica after a damp camp – one of the few things I haven't had so had nothing to do but bear it till in five days we reached Antalya. There a doctor has been dosing me with what I rather think are very drastic drugs and it is much better. This anyway is our last camp (and late in the year for it), so beautiful with the whole arc of Taurus around us and the thin wind tumbling about with small waves in the night. The shallow sea where Cleopatra's ships rode lies like pools of rosy milk in sunrise or set; and the limestone ruins seem as if the milk had frothed and foamed and set into its vague obliterated shapes of stone. We saw Priene, Miletus and Didyma, then by the coast to my little hidden village (now *well* hidden by badness of road); then down to Xanthus and over a possible Alexander route – honeycombs of graves in the rocks of the pass, the way cut by landslide, wanderings in night, ending at Al Mali where my old driver Ahmed and Ali gave a touching welcome; and so Antalya, where they left me for a day and saw Termessos, and on here by Aspendos. Today Alanya and up by Anamur and Mut to Karaman. Then Konia to Istanbul where I shall stay at least till 20th and hope for news. Longing to hear how the *Lion* goes.

Love,

FREYA

17 October 1961

Dearest Jock,

The day after tomorrow I leave for Ankara and two days later for Diyarbakir – rather doubtfully, for my sciatica seizes me at inconvenient moments and makes me almost faint away with pain. I have been to the hospital and it seems a small fibroma has settled on the nerve and the advice is to 'leave it alone'; but the real trouble is the back and the disc, and for that there is no remedy but a stiff backbone and patience. How lucky it is to be able to get about still, however maimed. Sitting in a car and jolting don't seem to matter.

I pottered about mosques in pouring rain to look at the election which went with a quiet and touching dignity, little groups of volunteers spending their wet cold day round the urns under the mosque arcades with the plane trees dripping on to the cobbles all about them. The result is filling everyone I see with dismay as it is 50/50 and means a coalition between the people who have been executing each other: one can hardly imagine a more uncomfortable combination. It confirms what I felt so very strongly in the 1954 election, that the Turks do think their choice out for themselves and come to their own conclusions. It would be a tragedy if such *good* material for a self-ruling people were to be suppressed under military rule or such. My own reading is that with one thing and another the vast Anatolian peasant stretches have been awakening to their power and unless the young intelligentsia gets out a bit and comes to know its Anatolia and be known, it will find that the rule of Istanbul is superseded. Menders was a farmer himself, and this vote is a tribute to his understanding of the peasant.

Meanwhile, apart from one little stroll in the bazaar, I have been sitting relaxing in this nice hotel, reading the Eastern Wars of Nero. Friends from the Long Range Desert Group of the Eighth Army are oil drilling in Eastern Turkey and have offered to lodge me in their camp and provide a jeep, so I shall visit those battlefields in comfort I hope and try and get a notion on the controversial site of Tigranocerta. Perhaps next year Simon and Mark and Henry may like to do the Euphrates. They are really good travellers now and one could go anywhere with them: in fact it will be *they* taking *me* at any moment. Such a dear letter from Simon, and one I enclose from Caroline (can you send back to Asolo?). It is such pleasure to me to think that it has meant something, and that they will remember it long after I have left the light of this pleasant world, and will go on, settling on their camps and talking to the people on the lines whose foundations were laid so long ago by

W.P.[38] and my father when I was young. It seems almost too comforting to be true that Simon talks of a *fourth* year together at his age of twenty-two. It is so charming to see them year after year, turning from boyhood to manhood.

I have had two very pleasant letters about the book from Tom Boase and Gerald de Gaury, both liking it. Let me have news of it, and of you, in Beirut on November 10th.

P.S. I find I can, very slowly, plough my way through a Turkish translation of the *Iliad*. Not however a very useful language for every day except possibly in times of massacre.

Love,

FREYA

JOHN GREY MURRAY Near Diyarbakir

22 October 1961

Dearest Jock,

Such agreeable things fall out of the blue. I lunched in Teheran with Peter Stirling who told me to tell his brother Bill about my coming here as he is interested in an oil drilling company. He recommended me to their care and a Mr. Wigginston met me in Diyarbakir this morning and brought me out here, along a desert road plastered with crude black oil for asphalt, to their camp on a high place in the middle of air and emptiness – a breadth and peace that seemed to feed one's soul. (Most of them don't feel it that way.) They have a dozen or so exquisitely sophisticated caravans and have given me one of them and are keeping me for a week to look at the battlefields of Lucullus. Electric light, frigidaire, bath, lots of cupboards, everything one can want is in the caravan – perhaps one day, when too clogged with possessions, I shall give up Asolo and *live* in one! The windows are netted and open so that one can always get a breeze and look out to sunset at night and sunrise in the morning. The wide Assyrian downs are all around below, clothed now in pale stubble and the bright poison-green of the fan-shaped euphorbias that spring up in the dark patches of the ploughed land. How I love this deserty spaciousness and the thin dry fineness of the air. Even the pain that has been pursuing me so tiresomely seems to be going. It took me twenty-nine hours to come by train from Ankara – very leisurely and pleasant,

[38] W. P. Ker, F.S.'s early mentor.

and I was able to realise and I hope photograph the great bend of the Halys river inside which we travelled all yesterday, and woke this a.m. in time for the Euphrates (the sudden vividness it brings to its landscapes, and wild strength) and was really able to disentangle a lot of the strategy of Lucullus' day and Nero's by looking carefully out of the window. There is a strategic height between three rivers – Euphrates, Tigris and Murat – which a Roman should have held and didn't, and the railway crawls up and round it with ample time to size it up.

25 October 1961

It is most fortunate that the rig which actually drills is out of work till mid-November so that a Land Rover and a charming elderly mechanic engineer from Texas have given me two long days – first to look at two passes northward (where Xenophon, incidentally, went up). There is a bit of a wall across one of these gaps – possibly Urartian, made of great blocks; and beyond is a natural tunnel which for centuries was thought to be the source of Tigris and has inscriptions (we looked for in vain) of Assyrian kings. But the landscape was very great and has made one or two campaigns much clearer to me than they were.

Yesterday we went south and found the Tigris running by a wall of cliffs sliced smooth as if they were butter – and there, with hundreds of rock-scooped houses, is a town now half deserted and ruined but once the great bridge and crossing of the stream. They are building a new bridge of three great cement arches so that it may once more revive – but is now a sort of cave-dwellers' version of Les Baux. There is here so often this fierce mixture of beauty and hideousness which makes one have to be strong to take the East: this nakedness and poverty and beauty in spite of all. An ex-cook of the camp here appeared in the ruinous street and insisted on inviting us to food – stew, grapes and watermelon – and made it a thirteen-hour day, so that I am resting today. It makes a great difference to come back to the comfort of a caravan, heating, bath, light, Dunlopillo bed – all turned on by a switch or two, windows netted for flies, easy to open – and light woods pretty and shiny, so that everything is here except the 'patina' of life. Breakfast 6.30; lunch 11.30; supper 5.30 – and the eleven inmates (with two wives and four children) are pleasant and simple and easy and read awful novels and go shooting partridges or pigeons on Sundays. The villagers make holes under their roofs for the pigeons' nests and they go about the stubble in wide droves, turning with wings *blue* when the sun catches them, so that it looks as if a shred of the blue distance had come near.

The 'rig' has been so very kind to me and have I think enjoyed a whiff of

Antiquity amid the oil. They take me to Urfa tomorrow, where Austerity begins (and oh dear, I have a tummy starting too!).

Love,

FREYA

JOHN GREY MURRAY Mersin

8 November 1961

Dearest Jock,

The adventure is over and tomorrow I should be in Beirut relaxing with nothing more than a bad cold and a few spasms of sciatica to pay for the last three weeks. The oil drillers at first and the Bank Managers from point to point of the Roman road this end helped me along with no permit and a *few* anxious moments, and I was able to do all I wanted except the scaling of a most remarkable and unexpected castle on a bend of the Euphrates (it was pouring with rain and the *kaimakan* who two days later was inspecting the bridge was washed off – no doubt in his city shoes – and rescued by his soldiers). I was prudent and also renounced the walls of Antioch, but climbed to a medium height and scanned them through my glasses. I went down to the old Hellenistic harbour, filled with water-flags and marsh and held in the decay of crumbled quays, and I have now followed the Roman way in the South from the sea to the Tigris, and should need only one more journey to where under Ararat Euphrates is born. I am glad to think of this, for I don't think I can do this travel much longer: the fact of being always in and out of some physical disaster, and the *moral* strain of nine, ten, twelve and thirteen hours either jolting in a jeep or talking – Turkish often – to strangers is much more than it used to be, so many years ago. Thirty-four years ago I was tossing off Mersin shore too rough to land: now there is a harbour, and a huge grain elevator (but no grain for export) and a white ship very spick and span, with apparently no passengers but myself inside it.

How kind the people have all been: kindness seems to blossom under one's feet as one moves around and the people who begin formally part with presents and kisses (their wives'!). In Mersin there was no hotel at all and they took me to their house to a bed with a pale yellow satin quilt and two endearing children, and drove me beyond Tarsus to where the Cydnus flows above a barrage of silver water, a slow green tree-lined stream deep enough for Cleopatra's barge.

I came away sad however, for there is a dreadful feeling of failure all about. Everything they do seems just not good enough, and the old world is

38

not entire in its aloofness and the new one too clogged to proceed. There is discouragement, and no visible prospect of a government that can function. And the very fact of this lavish kindness and hospitality is I suppose financially ruinous: the Turk is just *too nice* for the modern world. They took me to a French film last night so strident in its depravity in contrast to this decent conventional people that I could hardly bear to sit it out.

Love,
FREYA

JOHN GREY MURRAY

British Embassy,
Beirut
22 November 1961

Dearest Jock,

Your note with the B.B.C. talk came yesterday and the last before that was October 17th sent on from Diyarbakir. On the face of it, you are rather a poor correspondent, but it is possible that Turkey is scattered with letters and I dare not complain of anyone. I was very pleased with the *Lit. Sup.* in spite of its slightly Zionist slant. Unreasonable I thought to expect me to give the Zionist thesis when all I wanted to prove was that our policy was ruining us with the *Arabs*. However good the Zion cause, it would not alter this fact. There seems to be a great reluctance in the human mind to keep straight; and when you come to think of it, there *is* no straight line in Nature.

Stewart is by way of coming over from Cyprus, so the great meeting may occur.[39] My whole effort, like that of Canute, is to keep it so far and no farther: luckily Stewart is not exactly tidal. I am rested too, being cherished kindly by the Larssons[40] and unwinding. Two days ago I went to Sidon: old castle at the end of a harbour causeway, built of yellow stone larded with ancient columns like the bits of truffle in pâté, a huge marble pillar laid flat at a threshold, and the old town in bits of wall remaining, with its narrow markets under Gothic archways, almost unchanged, and piled with the fruits of Lebanon, the best in the Levant. The people are largely Shi'a and supposed to be very fanatic, with portraits of Nasser all over the place, but friendly enough. As for Beirut, it grows and grows. An American architect has built a huge hotel with balustrades of white open-work like lace and there is a shopping centre where you can get lost in neon-lighted streets and escalators and forget the existence of sky. It is all done on borrowed money they say and

[39] Stewart Perowne's plans were altered, so the meeting did not take place.
[40] The former Barclay Sanders and her husband, Theo, who now lived in Beirut.

seems perched on *Nothing*, no attachment to the landscape or geography except perhaps a whiff of the Banking Houses of Tyre and Sidon long ago and plenty no doubt of Sodom and Gomorrah.

I am so glad of the good progress of the *Lion's Paw*. You must feel it is as your own child after all the hard work you put into it and I feel its success is really due to you dear Jock – all that cutting and pruning. I now think of the Romans and read the *Odes* of Horace – what pleasure, that exquisite technique! – and am rather disappointed having taken lots of trouble to look at *both* the sites of Tigranocerta, to find that a book is just coming out to prove, conclusively, a third one I haven't seen. It is extraordinary in Horace that almost every ode has some reference to the Levant.

Love,

FREYA

Cairo

11 December 1961

JOHN GREY MURRAY

Dearest Jock,

It is so nostalgic to find oneself here again. The lawns are as green as ever though now cut off by a boulevard from the river, the old butler still here though no longer gowned in scarlet and gold, and the town as I drove in looking a bit more dingy and subdued though with flecks of newness.

I had six splendid days in Jordan – driven straight on arrival by Derek[41] to the Wadi Ram where the Lawrence film spent the summer: a fantastic world of rock and sand that takes its colours from the day – and evening round the coffee-fire under vast cliffs with the police and their scarlet sheep-lined coats and red and white *kefiahs*, sitting by a Beau Geste tower in the gap of Akaba and the waterless silence. It rained in the night, but not too much to hold us marooned, and the next day we had a ceremony in the sub-tropic warmth of Jericho – Musa Alami showing his training farm to the King. I was brought up to meet him, and was touched to recognise the gentle royal manner of the Hashemite. I told him I had known his grandfather and was told to come again and stay longer. I went again to Jericho and saw its oldest foundations – a little mound that held 4,000 people and has the earliest planned fortifications known, and an early Muslim palace nearby, with the Graeco-Roman ease come slightly barbarised down into it. We had another expedition to Kerak – the most splendid castle on the ruinous hills that rush steeply down to a triangle of the Dead Sea some thousands of feet below.

41 sc. Cooper.

'Too much past and too little future,' someone said to me about these lands; and it is a bit the feel of the Middle East just now.

I was glad to find your note and the good *New Statesman* review – and have two letters of yours to thank for from Beirut: such *riches*! Love and thanks dear Jock,

FREYA

JOHN GREY MURRAY
Porto Ercole
26 December 1961

Dearest Jock,

Christmas day over again: this slipping away of everything into the Past! It was very pleasant, pouring wet outside and fire and candles in; and lovely books with your Osbert – I *am* enjoying it. Thank you ever so much. How good the old jokes are: they seem to mature like wine.

Did I tell you that I was interviewed in Cairo and given a splendid write-up as the author of 'the most dangerous of the British Intelligence services during the War', 'the woman who made thrones totter and altered boundaries' etc. . . . and now 'an old lady of seventy' (a tiny bit premature) 'has come silently to Cairo.'?

Dulcie and Tommy are here in good form; Alan plotting book on Sahara; Rosie[42] with two daughters and a Russian; the Moorehead family coming to Asolo in two weeks' time. The Turkish squirrel[43] I long to keep as a pet, but it and Caroline have become attached to each other and can't be parted. Perhaps as well, as he does eat all the furniture and nibbles the electric wires; but you never saw anything so pretty.

Did I tell you how beautiful Greece looked? One vast mountain counterpane of snow as I flew over.

I think of you all at Cannon Lodge with love and wishes.

FREYA

JOHN GREY MURRAY
Asolo
30 January 1962

Dearest Jock,

How can I spend my birthday eve better than by neglecting my work and writing to you? So pleased I was to get two letters and hear your news –

[42] sc. Rodd.
[43] A baby squirrel saved in the mountains near Antalya in September.

41

though it must be a very worrying life just now to be a publisher and watch all our standards of literature (it seems to me) going downhill at a terrific speed – or is this the natural reaction of sixty-nine? I am hoping for you that John junior's entry into the firm will not be too long delayed: one does need to have someone with the sense of *continuity*. I wrote to him a day or two ago by the way suggesting he might like to come out for his vac to work. If Mark comes it will be a very 'dedicated' household, with perhaps a day off in the week but no more; and if it were possible I would gladly pay a godson's air ticket here and back – for what else are godmothers for? Especially as you tell me the *Lion's Paw* is doing well.

I am in the first chapter for better or worse. I hope to make the picture come humanly alive, but I myself shall be out of it, as it is essential for the history itself to speak. The plan so far is a series of separate chapters: the Battle of Magnesia (entry of Rome in Asia); the Wars of Mithridates (Lucullus and Pompey); the policy of Nero (fascinating on Euphrates and Armenia); Trajan's dream; Diocletian and the system of the border, etc., etc.; down to the entry of the Arabs. The chapters are not continuous in time, but the theme of the frontier is continuous. As the book is meant to deal with only one point – the preferability of a peaceful to a warlike frontier – I think it should not be a long book. It means a lot of reading. I have just dropped a line to John Sparrow to ask him if he can find out how I may get by without reading the *whole* of Seneca and Cicero and to tell me which bits are necessary.

The Kuwait album looks very well and I am going today to start the work of Iraq. It strikes me that a series of picture books might be done on the Middle East as I knew it, with quotations – a sort of illustrated anthology? A nice little event was Malcolm MacDonald's[44] arrival with a Government Chauffeuress, a wonderfully unkempt but endearing private secretary, and a little Indian girl called Tuki, for two nights, and a day in Venice. They were lucky in icy but brilliant sun and it was very enjoyable. What an agreeable person he is, with the zest of a boy and a very gay Bangkok tie, orange, yellow and vermilion crossed with black.

Much love, dear Jock.

FREYA

[44] An old friend. A former Cabinet Minister, High Commissioner in Canada in the war (when F.S. had stayed with him), and High Commissioner in India 1955–60.

Asolo
                                                      8 February 1962

Dearest Christopher,

I was so glad to get your letter, and now the photographer sends me this
rather jaunty production, you and I looking like two old cronies that successfully let the world go by – and so we are. The sun seems to catch my bosom
in rather a *protuberant* way; it surely isn't as extrovert as that? What is
perfectly obvious is that all the party has enjoyed a very good lunch, and so
I remember it.

I have started chapter I of the Romans, the miserable tearing up of the
Middle East by those brutal fascists. I must try and find a few nice ones to
keep me going, Pliny so boring, Cicero insufferable, Julian, I discover on
reading his letters, an appalling prig. Even Catullus jeers at a man *for being
poor*! What a relief to turn to Polybius who was Greek. I would have liked to
marry him. What a *decent* person. By the time you come next year the ms.
should be ready to be read.

                              Yours always affectionately,
                                                      FREYA

Asolo
                                                     18 February 1962

Dearest Jock,

I love to have you as my Valentine. The only man I saw on 14 February
was my dentist, and I believe he is a Communist. I drove to him, near Venice,
in my Topolino and was fined 5,000 lire for breaking too quickly into a
highway. I find my driving far more expensive than hiring, and now take a
chauffeur to sit beside me and give advice as it really is very dangerous in
Italy – and the chauffeur said I was 'a little absent-minded'.

I was so pleased to get a good proper letter from you, and very pleased that
John is coming. It looks like a reading party: Mark for a fortnight over his
Arabic; Simon a week (inadequate) with finals ahead; Skimper three weeks
with English literature; John I hope for as long as he can manage.

Chapter I is done and I now read for chapter II. The skeleton is fairly
clear: about ten chapters not continuous but each taking a bit of frontier
history when it becomes interesting. All with an introduction and close to
explain the thesis. I think it is a good subject, but the problem is whether to

[45] A wartime Middle Eastern colleague, now living in the Lebanon. F.S. had visited
him the previous November.

bring in any personal travel at all. It needs great skill to do so in such a subject. Anyway I will try, in chapter II, and send them both to you to see.

The U.S.A. by the way seem to me to have been fairly kind 'more in sorrow than in anger' over the *Lion's Paw*. I am so glad it is going well, and £1,200 will be extremely helpful; especially as there is to be a long interval before the Romans are ready.

Love dear Jock,

FREYA

MRS. T. DEUCHAR   Asolo
                                                              22 February 1962
Darling Dulcie,

This is the photograph you asked for, extracted from Henry, and Orvieto and Tuscania, a lovely memory. And here, too, are thousand thanks for the Classical dictionary. I spent a happy evening over it last night, and was pleased to find that I have been to practically every temple and theatre in the book. My Graeco-Roman world is becoming very *intimate*. Thank you, darling Dulcie. I am so grateful and so anxious to hear of you *well*.

Two little Turkish ladies have descended on me, mother and daughter, the latter a pretty little thing like one of those Turkish fifteenth-century miniatures. Has just left her husband because she wants to be more intellectual, and of course the tragedy is that she never will be but would be a sweet mother with little Turks toddling round her. Her own poor mama in tears and saying she feels it so because she left her husband, but only after twenty-seven years. I am distressed because the husband is so nice, and so devoted to the little thing (who is very spoilt but endearing). Anyway, it is dreadfully distracting in the middle of chapter II, which I find desperately difficult anyway.

Your devoted

FREYA

JOHN GREY MURRAY   Asolo
                                                                22 March 1962
Dearest Jock,

Your nice long letter has just come and I am so tired of those Romans. You will however be full of admiration (I hope) when you hear that I have got to chapter IV and Mithridates, poor man, endearing but not a family man,

44

is liquidated. How beastly the Romans were! I will send what there is back by John or else bring it – though it is still probably in need of vast labours.

I feel sorry for the amount of your comings and goings: you will soon be like me, reaching a time when some refuge is necessary and a bit of quiet.

I sometimes wonder if I ought not to go and settle in some austere little vineyard of Tuscany or Greece; but then those godsons might not like it, and their coming gives me so much pleasure. At the moment I have Teresa and her Bron[46] and they are a dear couple: he couldn't be more unlike his book. I am trying to persuade him that the fashion for de-bunking is *past*!

Love dear Jock,

FREYA

MRS. DEREK COOPER   Florence
                                                17 April 1962

Darling Pam,

I have to get away from my book to write a letter, and here I am for my one and only committee meeting, and expecting John Murray and Skimper to come for me, and for their first glimpse of Florence, in the Topolino sometime today. Tom Boase too turned up, so we we hope to foregather this evening. I had suggested their coming a day earlier, but am pleased to suppose that Asolo and Work held them! I believe they have both got through a good deal, though I still feel that English literature isn't Skimper's real line of country and wish he had taken history or Arabic. How difficult life is when all the most important things have to be decided before one knows anything about them. The thing about literature, of any country, is that it is not a thing one *learns*. It is a sort of climate that one breathes – one does it through ecstasy and excitement and the learning is a consequence; whereas history and most other things can and in fact should be approached from the factual outside. I should not be at all surprised if Skimper discovers this and switches – but have been careful not to suggest anything of the sort. Cambridge seems to me to produce awfully little communication between Dons and Disciples. When I think of what I owe to the few first-rate minds I met, like torches through a darkness; and darling Skimp says he can get it all from books – just as if one could use the dynamite without a match! He will get along, because he is so truly conscientious and will puzzle it all out, but I would have been happy to see him more truly in the saddle in a subject that suited him – like music for instance. He has been working away at my out-of-tune piano. He and John seem very happy together, and to me, you know I am sure, it is

46 Teresa Onslow had married Auberon Waugh in July 1961.

45

true joy to have them. I hope I make them as happy as they make me. They are both such dears, and very touching to come and spend their vac with a plain old woman.

I have written to Zara[47] asking her to enquire if June 23rd would be a possible weekend for Cliveden. It seems to be my only one, as I then go North, and no time when I return except to get to Asolo and back for Turkey. I mean to try and get along the Euphrates to Erzurum; one can anyway get to Malatya and along the left bank and then, if I can get a permit, I will turn towards Kayseri and the Black Sea mountains. But I hope for Erzurum and perhaps a dash to Isfahan for the sake of Mark, who says he is certainly, and Simon, who may be, coming. They are really good travellers now. I wish Derek could come. (Skimper can't as he has a job.) How is Grey getting on? I keep my fingers crossed and would like to hear what the prospects are?
  Love darling Pam.

FREYA

JOHN GREY MURRAY

Asolo
29 April 1962

Dearest Jock,

  I was glad to get your letter, cheerful and warming as the sun. Now I must tell you a rather sumptuous bit of news. I have sold my fourteen Prendergast sketches for £5,000! This relieves me of a sort of angst to which I am unreasonably liable (early poverty no doubt), feeling that if the day came when no one wants my books or I can't write, I should be unable to live here (and it is getting very expensive). I have told Mr. Punchard[48] that I mean to spend them slowly over the next twelve years, and by then I will be eighty-two and Allah will provide. It is a great relief to feel this little margin – and I shall travel to England first class and buy *three* hats in Paris.

Love,
FREYA

AUSTEN HARRISON

Dartmoor
30 July 1962

My dear Austen,

  I wonder if you are in England? I ought to have written before, because I have been here for quite a long time, but had only five days in London and all

[47] Lady Gowrie, previously Pam Cooper's mother-in-law.
[48] Alan Punchard, F.S.'s accountant and adviser.

the rest of the time scattered about from Sussex to Oxford, up to the island of Eigg in the Hebrides, and out to Dartmoor in the West – so there seemed little chance of our meeting. It was nine years since I had an English summer, and I had a fortnight of perfect weather before the usual drip 'with bright intervals' began, and there can be nothing more beautiful than a fine summer's day here when the roses are out in all the little gardens. I write from Dartmoor; the rain streaking down in a familiar way, but I have had two lovely evenings to see the views of my childhood and they are still unchanged and beautiful – not unlike the desert outlines in their empty brown gentleness.

Affectionately,
FREYA

JOHN GREY MURRAY

Abey,
near Beirut
26 August 1962

Dearest Jock,

I am up on the slopes of pine and limestone with Beirut below twinkling dusky in its summer haze. Here is the clear air and pure sky and one of the great terrace balconies that make the beauty of the old fashion of the Lebanon. A stone trough to be filled with earth and flowers and a marble seat inside runs all along – and the stone is the limestone yellow of the hillside which the masons can still cut as if it were butter. Moore[49] has saved this old house and made it a summer house for the Ambassador. He must have used great art with the Office of Works: one can't but feel it a much more secure memorial than most Ambassadors can leave. We had twenty-four notables – two from each of the village families – to coffee with messages of welcome; and then walked up the hillside which is just as wrinkled as some of their faces, and recognised all those delicious smells that push their twigs of thyme and rosemary out of the stones.

Mark is at Brumana (which is now a garish summer resort though still with the most splendid of the Lebanon views); and Skimper should come from Jordan tomorrow. We leave at six on Tuesday in the little train for Aleppo. We hope to be allowed the west bank of Euphrates in spite of Kurds, and I hope to find news of you in Malatya. After that there will be nothing before the Park Hotel, Taksim, Istanbul on 2 October.

Love,
FREYA

[49] sc. Crosthwaite, Ambassador to the Lebanon 1958–63.

Dearest Jock,

We have got so far – the ancient Doliche on the Roman road – with the usual drama. We got in by a little diesel train under the eyes of the police, running down into the plain of Homs, with a noticeable commotion of nuns, monks and orphans on the opposite-going train, and a lot of lorries empty of human beings in the sun. When we got to Aleppo we found that the border was closed for exit as a friend of Nasser's had just handed in a list of Syrian suspects whom they hoped to catch. Luckily I still found a friend in the old Baron Hotel and we spent an Oriental morning of coffee with the governor and tea with the police, and by the afternoon were wafted across to Antioch. So good to feel that most romantic landscape familiar in the gold of evening. An easy day next day, in a taxi on the reverse side of the hills of Issus, after seeing St. Peter's church. It is just a scoop out of the cliff of Antioch, with a poor modern statue and altar, but was truly one of the earliest if not the first church as likely as not, and gentle there with a whitewashed carved façade behind two olive trees. They are planting the steep slope of the Antioch cliff with rows of forestry not yet grown, and a factory is being built just below; but it is still a minaretted small town with bits of walls and towers, and it slides into a wonderful plain of various green. Here it is all red earth, bright vines, and square houses twinkling with windows over low rounded hills, an old Seljuk citadel mound with towers in its midst. It was the military holiday yesterday, so nothing doing but military processions and flags and circlets of light round the minarets.

We hope to reach the Euphrates castle tomorrow, to see another bit of its banks the day after, and then make for the great monuments on Nimrud Dagh. Mark is being a treasure as ever and learning his Turkish fast; Skimper learning, not quite so fast; all of us pleased with our programme so far. You can't think how lovely the sunset light on all the pencil minarets, glowing against the glowing hills from which their stone is cut, the selfsame colour. We have a roof terrace, with a scent of incense coming up unexplained from below and a splashing fountain whose tap one can turn to make a noise.

The idea is to reach Malatya by the most devious way possible, to be there anyway on 8 September.

2 September 1962

A splendid first view of Euphrates yesterday for those two boys. We crossed by Birecik and followed my last year route to Halfete down under the crumbled cliffs where the river lay small and peaceful like a python in the sun between the strips of trees. We had tea in the fisherman's garden, his nets hanging on apricot trees; and then up, seated on chairs in more of a box than a boat, the old man with a pole and two others pulling a rope barefoot along the shore. About one and a half hours to the castle, its walls Hellenistic, Roman, Byzantine, Crusader, early Muslim, its core far older with steps cut in the stone and the living cliff pared away in corrugations till it and the walls are vertical high above the green gardens and stream. A circular stair was cut by these early people in the rock for supplies and water in times of siege; a Byzantine church, and square Greek buildings still easy to see; and there is much no doubt underground. It was so hot we all wilted, and came down to fruit – white pomegranates under a tree, and then down again on the heat of the river. The day 4.30 a.m. to 8 p.m.

All love dear Jock,

FREYA

JOHN GREY MURRAY
Malatya
16 September 1962

Dearest Jock,

We got here safely on the 11th – only just safely, for the crossing of the Taurus coincided with a wind storm such as none of us had ever met before. It was an uninviting ridge anyway to cross, solidified hills of earth too high and waterless for trees (2,340 metres) and going on in a heartbreaking way for three hours up and down and three hours along the top; with the path not more and often less than eighteen inches, looking down into the deep and dusty valleys, and the wind hitting whenever we drew near the top. I couldn't possibly face it on foot, and three or four times nearly went over mule and all. The muleteers crouched along in the shelter of their animals – with some very alarming slips. The boys very good. Impossible to talk; *cold* such as we had forgotten. Once or twice I thought I could not make it. The men asked for rest, but we luckily refused and at last the ridge lowered and very slowly the climate became human again. We reached Malatya after five days' ride following the Euphrates windings – very grim and very majestic too. Wonderfully remote. Have got across to the forbidden side yesterday to see the site of Corbulo's battles, but otherwise we have had enough of the wilderness anyway and are ending up in a touristy way at the Byzantine chapels of Goreme.

Have a horrid chest, but still quite glad to cross Taurus in my seventieth year in a storm (and the young just as dilapidated by it as I am).

Love,
FREYA

49

S.S. *Ege*
20 October 1962

Dearest Jock,

It doesn't seem credible but I should be home tomorrow evening. Two months is about as long as I can bear to be away now and quite as long as one can go on living in the luggage suitable for one mule-load. The second half of this summer wandering was very different from the first – equally pleasant, but not so up and down. The only new site for me was Assos – a small Greek citadel where no memorable event was ever recorded, but all its enchantment still intact. In a very few years tourists will swarm: a chain of hotels nearly complete – Troy, Pergamum, Ephesus – just like boxes and one feels decanted from one to the other, but they are clean. The roads will link them and it will be like Greece. The poor people like us who like their landscape plain will be pushed farther and farther East. But we had Troy completely and Pergamum almost to ourselves in spite of the hotels, and it was wonderful to take anyone as sensitive as Dulcie about:[50] it was like opening door after door, ending with Priene and Didyma – the most impressive of all.

Ephesus is emerging fully armed like Athena from the head of Zeus: it is staggering to see a Graeco-Roman city practically *new*, the stone not rounded and weathered grey but bright yellow with sharp edges, every detail of Hadrian's temple clear cut as when it was built. The reason is that the whole city lay in a valley narrow enough for the hillside earth on both sides to drift down and cover it; every bulldozer load of earth has a column or two inside it!

Asolo
22 October 1962

Got here 1 a.m. this morning as the boat had an Oriental leisure in all its doings – but very amusing with all the Levant and a charming little Arab bride on board, born in a tent and brothers educated at St. John's, Cambridge.

Love,

FREYA

Asolo
10 November 1962

Dearest Sybil,

I am galloping through the books I must read for this Roman history at a very unclassical pace. At the moment it is Pliny and his Natural History:

[50] F.S. had joined Rosie Rodd and the Deuchars in Istanbul

it gives one, far better than any text book, the picture of the world that an educated Roman looked out on – full of surprising things that later came to be forgotten, like the roundness of the globe, and then with sudden gaps, such as the ignorance of the law of gravity, and the consequently puzzling problem given by the want of flatness of the sea. It is fascinating to find oneself getting gradually acclimatised to a new landscape – a world very brutal in its shadows. I invested your present almost entirely in little red Loeb classics, and think of you when I take them one after the other down from that shelf. They are a great boon.

I would like you so much to see my room: it has windows on all four sides, and a very tall persimmon tree is just below me in the south, with the plain of Padua and the Euganean hills beyond. Even now the warm rich Venetian colour comes through as their painters saw it. They have just closed a collection of Cima da Conegliano in Treviso, gathered from everywhere, and he appears a charming, easy, *livable* painter with enchanting backgrounds of all the country that I know.

Will you be at Houghton for Christmas, all gathered together? I love to think of the summer days and my last English weekend there. There will be no England for me for another year I fear.

Very much love, dearest Sybil, to both of you.

FREYA

JOHN GREY MURRAY   Porto Ercole
                                                      23 December 1962

Dearest Jock,

So very good to find telegrams, wishes and the most welcome book[51] all waiting for me here last night. I think of you all gathering together. I found an enormous batch of Roman books to read which I ordered from Heffer's and shall spend my Xmas over Martial (rather squalid), Terence and Plautus and Seneca. Kenneth Clark will be a most welcome break!

I had a night in Rome and a morning at the Diocletian baths noticing with no surprise that every single thing one wants to look at is either Greek or copy of Greek, and then lunch at Ostia. I was told a story of a man in Rome who took a pet stag around on a leash. 'But it isn't a dog,' the policeman said. 'Indeed it is,' said the man. 'But it has horns,' said the policeman. 'That,' said the man, 'is its own affair.' Very Roman.

Everyone here flourishing. Kash the squirrel with a fine winter coat, biting

[51] *The Gothic Revival* by Kenneth Clark.

right and left. I go home by way of Ventimiglia for two nights to see Cici;[52] then shan't move from Asolo and do hope you come.

Love,
FREYA

JOHN GREY MURRAY Asolo
16 January 1963

Dearest Jock,

I have been here a fortnight, in a very poor way, and have not yet been out at all, but working all the same and just finished chapter VII (half way). It was the worst to write, on Augustan Rome, and took forty-seven books to read. I had no idea that Augustus was such a complicated character – like Cleopatra, or Richard II, two completely different sides to him. Meanwhile I do hope to hear of your coming out. Do please, please manage it: so much to show you and decide, and this house beautifully warm.

My house problem is not yet settled, but Dulcie says she has a plan. I offered it to the Boyds but they say they have as much in Italy as they can do with. It is rather silly, for it is worth much more than I am asking and could easily let. I rather hate the thought of its going to strangers, but would love it to go to Dulcie or anyone she cared for. Anyway it will be settled this year I hope, and then perhaps I can afford a secretary – I do begin to need one rather badly. And I could also travel first class, and spend a little on useful things as well as hats. This year I have had to re-do the drainage and repaint the façade.

So delighted that young John is to be my guest on the Bosphorus. I think he will enjoy it, and see Istanbul from the right angle.

Love,
FREYA

MRS. T. DEUCHAR Asolo
27 January 1963

Darling Dulcie,

Letters take ages (why I can't think as the *insides* of the post offices can't be frozen), and I was so glad and relieved to get yours yesterday. I am beginning to feel cut off from all the world.

---

[52] F.S.'s niece, to whom she had made over a small property, L'Arma, near Ventimiglia.

I have just been reading that in Armenia partridges are caught at dawn, before the sun *melts their wings*. Here the sun is now out on the snow, and it is so good to think of your coming third week in February. There is no saying about weather, as often February is lovely and March rainy, or vice versa, but a rather boring old Colonel might be coming mid-March, so better not have it later.

My house, yes. I was just as surprised as you and now I am not going to hurry, because it seems sad to make such a good offer to strangers. I shall just let friends know and something will turn up. I can carry on while I write and (with the sale of those little pictures last year) can anyway manage for five or six years during which it is obviously going up in value – not that I should ask any more because I don't want it to do more than just see me through. Meanwhile, dearest Dulcie, if anything sudden happens to me it is yours, and even that temporary ghost of possession gives me pleasure. Perhaps, too, in five years or so you and Tommy might like to come out and share and that would be best of all. I would give you *lots* of work, and I think it would be a rich good life in its autumn way.

Now you will see your books worthily housed in the new book table which is rather splendid, with lion feet. All I do for this little town is to design something now and then and make them do it, and something they wouldn't do otherwise. Five of them brought the table and drank its health in a glass of wine.

I am writing like a slave, buried in those bloodstained annals. I hope you may find three new chapters and all the early ones gone over with bits added. Whether good or bad I have no idea, but it is like the discovery of a huge new continent to me.

Dearest love, darling Dulcie, also to Tommy.

Love,
FREYA

MRS. T. DEUCHAR

Asolo
29 January 1963

Darling Dulcie,

Jock has at last written and you have probably heard that he thinks the idea of a non-picture book is all his own.[53] I am writing to him that if, as he suggests, there are to be a *few* pictures, you will do the choosing when you come here. He is also going to write tactfully to Lucy suggesting a little

[53] Dulcie Deuchar was to edit an anthology of F.S.'s writing.

writing. His long experience of the more squalid side of authors' characters makes him wonder if Alan would mind?

Thinking over my house and its problems, I remembered an Oriental story that fortifies me in my idea of waiting a little. A king had a pet donkey and asked all his wise men if they could teach it to talk. All said no, except one, who promised to do so if given seven years. 'How could you promise such a thing?' said his friends. 'Well,' said he, 'in seven years, either I shall be dead, or the King will be dead, or the donkey will be dead.' So I think I shall wait seven years!

Dear love,

FREYA

CHARLES HARDING   Asolo
                                                      31 January 1963
Dear Charles,

How wonderful of you to remember this aged birthday – it gave me such pleasure to get your telegram this morning. Seventy is rather a step, and Jock Murray is celebrating it I hope within the year by making an Anthology out of those sixteen books which are my fleeting little monument. It is most enjoyable to watch one's book growing with no personal effort!

I am here, stuck deep in snow outside and my repulsive Romans within, till mid-July when I have a little house on the Bosphorus for the summer.

This funny little prayer I am sending to a very few intimate friends. It is a little egotistic perhaps, but who should pray for one if not oneself?

Love,

FREYA

A BIRTHDAY PRAYER

Grant, Divine Love, to this body, that now for seventy years has worn Thine earthly love, an easy stage at last: and if this cannot be, help it to remember how fast we travel to Thine inexpressible joy.

From Freya to Charles

54

JOHN GREY MURRAY   Asolo
                                                                  28 April 1963

Dearest Jock,

The exciting news is that I have bought a little hill.[54] I took the Gibsons[55]
there yesterday morning and they said also that there is no doubt about it;
so I went with the *geometra* in the afternoon and found the 'Nobile Martini'
walking about his fields a few miles away – rather a touching old man whose
sons don't care any longer for all the old things he likes. He was sorry at
having offered it but said he would stick to his offer (longing for me to back
out). 'You can always get back the price by cutting it into three lots,' said he
– just what one would like to prevent. Anyway the next thing I have to do
is pay, so would you send those £800 to my bank please, and do you think
an advance on the two books would be feasible? You have offered before but
I don't think I have ever had one? (Or possibly one.) I have six weeks in
which to pay.

Pat Gibson, who is good at business and houses, says I ought now to
borrow on the property and build a little house and let it. Anyway I shall wait
till something definite turns up about the future of *this* house before doing
anything. You can't think how stupendous that view was yesterday morning.

Love to Diana and you dear Jock,

                                                                  FREYA

MRS. T. DEUCHAR   Asolo
                                                                  3 May 1963

Darling Dulcie,

There is a lot of news. First of all, Larry Durrell is going to write a short
foreword for *your* book (what news of it, by the way?).

Secondly, I have had two sets of visitors and each has been trying to buy a
house. One has succeeded, and the other is still in process. They are those nice
Gibsons and would be pleasant neighbours.

Thirdly, I have bought a miniature mountain! While looking for the
Hodgkins, who preferred a lower little hillock, I discovered this stupendous
view and got carried away and bought it with partly the money of those little
pictures and partly (I hope and trust) an advance from Jock. It is ten acres
and rises in a steep grassy slope with a church and cypresses on one side on
another little hill, and all the Venetian foothills spreading to the plain below.

[54] Just outside Asolo.
[55] Pat and Dione Gibson.

Jock has seen and will tell you. I do so long to show it you! Now that this house is rather insecure (three people show interest in the reversion plan) it gives me a delightful feeling to have this, like an animal with a bolt-hole. It has no noise, and no one can spoil the view, and two lost little country roads, and water and electricity, pass by at its feet.

The only other piece of news is that I dined with Stewart in Venice, cordial and casual and left me very sad.

Dearest love,

FREYA

MRS. DEREK COOPER   Asolo
3 May 1963

Darling Pam,

With great joy I seized your letter this very morning – and here am writing at once. You have now a choice of decisions, not only whether to come at all but also whether you are more taken by this house or the Mountain, and I am longing to hear. If you prefer the Mountain, we could build it up gradually while continuing to live here – but I would then have to sell (delayed) this house. Derek might well prefer this as I believe he would love building up those ten acres with trees etc. Of course the essential thing is for you to come out and see it all and it fills me with gloom to think this can't be this year. I would much rather give up my English plans than put it off any longer: would you all come out for Xmas here and stay on? I shall be here from mid-October, and November–December would be perfect for me.

What I *don't* want is to share the house and still have to run it, and would like you to take that over and do what you like about it, and to become a cantankerous old lodger paying what I cost so as not to be a burden, but otherwise free as air. I have had friends sharing and worked out their expense at about £10 a week, and it seems to me that this would be fair, and the same for any guest of mine; but you would have to keep it going whether you were here or not, so I hope you would be here a lot. Even if you were away and I here, it wouldn't add to your cost as the household seems to eat just as much when one is away. The only problem would be if I were here when you wanted to let, but I think we could manage to choose the same periods, and share the rent?

Much love to all,

FREYA

56

Asolo

19 May 1963

Dearest Jock,

Here is the agreement signed and I am sure you have done all that can be done for my income and hope there may be huge sales. Another title has suggested itself to me: 'Darkling I Listen'. 'Traveller's Joy' is anyway *too sentimental*, like little things about gardens in *Home Chat!* Joy is a tricky word isn't it?

Rather distracted not only by my own mountain but everyone else's, I am yet plodding on and just reaching Zenobia. Fascinating new lights keep on appearing. The Christian revolution for instance – it was not Christianity pulling the underdog out of the mire, but coming in in a military-cum-proletariat revolution on the *winning side*, and getting a bit tarnished in the process. I have just read the letters of Jerome, and don't like him; but the Greek Fathers, Basil, and two Gregorys, and John Chrysostom and Origen, all superb and sane. None however better than Plotinus.

Peter Green[56] has written me a fine encouraging letter and I feel heartened to the weariness. And feel that I ought to continue my financial ruin by buying Tenney Frank's *Economic Survey of Ancient Rome*. He is very urgent on its importance and I might do a volume before and another during my stay in Turkey.

Pam and Derek are dubious about taking on Asolo: I think it is a rooted reluctance to decide to leave Ireland. Meanwhile I might build a *little* house and let for a few years and then think again? I went yesterday with the owner to see the actual boundaries.

Lots of love,

FREYA

Asolo

10 June 1963

Dearest Jock,

Bron Waugh – to whom I sent the titles as a guinea pig – writes to say he likes 'The Journey's Echo'. Did I suggest it? I had forgotten, but it does seem to me the best so far.[57] The word 'Traveller' should I feel be avoided. It will be so exciting to see the proofs: I hope the plans for the house will not get mixed in with them! The road, water and light, and a tiny cottage are

[56] Classical scholar and friend.
[57] It was in fact adopted.

to be attached (on proceeds of *tessoria*)[58] to the existing ruin. I am still trying to persuade Pam and Derek. How un-brave people are! I took Cocker (the gardener) up and he couldn't get over his rapture. 'How did you deserve such luck?' he says. 'By making up my mind quickly,' said I, 'and not losing the Common Market.' He is kindly going to supervise tree-planting in September – a little slope of olives which the government now gives one for nothing, and then lovely things like magnolia, tulip tree, American oak, and blossoming trees on top.

A fearful storm is slashing down on us, the lightning crackling as if in a frying pan. I have finished chapter XIV and hope to start on Julian.

Love,

FREYA

JOHN GREY MURRAY Asolo

20 June 1963

Dearest Jock,

I am glad you have taken the 'Echo' – would you think 'quotations/quoted from Freya Stark' might do for the subtitle?

This is sent you in a bit of housebuilding chaos as both Gibsons and I are in those throes. They are here for two days only and have bought five beds, seven mattresses, chairs, cupboards, etc. As for me, I am going to look at doors and balcony balustrades; and we spent a happy evening designing my dream-house on the hill – it grows round the little core which the *tessoria* is to pay for. I have offered, when the dream materialises, to build a little cottage for Caroly on the 'estate'! It is rather remarkable to concentrate at all on Romans under the circumstances, but I hope to finish the preliminary revising before I go. *So* grateful for Tenney Frank: it will keep me busy if not happy through the summer.

Alas! I can't get away – and really can't afford it either. But I would fly over in spite of that if it were not that some vital reason for being here happens every alternate day. And Dulcie lures me with three operas! So many cakes to have and eat.

Love,

FREYA

[58] F.S. had sold the *tessoria*, the small silk-weaving factory in Asolo, to Caroly Piaser for £7,000.

Asolo
                                                                    17 July 1963
Darling Dulcie,

It really is worrying about letters and how we seem back in the Middle Ages. I only hope Turkey is more civilised than Asolo in that respect. I can't believe I shall be sitting in our Bosphorus garden in a week.

The news here is that Derek and Skimper are coming for a fortnight on August 5th and I hope will deal with all the *agriculture*! Checchi refuses to be torn from this garden — 'La fidélité des chats,' as Napoleon said when he came back and found all his old servants who had deserted him, back in the Tuileries. But I have got a peasant with *three* young daughters as house-maids for the future. Emma *may* come! The contract with the builder is to be signed today. There is no real problem, as this house is bound to cover far more than the cost of the other; but I was thinking of your and Tommy's offer and wondered if I was wrong to refuse and perhaps you would *like* a share in the adventure? My top flat is to be yours for life anyway and you might enjoy to produce more marble bathrooms, or the swimming pool? Anyway you must see it first, and I don't want you to disburse for help, of which you do so far too much already, but for *fun*! Darling Dulcie, I think we shall enjoy ourselves so much with this venture. I may be quite rich, because this house seems very valuable, but I hope you will go on giving me your lovely presents because they warm my heart.

Such strange people now come to look over this house, rather touching, all with money from industry and longing for Culture so that I feel like one of those decayed Romans with the young and eager and uncouth barbarians pouring in. Do you know, I am glad to think of the place that has had such love and care going out into a new world and perhaps doing something quite fundamental to the unknown lives that will inhabit it; and am glad that it will probably be one of these children of the future that will love it while we sit on our little hilltop in the sun.

I have got a terrible list of books from Steven Runciman to read for my last two chapters, but they look as if quite unobtainable and most translated from Armenian into German!

Dearest love,

FREYA

18 July 1963

Dearest Derek,

I do hope I have done all I could to start you off, and long to hear what you think of everything. The house is supposed to be up to its roof by October, but all the inside unfinished: they want to know the lighting and heating and built-in shelves and cupboards now, however, and I have left you the plan with your floor only sketched in so that you can complete it. It is fatal, from a financial point of view, to change one's plans once they are estimated – and that makes it all very hard.

You will find a plan for a little bath house of which the tower already exists beyond the swimming pool. I thought it would be nice to enlarge it with a little bedroom, shower and W.C. for visitors, and a tiny tower room for *writing in* (me): and you will find the plan, with a shed in front for garden chairs, etc. Do you approve? The swimming pool is to have a stone surround of about five feet so as to keep one's feet (and the water) clean, the stone to be neither too rough (feet) or too smooth (slipping). I think the pool and bath house could be done at once, so as to get the workmen off that part of the ground. I have tried to urge this but you may find they need a push. The pool they say should not be wider and I don't believe the proportion will be good if you make it much longer. The exit pipes would go *through* the bank and come out in a stone sarcophagus (still here in garden) on the terrace below. I think one could make a lovely grassy slope up to the bath house, and plant the precious plants (*cornus floridus*, hydrangea and a bay of roses) with the background of the little wood. But you and Cocker will decide that. The urgent things are the trees, the transplanting from my garden, and preparing a nursery (for rose-grafts, etc.) and a large asparagus bed, as that takes three years. They do beautifully here.

I hope this is all. So far I am still, just, within my means as I wrote: but if there is any real need I will borrow – so don't let us omit anything essential.

Luck to you, Derek dear,

FREYA

25 July 1963

Darling Dulcie,

I thought I would spend two days in this little house before writing to tell you all about it; and here I am settling down, in extreme and rather unusual comfort, Mustafa the cook producing fresh fish and shish kebab (and I already look forward to the day when you will teach something better than pure oil by way of a sauce). Sevim came to meet me and Mrs. Arel handed the house over with every touching attention, sweets and cigarettes in *innumerable* little containers, scented water on the dressing table and pink soap carefully kept on every available shelf on upside-down nail brushes. More ornaments of an incredible ugliness than I ever imagined all at one time out from Europe and all kept with obvious enjoyment and pride. I shall put them away as soon as she leaves next week, 'for fear of spoiling them'. To me it is fascinating, the process that has gone right through history, copying fashions and civilisations; and what one lives in here is an apotheosis of the bourgeoisie, but so practised and enjoyed and refined that it is a work of art in itself. Here it lives and Anatolia, and all the world in fact, is scarcely even an echo. Nothing exists but the city and the great stream that runs through it. It comes lapping to the garden, hungry and wicked little waves that tell of the current below. They make me think of the hordes of Asia lapping for so long against the Roman bulwark and breaking it at last. And if you bathe here, darling Dulcie, you will be wafted away to Seraglio point in no time. I went gingerly and had a delicious very careful swim at Sevim's this morning and there is a little cove near here which they tell me is safe.

I hope you will not mind the calling steamers. They are wonderfully silent. Suddenly a shadow falls on one's notepaper and they are there, and a few people stroll on and off, and with a few gurgles they go, except that now and then they make a sudden noise like a cat when it is trodden on and just as disconcerting. So far the smoke all goes the other way, and in fact I enjoy the company, like watching a boulevard up and down this street of water. Yesterday I was puzzled by a German ship sailing from the Black Sea like that of the Ancient Mariner, not a soul visible on board, and they tell me that people often jump off and swim ashore from Russian or East German boats, so that probably they are kept below while in the Bosphorus.

I am staying quiet for a day or two as I really was very tired, and also I like to let this novelty sink in, to slop about in a dressing gown like the Levant while Mustafa heats the bath in the morning, and to think of the whole day ahead with nothing that needs to be done.

Dearest love,

FREYA

Istanbul

                                                                26 July 1963

Darling Pam,

Yours is the first letter – lovely to get, like old times. Yes, you can advertise my sale. I am asking £66,000 – glad to get £60,000 – and ready in an Oriental way to make rock-bottom at £50,000 if necessary.

I have been glad not to see the papers. I would write to Bill but don't quite know how as I have no idea of what he is accused.[59] Did he *know* of what was happening? I believe one can let a sort of animal quickness that senses danger fade out of one's system if one doesn't keep it alert. I know that if you travel among dangerous people you quickly become extraordinarily alive to every nuance of character, when your life perhaps depends on it. The only safety is never to let a false value, however conventional it may be, get away with one.

But as for asceticism, darling Pam, don't have anything to do with it. I have just discovered that practically every Early Father died at about fifty of dyspepsia: they never seemed to remember that the miracle of Cana was just to make a party go more cheerfully; and the only one who wanted to spend the box of ointment on the poor was Judas! There is surely a ritual of living, to use and spread the beauty of the world, thinking of it as the feast to which we have been invited. But you shall have your little church straight across a little valley from your bedroom window; and, why shouldn't you keep a pony (and one for me too in that case!)? It isn't very good riding country – but there is grass enough on the mountain. The name by the way *is* 'Mountain', 'La Montagna' – very pretentious for ten acres!

Bosphorus is pure suburbia of the Levant – the water a huge boulevard lighted at night on all its little hills – and round the Black Sea curve come ships of every nation: they skim down the wicked current and creep back along the quieter edges. Mark is due out on 16th and John Murray on 25th. Such a *comfortable* house.

                                                                      Love,

                                                                      FREYA

Istanbul

                                                                30 July 1963

Dearest Jock,

Your letter came – quicker than to Asolo: it took only three days and cheered me; I was feeling rather depressed with the usual tummy which one

[59] Lord Astor had been involved in the Profumo scandal.

never seems to get used to and also with the fact that not one other expected letter has materialised.

Meanwhile I am reading Tenney Frank in this perpetual Levantine atmosphere which hasn't changed, I'm sure. I took a gentle little walk in a valley parallel to the Sweet Waters of Asia – a shut-away world of grass and plane trees tucked into hillsides with farms – but have been only once to Stambul (with this tummy) and only twice bathed because the Bosphorus is so terrifyingly fierce – but there is a *plage* near by which Dulcie and I will patronise and I *hope* the boys also: I should hate to see them swept away.

Love,

FREYA

HON. MALISE HORE-RUTHVEN   Istanbul
                                                    28 August 1963

Darling Skimper,

I was so pleased to get your two letters and it all sounds O.K. on the mountain. The olives and cherries will be lovely, both above and under the path, and I hope I may live long enough to see their little blossoms. I am delighted at not having to build a farm house (which was entirely for the Cooper-Ruthvens as I am not very strong on animals and they do interfere with plants). If there is a man near by it will be perfect, and later on I feel sure that other bits of the hill will fall into our lap.

Mark is working at his Turkish like a Trojan and we have a charming and beautiful teacher called Leila twice a week. Mark's Turkish is just as good (or bad) as mine by now. John Murray arrived yesterday and Dulcie next week.

I do agree about those two Piero della Francesca paintings: somewhere or other Aldous Huxley says he thinks the Resurrection the greatest picture in the world – and I think one could take it as the embodiment of *European* civilisation, a sort of highlight.

Love and best luck,

FREYA

LADY CHOLMONDELEY   On way to Athens
                                                21 September 1963

Dearest Sybil,

Here am I on my way home, and the summer is over. How quickly they go! I am breaking the journey to go to Mytilene, where Peter Green has settled with his family and kindly offered to look at the footnotes of my book. Nothing should be easier than to cross over to an island fully in sight of the Turkish coast, but it is so uncertain a problem and my time so short that I am going to Athens and back, and hoping that the Common Market may make things easier next year. The Turks put out flags for three days. Are we the only people left out now? I do hope we are getting in on the ground floor with Russia and all her satellites?

The house on the Bosphorus was a very happy experiment for all. The two godsons swam across one quiet morning and saw a good deal of Istanbul and we drove to the Black Sea and the Isle of Princes; and had the drama not only of a luckily small earthquake but also of a Russian ship crashing in among the houses opposite and lying now like a huge whale among them.

I shall be busy with house and builders when I get back, but hope to be in England for most of January and possibly all February. When and where shall I see you? It seems a long time since last time, and I wish so much that you could see my old house before it goes. However, there is as yet no news of that.

You would have enjoyed Istanbul, with Soraya and film stars bringing a modern sort of Arabian Nights atmosphere into the newspapers.

Love always, dear Sybil,

FREYA

HON. MARK LENNOX-BOYD   Asolo
1 October 1963

Dearest Mark,

I was glad to find a letter. It doesn't seem possible that you were swimming the Bosphorus three weeks ago, and that I have since been all the way round by Mytilene. I left Istanbul with my carpet rolled in a huge bale.[60] I think it must have become invisible by magic, as neither Turk, Greek nor Italian breathed a word; and now it is unrolled and looks much more wonderful here all on its own. As we were wearying of the Piraeus police I said to a rather nice Frenchwoman, 'I hope it won't take so long to get into Heaven.' 'We shall have less luggage,' she said.

John turned up at Piraeus with a successful tour behind him and a Roman seal that I fear would make you very envious, a real beauty. He came here for a night and we went up the mountain, and there is the house growing like an Aladdin's lamp rubbing, the walls about four feet high and the little

[60] See final paragraph of letter following.

bath house almost complete. I don't believe there is anything wrong with my design at all and I feel rather conceited, so hope there is no Nemesis preparing.

Ibn Khaldun is the most difficult of all Arab authors I believe, so he mustn't get you down. What fun it was, dear Mark. I loved having you, and so glad it ended with that swim.

Love,
FREYA

DEREK COOPER

Asolo
2 October 1963

Dearest Derek,

I have just got here (yesterday) and was delighted to find your letter and hear of arrivals by 24th. Tummy O.K. again and now I suffer only from broken tooth, broken (?) finger, and general decay, but am still far more alive than anyone in Asolo who has to do a job.

The mountain however now looks like Knossos or something. They promise the roof on for Xmas. I had no time to look in detail, but the proportions seem very good, lovely wide corridors and a feeling of ease and space. I cross my fingers that you and Pam listened to my prayers and marked everything that has to be done in the actual masonry, as the estimate will go haywire if they have to undo – I mean things like niches for central heating.

The road has an Arab look and bumps all over, but is there, and Topolino went up beautifully. The swimming pool not begun and, dearest Derek, it is no good telling me to get Bernardi to see about it, as it is just because I don't think B. very reliable on this point that I SOSed you. There must be experts in England who can tell you. The lily ponds won't interfere as they have separate water, but according to Tommy Deuchar it is a choice of emptying once a week or so or keeping the same water there always, with a chemical inside.

I have written to Cocker – but there is no sign of anything having been done, so I believe you will be in time to do all the planting and transplanting when you come. I have a donkey's load of work on my book that *must* be done, so that I shall be hard put to it with the house and the Romans getting mixed, and I feel someone ought to be there all the time for the planting. Anyway it is raining now, so the end of the month may be better in every way.

A horrid tycoon has already appeared to look at this house – says he would like it with all its furniture and rather dashed when I pointed out the price of

65

a single carpet! (By the way, I bought a carpet in Istanbul, a ravishing Caucasian eighteenth century for £150 – twenty-five feet long and the God who looks after smugglers wafted it for me out of Turkey through Greece and into Italy.)

Love,

FREYA

DEREK COOPER

Asolo

4 October 1963

Dearest Derek,

It has been pouring for two days and so frustrating as all work stops – but I have had Ferrazza here and I believe we have covered every inch of that little bath house, which should be ready for anyone to camp in in November. My little bedroom is being demolished to furnish it!

On Monday I go into Venice to buy four baths and basins for the marble workers – that will be my present to Zara and you and Pam (who can let herself go on building less amusing things like cupboards and kitchens!). Zara's is yellow marble half sunk in the floor so she can step in easily and yours is green and grey – and mine a splendid dark red.

I hope to get all the *lilies* planted before you come.

Meanwhile, could you bear to bring out our Xmas – a *large* pudding and mince pies and perhaps a box of crackers? I have ordered a turkey to be fattened. The Deuchars *may* be out here but not very likely. Everyone looking forward to your coming. Hodgkins may be out too. The latest news is that Henry Berens and his Janet's little mountain is secured – they are due here on their honeymoon in a week so it will be their surprise.[61] It makes our *view* safe too. What a mighty little mountain range it is going to be. I do hope we may all like each other.

I am practically O.K. again so I hope Asolo may do the same for you.

Love till we all meet here,

FREYA

MRS. T. DEUCHAR

Asolo

19 October 1963

Darling Dulcie,

I hope you are not dead, but it is a very long time since I have heard from you – not indeed since Stambul. And I have been, and still am, far too busy

[61] Henry Berens had also been negotiating for a hill at Asolo. He and Janet Balfour had stayed with F.S. in June.

for a decent life, but I would have written again if I had not put it off from day to day hoping for a letter. Calculating eleven more years according to the Insurance, a letter a month will only give you 132 to write, so do sit down, dearest Dulcie, without letting this month go by.

Henry and Janet have just left, with their little neighbour hill in their pocket, blissfully happy with all their life before them. And *our* view to the west is safe. I feel like the boy in the *Arabian Nights*, who took the stopper off the bottle and saw Djinn emerging, bigger and bigger. The house looks enormous, and has reached the first ceiling, and now they are digging the portico foundations; the proportions do look very pleasant with a feeling of space and ease, and the walls look old and unobtrusive already.

My book gets neglected, but I have got it into the Julian wars and hope to bring it more or less finished to London, but am strangely exhausted with a perpetual headache and no memory at all. There is a financial crisis overhanging Italy, in which case no one will want to buy anything at all and I shall have two houses on my hands. But I am not crossing any bridges till I reach them.

Dearest love and please write.

FREYA

MRS. DEREK COOPER

Asolo
29 October 1963

Dearest Pam,
It was shattering, you can imagine, to be plumped overboard with a house just twice too big for me.[62] It has taken me these days to get over, for I felt I could not write. Now I have been thinking with sorrow of your distress over Zara, though not too unexpected at eighty-four – and more particularly hearing of you in hospital. One can't easily keep

> The reason firm, the temperate will,
> Endurance, foresight, strength and skill,
> The perfect Woman nobly planned

with a microbe in one's tummy. I hope it has *gone*!
There is not much I can do, except countermand the two lovely bathrooms not yet started on. I am so very very grateful for Derek's coming, to prevent total shipwreck. He says you might yet get away for Xmas and in that case I will stay over and get away immediately after so as to get back here a week after Derek's departure, as these people cannot be left! He will have written

[62] The Coopers had been forced to change their plans about Asolo.

67

all the news. He is making a little bijou of the woodlets on the hill. The house too is coming rather beautiful, though a shambles just now. It is sad to see one's little dreams in the dust, and sadder after seventy than before, though not long to go.

Love to you and Zara, dear Pam,

FREYA

T. DEUCHAR Asolo
10 November 1963

Dearest Tommy,

I have come to a very basic decision about that little mountain of mine: to give it to Dulcie as a Christmas present. It won't make any material difference to me, as I hope she would let me spend the remainder of my years there, but I feel she would get more fun out of it if it were her own; and I would be happier not to be encumbered by possessions on my last lap, so to say.

The Coopers have rather fallen through, partly because of old Lady Gowrie's illness, but chiefly because they are not really decided to leave Ireland and this leaves me free to do what I like about it – and thinking it over, I feel sure that it would give Dulcie, and you and me too, a great interest and many happy days – and be helpful, I believe, to her health. I am making all ready for a separate kitchen and maid's room so that we could be quite independent. It is such a *beautiful* place, dear Tommy, and even now could sell for far more than it costs, so that you need not fear on that score. Dulcie would not need to come out more than she wanted, but it would be hers, and she could put anything she liked into it, and it would be like our little house on the Bosphorus, a dream to play with.

Shall it be a surprise for Dulcie? Or would you rather tell her? Do fall in with this lovely plan, dear Tommy, and please your loving

FREYA

JOHN GREY MURRAY Asolo
15 November 1963

Dearest Jock,

Things always go wrong all together and now there have been: Italian crisis; Lady Gowrie and all that; Derek sick in tummy and I in *head*; and last night a burglary! Someone walked around, took two teaspoons and four little bijou boxes and all Annamaria's money – and I now wait for the Carabinieri,

68

who never do anything at all. In all this your letter with birthday dinner idea comes like a ray of sunshine and I think it is *most* enticing. Have I got eighteen men friends – or sixteen with you and me not counted? I hope so. The 14th January would suit me, as I must leave by 21st or so. Whom will you ask? Osbert of course; Charles Rankin, Michael Stewart (I may be staying with them in January and also in Rupert Nevill's flat); Jim Bowker and Bernard Burrows to represent Turkey? – and Seton Lloyd; godchildren: Simon and Mark Lennox-Boyd and John Murray; Skimper, I fear may be away; Hugh Euston; David Cecil; Henry Berens; John Sparrow and Tom Boase; Gordon Waterfield; Harold Caccia; Harold Ingrams; Patrick Kinross; John Julius Norwich; all those are friends to choose from, whom I should love to see, and it will be wonderful to have a whole evening as I shall be too rushed to see them separately.

Love and thanks for all, dearest Jock.

FREYA

LADY CHOLMONDELEY   Asolo
18 November 1963

Dearest Sybil,

Too horrid – whooping cough. How boring one's body becomes! I have to spend a fortnight without using glasses (and am writing this rather by guess) because the muscle of the eye has got tired of too much Roman history, quite understandably. Apparently it is good for it to try and read without glasses so I spend an hour or two over a page and it is most extraordinary how the letters vary in a line of print, appearing and disappearing as if it were conjuring. I am of course desperately bored with no reading and so frightened that I do all the oculist says.

Have you read *Layard* by Gordon Waterfield? It is so good, and the only non-Roman thing I have touched except Auberon Waugh's new novel, which is a great improvement in human feeling on the first one and I think shows promise.[63] When I wrote to him I told him I thought compassion is one of the essential ingredients in English humour or satire, and there is a trace of it in his novel (none in the first one!).

It is good to think of you and England so soon.

Dear love, dear Sybil.

FREYA

[63] F.S. had not liked Auberon Waugh's first novel, *The Foxglove Saga* (1960). The second novel was *Path of Dalliance* (1963).

Asolo
                                                    30 January 1964

Dear Sir Reader,

I am not a protester against reviews and I don't think it is usually a good thing to be, but I feel that a private word may be said against misrepresentation from someone who had been, even mistakenly, considered a friend. You have given a twist to make my words into a general criticism of government officials. I can only think, without any blame to you, that you have never read any of my books, where affection and admiration have been constantly and always expressed over a period of thirty years. The quotation (I did not choose any of them, I may say) refers to the young Iraqis and merely tries to say that a competitive profession is an added difficulty among the many that beset them; I never say the artist is not jealous, I merely say that he ceases to be an artist in that moment. The quotation is from *East Is West*, page 175. This is not a matter of any moment and requires no answer.

We have perhaps different codes, and it would be as unthinkable to me to take private animosity to the press as it would be to you to smuggle rose bushes across a border; but it is rash to feel sure that one's own code is best, and your spleen, and my friendship, must be twenty years old. We are both due to be dead fairly soon I take it, and hope therefore that you will take as friendly feelings as you can into that anteroom.

                                                              FREYA

JOHN GREY MURRAY   Asolo
                                                    1 February 1964

Dearest Jock,

What a month! I feel I need quite another one to digest it and think over all the days – Houghton and Cornwall and Lancaster and Sussex, and friends in London, and plays and Callas, and that memorable evening: who ever had such a birthday at seventy-one? Thank you, by the way, for the telegram. The birthday in fact has made me feel younger rather than older.

As for the mountain, a lovely white stone cornice is being put round it by way of eaves and the roof goes on as soon as nights stop freezing – and you want to hear its story from the beginning. Looking back over the last two or three years I can see that I had a feeling of constriction in Asolo, apart from the fact of its being too expensive. That could have been got over by sharing,

[64] Sir Reader Bullard, Ambassador in Teheran 1944–56 and a diplomat with great experience of the Middle East, had reviewed F.S.'s anthology, *The Journey's Echo* (1963).

but it is no home for young people to share as there is nothing to do or make, and if it were old people, I would still be housekeeping to my ninetieth year if spared. Even more so, though I realise it only now, was the spread of the *asphalt*: every road is being smoothed with it and even now I often renounce a walk because of that preliminary dullness. In a few years I would be like dear old Herbert Young, a prisoner in my garden:[65] it is so beautiful and old now – even the rose bushes are like small houses and the trees are closing it all in, mercifully, from noise, or sight of other houses: the views are becoming vistas that one has to pick out between them – in fact one is enclosed. One of the great divisions of the human race is between those who like enclosure and those who need openness – and I believe I am very strongly one of the latter.

I hadn't thought about it however, and the mountain came by accident – by those £5,000 from the sale of my fourteen little Prendergast sketches. They were waiting to be prudently invested when the Hodgkins came here on a visit, fell in love with the countryside, and planned to buy a bit of land and build a cottage. We sent for the agent and he took us to my mountain and to theirs, which is half the size and has a lovely but less generous view. I urged my mountain, but they wanted something small and easy and bought the other and it was only in a day or so that I felt that such a view *must* be bought; and 'Just as good an investment as an annuity,' I said to myself in that hypocritical way in which one deals with one's subconscious, knowing of course that one would never sell. The little hill was all green then, full of wild orchids in its summer, and nothing up it but a grassy path: always a little breeze, and noises of farms, sharpening of scythes of haymakers, geese cackling and cocks crowing, creaking of ox-carts, all faint and drenched by the sun.

There was the shell of a cottage that had been ruined in the war and I thought – and so did the masons, optimistically – that one could use it and build on a room or two and enjoy it meanwhile and in a day the whole thing was done. It belonged to an old country squire whose ancestors had gambled away most of his money. 'Some families grow and some dwindle,' he explained, and his son has become a chemist and cares nothing for the land. They live in a roomy unpretentious house, with tractors and such under its portico and busts of the Roman emperors in medallions over the windows, and open a little-used room with good furniture and hideous bric-a-brac and tessellated marble floor to receive visitors. There we made our bargain and went to buy a 'carta bollata' to write it out legally, and I handed over

[65] Herbert Young, artist and long-standing family friend, had given his house in Asolo to F.S. to make a home for herself and her mother.

71

£5,000, which was what he asked for – for he was already regretting his mountain and longing for me to say it was too dear. (It was about double the price of agricultural land at that time but the old man loved the place because it is full of birds and he liked to go and shoot them: such a strange way of 'loving birds', as he said.) He had excellent wine and the agent (Bernardi) and I drank with him to the little hill and its new fate and a month or so passed with a lovely free and unencumbered feeling of possession. I had no plan for living there, but began to make drawings of a room or two added to the existing ruins.

Must stop this, dear Jock, as I have a *pile* of jobs waiting, but will go on if this is what you want to hear? Love and thanks for all,

FREYA

JOHN GREY MURRAY   Asolo

JOHN GREY MURRAY   Asolo
2 February 1964

Dearest Jock,

One day after the other sunny and frosty; the tiles are going on but can't be fastened with cement till the weather gets warmer – but in a few days it should all be rainproof. The tying on of a roof looks very fragile to me and I can see how a tile dropped down and ruined the family of Ben Hur – but they say it is always tied up with bits of wire.

I left off when the hill was bought and the old owner took me over its ten-acre boundaries – a little wood at the bottom by a stream, and a round woodlet on the southern spur that was once the decoy place for birds – a labyrinth of hornbeam with box hedges and a tower to shoot from. All is overgrown and Derek has now cut paths through the thicket and we have planted two glades of hydrangea and peonies (they are budding already). On the north the hill slopes more gradually and there is a circle like a druid circle on Dartmoor, only of trees, not stones; all the rest is grassy terraces, with one smooth bit where one could put a cottage if necessary. When all was settled I left for Istanbul last July and was away for two months, rather shattered when I came back to find that the old cottage had been pulled down and new foundations laid without a word to me. Drama was here and there: the Italians suddenly realised that their lira was unsafe and sent all spare cash to Switzerland (priests took notes under their cassocks and made large profits I heard); so it suddenly became much more difficult to sell Asolo and months went by without an offer and everyone began to say how silly I was to have rejected £42,000 for it. Now the spring is round the corner and we look like a steady government, and all seems hopeful again. That Kipling poem 'If' is full of good advice and I clung to the first verse, and decided not to build gradually but do it all and finish it before the prices rose: they have now gone up to nearly half as much as the contracts I made three months ago.

The walls were above the first storey before I left for England. They are made of old bricks and irregular stones that melt into a gentle colour of warmed earth like the peasant houses. Only the young peasant boys who do their own building still know how to do this work, and it is about three times as slow to build as the modern wall; but it is nearly twice as thick, warm in winter and cool in summer, and the portico melts into it with brick arches – quite plain without capital or keystone and no rigid line but the bricks irregularly drafted in among the stones. Austen Harrison had told me that it is vital for the vertical line to go up beyond the capital even for an inch only before the spring of the arch begins; but when we tried, the portico looked better with no capitals at all, and the only decoration of the façade will be a balcony now being cut in stone.

The autumn went by with all its little dramas and events: driving to where the stone quarries are, near Grappa, to choose slabs of marbly stone for the window sills, floors and stairs and swimming pool border; driving to Bassano for a modern kitchen to dangle before Emma's eyes. Emma has sparks of adventure though she is now round as a barrel, and is delighted with the prospects; Checchi wants to stay in Asolo with his garden (near the pubs I suspect) and work for the unknown buyers. One waits to see whether it will end in compromise or divorce. But meanwhile I have got an excellent man about forty called Giuseppe, with a charming one-toothed smile and an enthusiasm for digging, who lives nearby and will I hope sleep on the mountain when the house is left empty. And Lorenzina has her family nearby and is all agog to move up there, as tough and gay as a young pony, and I will have to buy her a Vespa to shop with. A major decision was the central heating. A persuasive young firm of two brothers living in an icy medieval house in Vicenza urged hot air as against water, so I asked the architect who looks after the Doge's palace and went to see a house where the owners had lived with it for seven years and found it working nicely. Everybody was clamouring for a decision and prices were rising, and hot air for better or worse it is to be.

We then had our major drama of burglary. This has been growing in Asolo over the last three years or so – beginning with cigarettes or food, and then a few trifles, and now 100,000 lire from the Mother Superior of the Infants' Asilo (knowing when the nuns were at mass and the one at home in bed with cold), and at last masked men with a tommy-gun rifling 300,000 lire and all the tobacco from a tobacconist in Casella. Between these two raids they came into this house from the garden (Emma *can't* have locked the door), and took away two teaspoons, two cigarette boxes and a watch, and 2,000 lire from Emma: and Bernardi came round the day after with a charming sheep-dog called Zeno to guard us. He has straw-coloured eyes with pink veins, and a long coat smooth to the waist and then bagging out very shaggy and full like a pantomime clown – and sits like one too, with his toes turned out and his head on the side – and I walk him through Asolo on a leash so that everyone can see how well we are guarded. I also remembered a revolver given me by the A.M.G. after the war, when bandits were about, and found it – filled with live cartridges – in a cupboard and asked Bernardi to get a permit from his friend the 'Maresciallo'. That, the 'Maresciallo' said, was impossible, as I would get into trouble by declaring a revolver only after seventeen years; 'but tell the Signora not to worry,' he said: 'she can freely (*liberamente*) use the revolver and we will not incommode her.' We now carry the silver up every night in a basket and hope that one of these days the burglars may be found and removed.

Love dear Jock,

FREYA

AUSTEN HARRISON   Asolo
                                                              2 February 1964

My dear Austen,

How wonderful it would be if you were here! I only got back three days ago and find half the roof on my house and ever so many things waiting to be decided. Such doubts as to the sizes of windows, for instance.

I, too, heard the Requiem[66] in London last month and was impressed like you, listening to it all night in my head with its sorrow and the awful insistence of the tolling bell. 'Only the monstrous anger of the guns.' What a line! I knew that poem of Owen's: it is a tremendous marriage with the music. That war was the thing that counted most, I suppose, in the lives of our generation. Like a page turning over, it shut off what was before. It made more difference than anything that came after could do. The other great impression in London was Callas in *Tosca*: such acting I had never seen and I did not mind what she did with her top notes.

I spent a month in England and now am immovably here till the house is

[66] Benjamin Britten's War Requiem.

settled and finished – not till the late autumn. So please wish me luck and stop *en route* if anywhere near.

Love,

FREYA

JOHN GREY MURRAY

Asolo

16 February 1964

Dearest Jock,

Enormous transformations are now happening with almost frightening swiftness; the gutters are to go on this week, and the beautiful stone balcony is promised. Yes, I just look around and then draw, taking the bits I like and changing the rest, and getting the measures by using squared paper, four little squares to the metre. Then I give it to the *geometra*, who is far too interested in Demo-Christian politics to take any notice, and leaves it to a very young assistant to draw properly; but I have to get him here to do it, or he adds little pieces of his own, and anyway is flummoxed by curves which can't be done with a ruler. The difficulty, I find, is not to get the design, of which there are any number to choose from in this Palladian country, but to reduce them and not spoil their harmonious proportions. I am sorry now that I threw away my own little bits of paper, as you might have liked them. I went with Ferrazza to see the people who get their stone out of the Grappa quarry at their back and carve it, to see that they are not altering the balcony, and found that it had reached its third stage – from my and then the young *geometra*'s drawing to being cut out in cardboard; and by the end of next week they promise it in stone. 'Do you want it smooth or rough?' Such decisions all the time! Smooth on the balustrade, where one might put a book or a glass or an elbow dressed in chiffon, and rough for the rest. As we were coming away – with a pink sunset veiled in white mists and frosts like a young nun – Ferrazza told me that he has the Finanza (Inland Revenue) for a week in his house looking over five years of his accounts and asking questions. 'And I suppose,' said I, 'that you go to church and confess as soon as they have gone?' 'Oh, never,' said he: 'Lies to the Finanza don't count as lies. One tries to redress the injustice of government.' His sister is a capable tall young woman who keeps all the accounts, and came to me with a bill to show to the Finanza 'and mind you show only that one and no other'.

We have been planning four stone copings for the roof top, holding up stone balls, and two of them with lightning conductors, as I think the little mountain will attract every storm round about, especially now that it is to be two metres higher. Giuseppe has taken all the good earth off its top and surrounded it with a rampart like the Lines of Torres Vedras, and next week (if it doesn't rain) the crane will pile it up with cages of useless yellow clay. It gives one a Semiramis feeling to be changing the landscape contours. Oh dear, I am at my last five million lire, and must find a bank to lend me another twenty million which ought to see me through. The *geometra* brought the Minister of Agriculture's secretary and two members of the County Council of Treviso, who have bought an old convent here to make it into a Duse Foundation. It isn't nearly as suitable as this house, and he hopes they may see their way to change; and that would be really very satisfactory, and I would put a stone seat for them in the garden with all our names. But this waiting is very *nervous*, chiefly because I have never borrowed money before.

Ever so much love, dear Jock.

FREYA

JOHN GREY MURRAY   Asolo
                                                   25 February 1964
Dearest Jock,

The great event of this week was the 'Torta', a dinner with all the work-men when a small pine tree turning about on the high crane celebrates the completing of the roof. I waited for Pam and Derek to arrive, as I knew they would enjoy it, and we then gathered (twenty-nine) at the Sole and had a huge meal – risotto, boiled meat, roast meat, the 'Torta' itself and wine without limit – which I hear went on till 1 a.m. as there was an 'Alpino' ex-soldiers' gathering next door and they all vied with each other in song. We left at a reasonable time after supper. It was such a friendly affair, all of them combed and pressed and washed but not at all shy or embarrassed and we discussed the mountain and all its aspects. The rain has now started so they are doing what they can indoors.

My eyes really seem to be on strike; I *must* find someone and am going to the oculist again. You can imagine how very upset I am about it – hoping it may be rheumatism as it is worse in cold. But it is preventing my writing almost altogether. A short chapter on Julian is nearly done and I will send it tentatively.

Love,
FREYA

Dearest Jock,

I have dropped behind with my letters (a little heap is collecting) but by hook or crook have finished the last chapter and am typing it – very frustrated as I work only about two to three hours in the day. I am so delighted and *relieved* that you like the early Christian one, and now feel I know the mood, so to say, and can do the same for the earlier ones.

My house is full – two Trevelyans, Mark Lennox-Boyd and Michael Stewart – and we all went yesterday to the monticule (Topolino of course refused to start: the battery gone dead after three weeks in stable, as if it were a horse needing constant feeding). Well, Michael thinks it just as good as I do and wants to rent the bottom floor for twenty years. I am delighted, and we have agreed in principle subject to the Deuchars' and his wife's approval. I hope Dulcie will be pleased: she will like them all I feel sure, and neither she nor I will have any of the bothers of dealing with sub-letting, or the difficulty of going away and leaving it uninhabited – and will just be able to be happy in our upper flat. Michael particularly wants a long let as he will not be there much till he retires in eight years or so, and I am delighted to think of something permanent (after all the trouble with dear Coopers).

Must go down to guests. I am so happy to think of you on the Moor:[67] loved the card – and look forward to 21st or 22nd.

Love,

FREYA

Darling Dulcie,

By now you and the Stewarts will have met and I long to hear all about it. Here the daily drama goes on like one of those long Chinese rolls with one incident after another. The most harrowing was the loss of Zeno, whom we took for a picnic and walked home, and he went ahead and we forgot all about him, and he vanished. Police were warned and every bark all night kept Emma and me awake. And next morning he was rescued by Checchi from a little boy who had found him and tied him by a string and brought him; but sad and I believe *beaten*, for he walks about as stiff as a Poona

[67] On Dartmoor, which F.S. had known since childhood.

colonel and has developed a sort of Timon of Athens complex, so you will be pleased to hear that he is now lying (and scratching) beside my desk.

The yellow earth you saw at its worst is all in place now and the estimate for the swimming pool is *just* inside the boundary and should be begun next week. The two bathrooms also. Rather a conflict over price of doors, otherwise peace.

Dear love to you both,

FREYA

MRS. T. DEUCHAR   Asolo

11 June 1964

Darling Dulcie,

I am sure some awful thing has again happened in the post here, as I have had no news since Damaris left three weeks ago, except the sad little note from Michael Stewart, and am feeling rather like a starfish left on the beach. No news of your reactions to the Stewarts. No news from Mr. Punchard of Tommy and his kind loan. The only news that I have got is from Lord Dunalley, the Irish agent, who is coming to see this house in a week's time (just when all the roses are dead) and seems hopeful, which is more than one can say of the Italians, although the banks are optimistic for after November.

The house is going on with the usual daily drama, *three* strikes having stopped the installing of the bathrooms. In spite of all, however, it goes on and the walls of your drawing room are up. The rooms both look very pleasant and just right size and the corridor too is wide and easy. How *strange* when it all turns out just as one thought it might!

Biddy Monckton[68] is here for a few days' rest. I am so happy when some friend comes here as a refuge. She has been nursing her husband for the last two years and is worn out, and also talks of settling here. Would buy this house if smaller!

Alan talks of coming for first fortnight in August, and the Reynolds Stones[69] may be *camping* on the mountain. At the moment I have an interlude of quiet and have reached chapter VII of the book, with many alterations and a desperate revising of footnotes. I hope to have it done by Xmas.

I wish I could fly over and talk it all over with you. I feel a bit *deserted* at the moment. It is extraordinary how the human being longs for certitude,

[68] Second wife of Walter (Viscount) Monckton, the lawyer and politician. He died in January 1965.
[69] Reynolds Stone, the wood engraver and artist, and his wife Janet.

which is nothing anyway but illusion, uncertainty being the very substance out of which life is made.

Dear love to you both,

FREYA

T. DEUCHAR Asolo
25 June 1964

Dearest Tommy,

I wish you and Dulcie had been here last night. It was the great moment of pouring the cement into the swimming pool. Of course it rained in torrents all afternoon, but cleared just in time about 6 p.m., but too wet to camp out. So we drove out with four *fiaschi* of wine to distribute to the workers and found a wonderful scene about 9 p.m.: four electric lamps lighting it all up, the moon sailing into a clear sky above the Folly, and the swimming pool like a ship, all timbers, with thirteen men and Piero working on her, rushing along with barrows of cement while the two best workmen smoothed it out in the hod and Piero prodded with a drill that shakes it solid. Emma, Lorenzina, Checchi and I were there, and the boy who is doing Dulcie's marble bath (very fine!) and the plumber came to see.

Very dear love,

FREYA

LADY CHOLMONDELEY Asolo
14 September 1964

Dearest Sybil,

I wish I were with my niece at Mortola, with nothing to do but to swim about, and cross the border to see you. I am hardly ever here at this time of year and it is all very hectic even though I keep out of most things. But I had a houseful of eleven for the ball[70] and enjoyed dressing up four lovely girls and two godsons and a friend. It was beautifully arranged (except for the fact that one couldn't approach near enough to see the dancers without sinking one's little heels in the lawn). They had a white marquee at the back, and it was a wonderful décor, but of course Maser is so *much* more beautiful without too many people: an evening party when people wore almost crinoline

[70] Given by Contessa Marina Luling Buschetti at Maser, a villa near Asolo famous for its Veronese frescoes.

dresses, and not more than sixty or seventy, and a long table of supper down the central hall is much more decorative.

As soon as this was over, I was surprised by a telephone from John Russell to say that Princess Margaret was coming to lunch, and that was pleasant and easy and I enjoyed talking architecture with Lord Snowdon; and drama was provided by an *army* of photographers who followed them from Malcontenta[71] (we kept ours in Asolo in perfect order). They had a dotty scheme to throw them off and come back to see my little hill, but it miscarried and ended in a sort of motor point-to-point across the Venetian plain. When I reached the rendezvous, there was a television lorry already ensconced by the swimming pool, and a policeman polished till he shone.

I keep on at my house quite steadily in spite of the crisis and hope like Mr. Micawber that something may turn up before the day of reckoning comes.

My book goes very slowly but I hope to get it into shape by Xmas and out next autumn. No prospect of a visit to England I fear till my problems here are disentangled. I wish I could show you *both* houses.

Dear Sybil, so much love,

FREYA

MRS. T. DEUCHAR   Asolo
                                                    15 September 1964

Dearest Dulcie,

It is good to get your letter, safely here in only four days this time. The Asolo world has been subsiding since you left, and the only excitement at present is a cinema company doing the arrival of the Martians of all people, in the *piazza*. I have one of them sleeping here as there was no lodging to be had. The other arrivals are the Bill Astors, spending ten days at Cipriani's[72] and sketching in my garden. He is such a poor little waif of a man. I sometimes feel it is just some rather expensive clothes walking around and no one in particular inside them. But she is rare and beautiful, and *good*, with lovely honest eyes which she never plays with. They are a rather touching couple, he always with a well-intentioned but silly value and she quietly putting it right.

I got a very cordial little note from the Princess, saying she was sending flowers (which never came, bad A.D.C. work!), and only hope that all this

71 Palladian villa outside Venice.
72 Hotel in Asolo.

publicity will sell the house. Nibbles come and go, otherwise no news and my solitary little furrow pushes on to the dip of its horizon, good or bad.

Dearest love, to Tommy also.

FREYA

JOHN GREY MURRAY   Asolo
20 October 1964

Dearest Jock,

It seems a long time since I heard from you and I believe I have not yet told you that (crossing fingers) I hope the lower Montoria is let for eight years to friends of the Moncktons – a just retired Q.C. called David Karmel. They are a gay little Jewish couple and wrote to offer £1,000 p.a. which I have written to accept. I suppose one now has to do this with lawyers to tie it up properly? It would be very kind if you thought you could give them a ring and ask them to look in and see you so that I may hear what you think? I am so demoralised by the unreliability of most of my friends that I shan't feel happy till the document, whatever it is, is signed – but they were ravished with the place and offered to *buy* their half: this of course I wouldn't do, but if a crisis became urgent it is rather helpful to feel they might even be buyers? The £1,000 p.a. will I hope just save me from having to decide whether to pay the Italian bank interest or eat. It is all very aging. We have agreed to share Emma at Montoria (though I pay her), but to have separate kitchens if either side wishes. I do hope it may work. They are nice *warm* people: I feel we should get on together quite happily.

Dearest love,

FREYA

JOHN GREY MURRAY   Asolo
7 November 1964

Dearest Jock,

It is such a sorrow – this dangerous world.[73] Somehow that dear house with the two of them fitting so happily and so independently had seemed more stable than most things. I can't bear to think of it, and Osbert with no Karen to find always there. Thank God always for the happiness that one has had. I wrote him a little incoherent line, but tell him I think of him constantly,

[73] Karen Lancaster had died in October.

and tell him to come here when he feels he can: that little hill of mine is wonderfully consoling. Thank goodness he has Cara who will probably be very dear to him. Such sorrow for you too dear Jock.

I can't do Xmas – but *next year*, an Ireland-Hampstead one? *Inshallah*. I think I will have to get to London, but only for a few days and those must be working ones: tenants, finance and Alan Punchard, dentist, at least two London Library days if you can wangle that for me (or procure the books), and No. 50: can it be done inside a week?

No whisper of a sale anywhere except the myth of the Treviso Council (*may* mature after their elections on the 22nd). I get rather a nightmare with lots of little dancing figures *all red*, but cannot help feeling serene and happy when I get up to the loveliness: out of this world, these autumn days – and the grass is growing round the pool and the electric people are (I hope) kindly going to paint their pylons brown all the way up the little valley. The floors are being scraped and polished this week; and the house with its thick walls seems beautifully warm even with no heating.

I have no word from *Venture* and probably that means they don't like the article. The American way is hopeless as the author is merely wanted to dress the ideas of the editor – what was expected of an old-fashioned and Victorian wife.

Dearest love, dearest Jock. How could I ever complain of friends when you and the little band of No. 50 are about? Tell me about Osbert when you write.

FREYA

HON. MARK LENNOX-BOYD   Asolo
11 January 1965

Dearest Mark,

I was so glad to get your letter and all your news and meant to write ages ago – but then Xmas, and then 'flu, and then New Year (very pleasant with all the Moorehead family and we talked affectionately of you). I read all about your difficulties with great sympathy, remembering them well and the almost impossibility of getting to *talk* a language. I don't think there is any way except going doggedly on with infinite boredom to yourself and others until suddenly one day you find people forgetting to speak to you in English and then you know you have made the grade.

I have just finished the book and am going to take three months at least off before thinking of anything new.

I am going to be stuck here for the spring anyway, I fear, and had only a vague idea about March being a good month for the Euphrates. I rather hoped that you might be able to hear what the boating season is: it all depends on the rise or fall of the river. May would not I think be too hot if that suits the river (may be in raging flood, and if so nothing doing till the weather cools off a bit). I might get off for three weeks even if this house is unsold.

Whatever happens, dear Mark, come and see this old lady as you fly north or south.

Ever so much love,

FREYA

MRS. T. DEUCHAR Asolo
23 January 1965

Darling Dulcie,

I feared from your letter that you couldn't get here so the telegram was no sad surprise. I wished so much you were here yesterday as Lorenzina, Emma and I went up for our first night, an adventure which filled them with rather surprising pleasure over the 1) failure of the ventilator to heat, 2) flooding of the hot water over the boiler. I lay wrapped in wool like a mummy and was comfortable but worried in my lovely room; and in the morning reassuring plumbers told us these things are trifles, soon to be adjusted (how frightened I am of machinery). Giuseppe brought his wife and son and we gave them a glass of wine in the sitting room; and slept in a *silence* whose magic I had forgotten, that wonderful country silence which only the absence of asphalt in a wide neighbourhood produces. Such peace, getting up in the morning with the little hills and their small life spread out below. It makes up for the unceasing nag-nag of problems pouring in. I sometimes think I am exhausted, but have long ago discovered that one thinks that long before one *is*.

Your poor chairs! The carpenter (you will be shocked) has taken one away. How much to copy? I asked. 15,000 lire (as against 500,000 for the original) because he says 'It costs rather a lot to make the worm-holes.' 'No worm-holes,' I said firmly; they must look beautiful but not old. I can't help thinking ethat it is the *dishonesty* of copies that you dislike? Mere copying in itself can't be objectionable or we couldn't be justified in using a sonnet form in poetry, or an Ionic column. Surely all *tradition* is copy, and it is only bad when it tries to pretend to be different from what it is. My lovely writing desk is a copy, and it is only changed and adapted to my needs but still not

83

able to be invented but for the fashions of the past. The trouble begins when the feeling and the object don't coalesce.

What a scrawl, dearest Dulcie, for a Saturday morning. A feeling of leisure comes with no writing to do.

Dearest love,

FREYA

HON. MALISE HORE-RUTHVEN   Asolo
                                                31 January 1965

Dearest Skimper,

This is my birthday (seventy-two!) and my book is written, so I am taking an easy morning and looking at letters far too long neglected and yours among them. I was so glad to get it, and have not only your news but what you are thinking about and feeling. Of course you feel cramped in Lebanon. I can still remember the excitement of getting (by train) across into the Beka'a and on to Damascus and feeling that at last I was really *there*. I am sure there is no way of learning the colloquial Arabic except by getting right away from anyone who can speak English at all: just a teacher is no good, once you have got the grammar, etc. Travelling as we did and talking to villagers in the evening, or attending an Arab school (that is what I did in Baghdad, and that was a good way, I discovered), or, probably, taking on an Arab job where you *have* to talk – all these would get you away from the sophisticated *effendi*. Lebanon is Levant and not Arab; I like it, just as I like Baalbek or the Baroque – in fact I think you are all too hard on Baalbek. But I like it to go and relax in after or before a proper journey. Will I ever do one again, I wonder? I can't get away this year as the crisis goes on and seems to be spreading to England (a letter has just come opened by censor if you please), and I think I shall spend months more with two houses. Montoria is practically done now, and everyone falls in love with it. I hope you will see it all in July, and if you are here at the end of the month we will go and see *Petrouchka* in the Verona amphitheatre.

What happens to you after this year of Mecas[74] is over? Have you got plans for the world your oyster? My love dear Skimper, bless you. I do look forward to seeing you.

FREYA

[74] An Arab school above Beirut.

Asolo

3 February 1965

Darling Dulcie,

Such a happy birthday began with a telegram from you and next morning a letter came from Lucy not even offering but just informing me that a loan of £5,000 is on the way. I was so touched that I wept! I know you and Tommy will be so pleased. His dear offer to help if things came to the worst had already lightened my load a lot, and now this is like a lifeboat sent out to sea where for the last year I really had felt like drowning.

I realise now by the reaction what a strain it has been, and I think it will take me a few months to get normal again and get over my strange feeling of fatigue. I shall pay the bank and get rid of that awful 10%, and dribble along with the masons, who are very rich, till in the course of ages this house is sold.

It is such joy to be reading for pure pleasure again and I have discovered a young American poet, Ned O'Gorman; at least he discovered me and called on me once in London and has sent his little volume, *The Buzzard and the Phoenix*. It is modern, and bits of exuberance are too frequent, but there are images of thought and power. With any luck he may grow and grow and one feels there is something to grow *from*.

Crocuses are out. The house continues to develop problems but is nearly finished. Anyway I feel enabled to cope. It is wonderful to have friends and in that I am so lucky. Bless you both, dearest Dulcie.

Your

FREYA

JOHN GREY MURRAY Asolo

5 March 1965

Dearest Jock,

If you come out before this house, if ever, is sold, you will find a very peculiar eclectic atmosphere among its furniture. I have had an inspiration and offered to show furniture for the Antiquary opposite, so that quite a number of my own things can travel up the hill: little parties come and look at chests of drawers etc. and incidentally get to know this is for sale. There is also a Chinaman from Hong Kong in the offing – hope springing eternal.

The most shocking drama happened to Henry's property: a posse of small wicked boys pulled all the tiles off his little roof and *smashed* them; I have spent the morning with the police, who seem quite helpless with 'minorenni': all one can do is to promise them prison when they grow up. They come and tear up my crocuses by the roots and have removed a newly planted cypress tree. We seem to combine all the disadvantages of bureaucracy and anarchy. Checchi was stopped by the police for carrying a marble washbasin in our own Topolino: only *clothing* is allowed – in one's own car! I wonder if that splendid Russian, whirling round the world in space, saw it as nasty as it seems to be getting?

Dulcie is due here on 31st and I hope will not waver, as all sorts of nice questions of curtains etc. await her. Do you think that providential help of hers and yours will get to me in time for April 16th when the bank loan falls due? I still live from hand to mouth but no longer feel that impossible barrier between the two of them. My nice p.g.s. too provide all Beppi's wages, grass seed and manure. With all this strain and labour, Montoria gets lovelier week by week. Mrs. Karmel enraptured, and bought Emma her dream of pots and pans, mincing machines and gadgets: she was given two hours (which nearly killed me) in a household shop.

I am saving time for you when I am dead by finishing the two scrapbooks of photographs, one of me, the other of Asolo and friends. It is nostalgic work – so many years even since 1945 when the book begins: Murray visits there, too few but nice to look at – and children growing up.

Love dear Jock,

FREYA

MICHAEL STEWART Asolo
2 April 1965

Dearest Michael,

I have written all the business to Damaris, so this is just for fun and to tell you that Montoria is now like a little convex sky of daffodils all over its top. Two little lakes of white ones on either side below, and jonquils scattered round the pool in the (still rather mingy) grass.

I am glad you feel like this about the U.S.A.: I would have been very worried if you had really taken to that ghastly way of life.[75] Nothing in this world that I can think of would make me live there for very long. Have you read George Santayana's autobiography? He describes the struggle in his soul between New England and Avila in Spain – which eventually wins. It is a very good book; but have you any time for reading?

I have very little: all is house furnishing and terrible finance and the odd bits of my book: I feel it will not be meticulous enough for the historians, and am now struggling with bibliography and maps.

[75] Michael Stewart was now Minister in Washington.

Leila Gencer the prima donna – after great triumphs as Norma at the Scala – was here for a few days. Wonderful glimpses of life behind the Sipario – more like Ouida than real.

You must let me know when your leave is due – or I might be in Samarkand next year.

Love,
FREYA

MRS. T. DEUCHAR   Asolo
6 June 1965

Darling Dulcie,

I *do* miss you so, and I have no one to take a sympathetic share in the dramas as they continue to pour on my dedicated head. I can't get *near* that article I should be writing.

Yesterday I made a power of attorney and that new *geometra* from Feltre is my 'man of affairs' now. He has got out advertisements and is bringing a new nibbler to Casa Freia and has got a month to study my builder and his ways. I give him a good mark because when I asked how their interview had gone, 'Very well,' said he, 'but I felt that he was just a little more amiable than he needed to be.' I rather hope that he may be steel-gentle under that lamblike smile.

The poor Karmels are bearing up in the worst June we have ever known: sheets of solid water blotting us out and fires every evening; the hay rotting and our road as you can imagine. They are a gay little couple and so far all is well, and when I am here by myself it gives me a pleasant feeling to think of them sitting by their fire downstairs. I join them there for lunch and they come up for dinner while we are alone. The house is full of untrained girls thinking of Young Men. Emma cheerful, however.

Much love to you and Tommy,

FREYA

MRS. T. DEUCHAR   Montoria
7 July 1965

Darling Dulcie,

We have just added to the incidents of this difficult year a hurricane. It came down from Grappa rather like Jehovah, spiky with lightnings, and scattered my lilies and burnt out the electric light, the pump for hot water, the motor of the hillside pump (so that no plugs worked) and the telephone. It also smashed a window here and four in Asolo, through whose poor old house the water gambolled as if it were a sponge. With all this, we have been lucky. The Bonniers have their roof half off, their road a wreck and their garden ruined for this year. And in the plain it was worse, and the Treviso–Venice road has huge trees of its avenue uprooted, while Francesca came home with stories of a woman being pulled dead out of a smashed car. My six tenants are bearing up however and we have light, telephone, and cold water (the swimming pool a great resource) and hope to get the pumps working this week.

In spite of all I am trying to write and have been asked by *Holiday* for another article, on Smuggling. I hope it may not cramp the future travel style?

How are you, and Tommy, and whom have you got to replace Joan? You *may* find it a blessing: nothing so angst-producing as a faithful old retainer. I sometimes feel Emma a Trial.

Dear love,

FREYA

JOHN GREY MURRAY
Montoria
15 July 1965

Dearest Jock,

I am so looking forward to John's arrival, to hear all the news, and see what notes you made on my typescript. So very glad you like it. I wish it were as lucid as Steven's *masterly* book[76] – but eight centuries is a very huge mouthful to boil down.

You nearly lost your little friend of thirty-three years' standing yesterday. The nice doctor tenant prescribed some nicotinic acid for my state of near-collapse and I took a little pill not noticing that the Italian has four times the dose of the American prescription (in a tiny little white pellet). I sat at lunch, felt very peculiar, and knew no more till I found myself on the floor with Emma and Francesca pouring water on me and Francesca's little gold madonna medal in my mouth. It seems I had gone purple and then white and heart almost stopped, and remained to all purposes dead. What an *easy* departure too!

Love, dear Jock,

FREYA

[76] Sir Steven Runciman's *The Fall of Constantinople, 1453* (1965).

88

24 September 1965

Dearest Jock,

My friends,[77] all perturbed to see me worn and wan, take me off on little mind-distracting tours: I have been carried these last days by Aquileia to Jugoslavia where you are now allowed in for three days with no visa. An adorable coast of bays and inlets, all shallow with a scatter of small round islands covered with thick bushes and pines as if they were the curly tops of negro heads emerging. It is all poor: no fine villas as here, and fields insufficiently tended. The young get away to Canada or Italy; and people walk with baskets on their heads, or drive in buggies, and all the roads aren't asphalt. We went to Parenzo where a magnificent sixth-century mosaic apse has been over-restored; then on to a pleasant camping peninsula called Vrsar (awful words to deal with), and back by Pirano – a little medieval-Napoleonic town of sailors where Tartini's violin is kept in a museum. All along one can easily speak Italian.

When I got back yesterday the Consiglio had deliberated and ratified the buying of my house so that I feel in the straight at last – too tired to be buoyant but immensely relieved. I have been totting up accounts and think I should break even – which means that it will be a bit easier than Asolo was and that I might replace part if not all my little fortune of £16,000 that went down the Montoria drain.

Must stop dear Jock. I know you will all be very happy to think your author not due for bankruptcy just yet – and will drink a little health to Montoria and lots of Murray days there.

Love,
FREYA

30 October 1965

Dearest Jock,

An unexpected blow has now fallen and I am back in the old soup again because the Provincia (with three signatures to promise immediate payment) now discover they may not have authority to pay for months, years, anything. I am waiting for the All Saints (three days' holiday) to be over before trying to get to the bottom of it, and will put the whole thing into the hands of

[77] Lyndall Birch and Wolfgang Reinhardt (F.S.'s p.g. and son of the producer Max Reinhardt).

Pat Gibson's lawyer whom he thinks well of. If I had known of this before I would not have gone for my 'cure', but am glad I did so as I don't believe I could have stood up to this blow on top of all; as it is, it puts everything into uncertainty again as far as plans go.

Mr. Milliken is a colossal, slow, story-telling man but I should think extremely reliable as he was head of Cleveland Museum, Ohio for years and years. I met him at B.B.'s and he comes here to work for a month or so. I was pleased with him because, describing the awful discomforts of Greek islands, he said to me: 'Camping is a thing you would never enjoy, Mrs. Stark!'

Love,

FREYA

MRS. T. DEUCHAR Montoria
7 December 1965

Darling Dulcie,

The story of my house and the Provincia would really be comic if it weren't wearing me down to a frazzle. What do you think they have started now? Decided that nothing can be done because I am still *requisitioned by the Fascist government*, long since damned and defunct! This has not been told me, but one delay after another continues and this was let out in private by one of the assessors to a friend here. You can imagine Asolo buzzing with it all. What the real reason is goodness knows. The wicked *geometra* is away hunting bears in Austria – 'and I wish one would eat him' the provincial secretary told me over the telephone.

I have, meanwhile, decided that house or no house I can do no good here over Xmas so will be in Rome from the 13th. What a dream if you were to join me there? I believe it is a large and beautiful flat, kindly lent me by unknown friends. If you were to come, Jock might be induced to let you bring my picture book which he wants me to write more for. He seems to want something different from the sort of dream-book I plan, and there is going to be a little tussle I rather think, of the sort that has often enlivened our long friendship.

Telephone interrupts to tell me that it is not the Fascists but the British Army in 1945 which requisitioned and never de-requisitioned my house. I have just got at our Consul in Venice. Every other house in the province was de-requisitioned except mine!

Your

FREYA

Montoria

5 January 1966

Dearest Jock,

I am being a Prima Donna these two days with a television crew of about ten men running me round between Asolo and San Zenone. They are giving a fifteen-minute compression of my life, which makes it feel very hectic: the last of Casa Freia, the road to San Zenone with Zeno (who steals all the limelight) running ahead of the car, and then the whole panorama of Montoria. It is just possible the B.B.C. might take it on from the Italian, and then you could see it: the prima is not up to much, but the views should be splendid!

I have just got your letter, and of course 24th January will do if 12th doesn't – *any* date will be made to fit such an Event, though I have come through the Provincia crisis with rather an inhibition about postponements. I don't think anyone will be here except Michael Stewart till 15th (but busy on his own), and Dulcie so vague as not to count.

The Fascist requisition of my poor house was dated 3.9.40, a pre-fectorial decree appointing the Credito Fondiario of Venice requisitioner. The Allied Military Government abrogated all *their* requisitions 1.2.1945 – but no one had cancelled them so that all the English and U.S.A. Asolo houses, four of them (and all except mine happily sold and resold twice), are still under nominal requisition, and are now busily getting it undone. It reads like Ruritania or your friend Parkinson![78]

Whatever you do you must come this month: I can't *bear* any more disappointments just now.

Love,
FREYA

MRS. T. DEUCHAR   Montoria

7 January 1966

Dearest Dulcie,

I believe, like the Lady of Shalott in fact, you have no feeling for the passing of time. One needn't bother much about clothes after eighty and that is why I try to enjoy this little decade while I can; I don't dislike the prospect of eternity, but it is nice to enjoy the ephemeral, which one is presumably

[78] C. Northcote Parkinson, a Murray author and evangelist of bureaucratic absurdity. His celebrated 'Law' states that the amount of work done is in inverse proportion to the number of people employed.

intended to enjoy. So small a fortune of years, one must be careful in the spending.

I have got to work at last, on my article on Palmyra. I can't do more than an hour at a time, but even that gives me back the lovely feeling of being alive in my head. As for health, I am glad after all to have been to the Swiss and wish you had joined me because they have narrowed the field down to two things (which are nearly related) and I needn't worry about anything else. It is pretty certain that the trouble *is* circulation though I take a heart tonic because the poor pump has all this extra work. Meanwhile I am trying to lose one more stone; I *brush* my arms and legs, I splash myself all over with cold water, I walk for one to two hours, and lie as much as I can with feet up in between, no pastry, no alcohol, no salt. I merely tell you these dreary details because I feel it just possible that yours may be circulation too and my procedure might tempt you? It is a real comfort to have got down to what really is the matter, even if there is little to be done.

Karmels left today, getting wonderfully mellowed. I think we have a *humanising* atmosphere. I miss you and would love to have you in all these small vicissitudes which are fun if shared – everything is fun if shared. I think of the war with nostalgia, when England was not decadent and we all stood banded together.

Your loving

FREYA

P.S. I read Bowra in Oxford,[79] very amused. John Sparrow said he saw a review title 'Dear Old Soul Looks Back' and thought it was on Bowra's book. Everyone wonders what he left out!

MRS. DAVID PAWSON   Montoria

13 January 1966

Dearest Pam,

The house is sold! Also paid for! And though there doesn't seem to be much left by way of income, I am free of all my debts! After all the strain I feel a bit battered, but like a ship in harbour, a very restful feeling. I don't think I shall be up to Samarkand (though I hope for next year), but I do plan to reach Turkey and to linger in Greece on the way and perhaps go and bathe off an island? Would you be about in June? – and ready for what? I think I shall be rich enough to travel in comfort and leave the Istanbul bus for strong godchildren.

[79] Sir Maurice Bowra's *Memories 1898–1939* (1966).

My book, too, is in proof and should be out in April,[80] and I plan to be in England for six weeks or so. So you see, life is getting into gear again and those moments when I thought *why* the devil did I ever think of building a house are quite forgotten and disowned.

Much love, dear Pam,

FREYA

JOHN GREY MURRAY   Montoria
                                              22 January 1966

Dearest Jock,

Your coming and going seems rather like a dream, and both of us too exhausted to have enjoyed it as we might; and I feel that what we both need is three weeks at least on a Greek island with nothing to do but swim. Will that ever be possible? How lovely it would be. Meanwhile I feel I was a bundle of nerves and never thanked you properly for coming all this way; but glad to think that you did and were able to start what I hope will be a long, at any rate fairly long, sequence with Montoria. It is snowing hard now, but we have a new supply of oil in the cistern and can take what comes.

I have my horrible sinus and you will be glad to hear have really decided on a quiet year with two months sea-bathing somewhere and no Samarkand till 1967. When I get to London I will ask you about that operation, as it seems to me that Eastern travel, dust, heat and cold, is going to be dished if I can't do something about it.

The will is done and I will send it as soon as signed. I went to Padova yesterday and ordered a new dress as I felt in need of a tonic, and got the dressmaker as one signatory of the will. One should never *assume* in January that one may wear summer clothes?

I leave about February 20th by way of Portugal to Nuri Birgi in Paris (new hat) to London March 10th. Is it possible? I feel like a barnacle thinking of running after *two years*.

Meanwhile the Romans seem splendid and poor John is a hero over the references. Do please put his name among the Thanks. What fun if we succeed in debunking the Romans! I think Aldo Martelli might do an Italian translation if you send him a copy and a note?

Best of love, dear Jock, and forgive impatience from your loving

FREYA

[80] *Rome on the Euphrates.*

Montoria

17 May 1966

Dearest Jock,

I had a charming three days with Birgi – a Mozart concert, a French evening party, a NATO evening party, and (by far the most agreeable) a supper on the quay opposite Notre Dame – a meal entirely of raw vegetables and cheeses, about twenty different kinds. I then found an excellent train that trundles through green, river-fed French landscape from 8 a.m. and gets one home in time for a latish dinner. In all the years of my life going to and fro from Italy to England I had never managed to look at this bit of France before, so soft and sleepy.

I have been sitting up late over those beastly pictures and have now found tentative substitutes for all those marked 'No' or queried – rather horrified to see that this is more than half the total number. It has made me sad, as I loved my photographs and thought well of the poor little nonentities, and now that I know they are poor I get no pleasure turning them over and over. For this reason among others I do hope they can be chosen before I leave; if we have to wait till October when I am here again, it will be *a year and three months* since I began to plead for a choice of these miserable pictures ('your splendid photographs' I see you wrote me in October last year!). I am all in favour of choosing better ones however, and you are quite right to want the best, but I simply can't bear the thought of more months going by and at last coming back to the same old problem.

Montoria is a paradise of greenness: it looks as if its little woods were cushions one could sink into. All except one oak tree seem flourishing and the roses begin to pour down their hill. I shall be so glad when it belongs to the Gowries and is no longer likely to be orphaned. Zeno nearly made me weep, he was so overcome at my arrival.

Well, dearest Jock, I *do* hope you are coming. I will write a less harassed letter in a few days, to Diana too – and a baby cap must be looked out for Joanna.

Much love dear Jock,

FREYA

Montoria

23 May 1966

Dearest Jock,

I have managed to do the preliminary selection of the other two themes just in time before Dulcie arrives tomorrow. She is here only for a week, but

I will try to get her to go through the whole lot with me. If we have got it right as far as we can see from the literary point of view, there is nothing more I can do till the technical eye is given to the pictures, and I am living in anxious hope of your arrival or if that is sadly impossible, John's?

I am now going out with a note book to write down names of roses. About eighty out of a hundred of the plants grafted onto small wild cuttings have taken and I try to recognise them as they put out their first feeble blossom. But about thirty plants are already out and look wonderful. A series is slowly being put out along all the western terraces, and three rows are there now, looking like jewels on the grassy banks. Grassy steps will connect the terraces, so that I can spend my old age getting quite a long walk looking at every variety of rose on the way. It will make it impossible ever to leave Montoria in May.

I am beginning to read for Samarkand — a charming book of stories. One of a holy man whom a disciple accused of drinking wine: he was taken to the cellar and lo, as the holy man stepped in, all the barrels were filled with honey instead of wines; whereupon all the other disciples complained and asked 'What is the good of purifying our cellar if you have not purified our hearts?'

I am harassed by uncertainties everywhere. Francesca's marriage, now on now off; Emma very problematical with Checchi still living in uncertainty in Casa Freia, whose fate is still uncertain.

Much love, and hopes,

FREYA

MRS. DAVID PAWSON   Montoria
                                                       1 June 1966
Dearest Pam,

How difficult the summer always is! I am sad about not seeing you at all, unless possibly for a day in Athens on the way from the island to Turkey end of August; but meanwhile this is to catch you before you leave Athens and beg you to stop off here as you go north.

I am just back from London after two very social months ending with a ball at which everyone except me was wearing a tiara. I didn't dance but saw several godsons at it, and enjoyed the rare sight of Splendour.

Dear love,

FREYA

Montoria
4 June 1966

Dearest Jock,

The pleasant event of these days is the building of my little shrine: it is going to look so pretty, between a cypress tree and a magnolia, both still in their infancy. When it reaches a pilaster, or cornice, Zeno and I trot down the hill to decide on its proportions and all the country people, walking by with their scythe on their shoulder, stop to talk about it. I thought I would write to Reynolds Stone and ask if he would like the loan of the house in July on condition of painting the Angel. There will have to be a *festa* day for him/her and I suppose one's guardian angel should share one's birthday – but it is a poor time of year and I often away, so I thought of giving him my sister's on 4 May instead.

The other bit of news is that I have been forced to buy three acres of grassy hill which were being sold just below my little secret garden. I am now trying to get Caroly to take them as a gift and build herself a little house there; she longs to do this but has domestic obstacles in her way. She *may* get her husband to consent if he is allowed to breed pheasants, which would be delightful.

Dearest Jock, of course all is well for you and me, it is only that if too much time goes by the gilt does wear off the gingerbread and one gets impatient in one's seventies: in one's eighties I don't believe one will mind any longer, and they are only just round the corner. I am reading a charming book of the eighth century written by a Spanish Arab on the Art of Love and he begins with asking God to 'preserve us and you from bewilderment, and may He not burden us with more than we can bear'. I am sure you must sympathise with this prayer now and then?

Very dear love,

FREYA

Montoria
7 June 1966

Dearest Dulcie,

You and Tommy still seem to be hovering here in some strange way, though it is a week since you left. It has been very quiet, just the sun going over our heads and the misty heat on the plain. I have trotted down the hill two or three times a day to watch the Angel's shrine. It is built now and looks very right, between a baby cypress and magnolia; and the long Sisyphus job with Caroly has finally ended with her accepting the slice of the

an expedition to Cremna, a ruined colony of Augustus' veterans in the hills behind Antalya (also about four days); and a stroll along the Cilician coast (stopping to bathe) to Anamur and a week's tour by Mut, Ermenek, Karaman, and back (another way). I hope this appeals to you? Jock Jardine[82] suggests Side as a base to begin with, and if you agree I will ask him to fix rooms in his cottage which seems to have been so successful.

Let me hear soon. I am looking forward to it. Hope you will brush up your Turkish before September!

Love,
FREYA

Montoria
3 July 1966

JOHN GREY MURRAY

Dearest Jock,

I am feeling a little less sad over the waste of another summer because I have started to draw again – and I am taking the paraphernalia to L'Arma to see what I can do. I am trying a combination of wash (Chinese ink) and pen. I never thought I would have three months with nothing to fill them, and it is just possible I might be able to draw tolerably by the end: anyway it is fascinating and so much *easier* than writing. The arts are the same, only the channel is different; and all one can do in this world I believe is to improve and smooth that channel: the art itself comes from goodness knows where. It seems that Socrates, in his last month in prison, began to learn the flute!

It looks as if the young Gowries are to be owners of Montoria this week: this is a big step and I hope it may be a happiness all round. I feel wonderfully *lightened*, as I hate the feel of property and might become a Dervish at any moment (except that I like my Paris clothes). As far as I can see, I now have no capital left at all, but my income (next year) will be more than double what it was before, and that seems a perfect arrangement. I think it is so intelligent of Alan Punchard to grasp the situation and recommend the conversion of everything into income: the old firm would have implored me to go down the drain with the gilt edges. It was he too who recommended sticking to Switzerland.

I am so very glad you are taking a fortnight off. But it isn't economical. Two months would do the trick and fifteen days is just a palliative. I don't believe there is any quicker cure for real fatigue. Archie Wavell went and

[82] An old friend who worked for the British Council.

lay on a beach in Palestine for two days in the middle of a battle – it takes a very strong nerve!

It is so lovely here now: *breathing* peace, except for the NATO aeroplanes which strengthen my anti-atom-bomb feeling twenty times a day.

Ever so much love, dearest Jock,

FREYA

JOHN GREY MURRAY L'Arma
13 July 1966

Dearest Jock,

It is sad in a way to come here like a Rip Van Winkle – so many memories in every corner and all the faces changed. I don't think I will do so again, but am glad to have come, and to see it prospering, and my niece happy in her own way – one of those strange people who are only contented if they can make themselves believe that they are suffering. The nephew is now nearly eighteen and good with his sailing boat but not his Latin – but a mother-and-son strain that gives this little corner an atmosphere of tension and masses and masses of nice but bourgeois Italian friends. One has to shake hands with about twenty when going down to bathe, but I now go early, and find the bay smooth and cool, with only a fisherman or so standing like a Victorian foreground, and the Australian sculptor who did my bust to talk to. I am swimming quite a long way again and it is doing me lots of good, and I can't bear to think of your struggling with my pictures while I have the holiday. I do a little sketch every day: they seem pretty bad to me, but some people are encouraging. Perhaps I may dispense with photographs altogether, if I can stick to this exercise all summer.

I hope you are resting in Ireland – wish it were here. The spices of the hillsides are wonderfully life-giving: it must have been wonderful when Aurelian was cutting his road and the hills were only touched here and there with vines.

Very much love dear Jock,

FREYA

MAXWELL ARMFIELD Montoria
14 July 1966

Dear Maxwell,

I will not be back till sometime near mid-October: but that would be time enough for my Angel if it suited you and when I get back I can send the measurements of the niche. It is on a shallow curve – and I am so glad that you are allured by the thought of doing it.

It is a very quiet and rural little shrine so I don't think the Angel has anything to do with swords; standing lightly (as he is an angel) but on a stony road (as it is mine), with a pilgrim staff in one hand (for the poor thing comes on all my journeys) and with my house (which he is carrying carefully) in his other hand? A rather Byzantine angel perhaps, quite straight with his wings behind him? I feel sure you will like the country you look out on: all little paintable hills! I hope it can be managed.

Yours ever,

FREYA

LADY CHOLMONDELEY

Amorgos

6 August 1966

Dearest Sybil,

I got here yesterday and am enchanted with my island which hasn't a hard road upon it and is therefore still quite unspoilt. All I have seen is its great north-east bay, shut in all except north-west but so big that the enclosure seems open: its sides are bare brown terraced slopes with a few little white clusters, villages of flat-roofed houses. The little port has a jetty at which nothing bigger than a caique can tie, and they can be watched all day (there are only about four) seeing to their nets till they set out into the sunset. Otherwise there is nothing except a church, about twelve houses and this hotel, and the island life comes drifting in and out as it has always done, with mules from the inland villages bringing down their grapes and beans and cheeses, and people beautifully healthy and friendly. The hotel has only six rooms, and minimum of furniture, but clean as a new pin, with the proprietor cooking excellent food and two lovely maids in blue cotton and high-heeled shoes, most anxious to talk if only I knew Greek. There is the feeling so native to Greece as if the elixir of life ran through its poverty and hardness and everything it touches is beautiful.

I am writing, dear Sybil, because it is your wedding day and I have been sitting on my balcony watching the sun sink over Naxos and hoping that all is well with you both – that Rock is getting better, however slowly. These long anxieties are terrible for wearing one down.

I have a book which tells the tragic story of Samarkand and the Mongols, written by a contemporary who became a Minister and was able to help in reconstruction – *The History of the World Conqueror* by Juwaini, translated

101

by J. S. Boyle (Manchester University Press). All the early part should be read by anyone who wants to know what happens when one is really conquered by the barbarian. It explains how the most flourishing part of Asia was turned to desert not from malignity but because the Mongols' only riches were sheep and they wanted grazing and no towns. There is a description of how town-walls or houses were destroyed by ropes threaded through them in two places and then tugged by the army till the wall came down. It is frightening because the barbarity is so *abstract* (as well as appalling). Anyway it is quite a book to be read before going to Samarkand. The monuments left there are due to the Mongols preserving the *craftsmen* when they massacred a town.

I must stop as I am falling asleep. I hope to be curing myself with swimming, and took two good, heavenly swims today: the sea here like an elixir.

Very dear love,

FREYA

MRS. T. DEUCHAR   Amorgos
                                                              18 August 1966

Darling Dulcie,
Far away in the north-east yesterday I saw the outline, very faint, of the island of Ikaria, where Metaxas used to imprison his political exiles, and I thought of how they would see the months pass and look with what longing at the little steamer that might bring them mails. Here, I have just discovered, that though there are three steamers a week, one only brings letters and that should be tomorrow.

Meanwhile I write but have no idea whether to think of you in Australia or at Standon. I would have liked to have had my magic carpet and wafted you with me yesterday across the back of the island. Such a day! I left on a mule at 6 a.m., up among vineyards from the two villages that hang above us with five or six hundred steps (I lost count) above them and below, vines and fig trees throwing their heavy sweet scents across the path; and then the thin ribbon-terraces of stubble propped on walls, centuries of labour, that make the island hills look like hieroglyphs in patterns of walls; and round these austere enclosures the thyme now blossoms, thorny and purple, a scent of marvellous splendour out of the stones. No riches can speak like this poverty to the heart. I was so happy. I had thought I could never do this and am doing all the doctor says no to, on the theory that the general health which flourishes on days with a mule may conquer the particular bits of me that are going to pieces. Anyway, it was heaven to be sitting on the wooden saddle in the sun, up and down, high above the bays and inlets and their rare paths and whitewashed chapels and sunny winding jewel-depths of sea. Naxos rising in the west until we cut across the waist of the island and saw its fearful eastern wall, curving sheer with dark outlines in the morning shadows, and the dark Aegean flecked with foam. On and on, and no other traveller on the path, to the highest mountain which has St. Elias (from Helios the Sun-God) in its chapel; under its shoulder the precious side, where halfway up the sheer face a monastery is dedicated to the Virgin. Two monks only are left, and it was only trickling on from its great days when it was the jewel of the island, but masons were at work and no doubt it will be resuscitated for the tourists. Already a road brings cars to the village a half hour away on the south.

There were a few pilgrims, all Greeks, and one busily photographing the pages of an eleventh-century manuscript. The little rooms cannot manage more than nine or ten feet width, their precipice platform is so small; their dazzling white walls slope to it in great buttresses with little windows high for safety. There was no shade except two scraggy almond (?) trees (for the mules), and so when I had drunk coffee and visited the little church crowded with all that furniture, a chandelier in a nylon bag and silver lamps and ikons and many little models of arms and legs of all ages, I decided to go on to Amorgos, the capital of the island.

There down a whitewashed street was a *taverna* and the muleteer and I lunched on its terrace and I found a sofa for a siesta. The whole south of the island drops away, and I saw a motor car again as the road reaches (but doesn't penetrate) the village. Only the clip-clop of hooves, donkeys or mules. At three in the afternoon we started back as it is a four hours' way over the Elias shoulder, very high. From there one looks far out and sees how we lie as it were in a nest of islands, Astipalaia and Anafi and Ios, Naxos, and Dhenousa, and far Ikaria, and Santorini the last of them visible only to the imagination on the edge of the Cretan Sea. The afternoon lay like sheaves of gold, and the sea had turned soft, bluer than anything in the world, and swathing all except the summits of the islands in misty veils that held their secrets as if they were brides. The horizon itself was lost, all blue water and white sun. Our island too lay there like a brown leaf in the sun veined by its laborious little walls of stones.

We got back at seven after thirteen hours, eight and a half on the mule. I was so pleased to find I could do it and feel none the worse, and the legs which had grown by a half an inch have today subsided. Anyway, the day was worth whatever the cost may be. I was wondering as I came down what the islands must look like in spring; am told that in March and April they are a paradise of flowers and the little terraces are green with the young corn, and they would not be very hot then. Why not choose an island that doesn't require eight and a half hours on a mule and come and look at this loveliness? So small a time is given, so much to see.

Ever so much love, darling Dulcie, and to Tommy,

FREYA

SIR MICHAEL STEWART
Istanbul

2 September 1966

Dearest Michael,

I am now sitting with Bosphorus flowing under the window and Rumen Hisar opposite. Did you ever hear the Bosphorus *grunt*? It makes a noise unlike any water I know and throws itself against my bedroom wall as if it were a huge living creature throwing itself like a sack full of loose pieces, in short whacks: I can't think how the banks have stood up to it so long.

My trip to Erzurum is sadly smashed by the earthquake, so I have nine days here and then meet Mark and his girl[83] at Antalya and hope to ride about round Anamur.

Turkey, or anyway Istanbul, looks very much more prosperous and everything can be found and many things made here. If given time, the Turks will get on very well I believe, running their own country. They are ominously intent on tourism at the moment.

Tell my goddaughter that I love her, not only when good (which might mean rather a short time) but also when naughty.

Love to you all,

FREYA

MAXWELL ARMFIELD
As from Cilicia

10 September 1966

Dear Maxwell,

Just as I was leaving the Bosphorus yesterday a huge heap of all the overdue letters arrived and yours of August 8th among them.

Angel: colours, blue – indigo – very good. Not gold I should say in the very rural surroundings. I like the stars, and the house held in the crook of the arm. The right hand and bent head are a bit *ecclesiastical* for my Angel

---

[83] Elizabeth Bridgeman.

who is, I feel sure, a bit of a pagan at heart. I think of him facing us squarely with a staff in his hand, ready for anything, and particularly for all the shocks I must have given him. I don't on the other hand mind his standing on a sword, though not very comfortable, if his rocky path is difficult.

The only motto I have thought of so far is from the *Georgics* (Book II): 'Sacra fero ingenti percussus amore' – but we are sure to find a number of good ones in the *Divine Comedy*.

I am on the way to Cilicia and out of reach of mails till I get home. So *au revoir* at Montoria where I may possibly find you?

Finance compromise sounds O.K. and I can certainly do all in liras.

Yours ever,
FREYA

JOHN GREY MURRAY Side

19 September 1966

Dearest Jock,

We have spent three days in this old city, its theatre and streets and walls all crumbling round us, its two harbours sunk and shallow in its sea, and a few inhabitants originally Cretan living in charming stone houses with wooden porches in and out of the ruins. There is a little square with the two pubs we knew before now a bit painted up but still standing on crooked poles above the bay, and a new restaurant named after Cleopatra in which we are writing. We have rooms in the barber's house, covered with embroidery and beautifully clean; we have nothing to do with the new motel, nor meet the Americans who – very imaginatively – have bought a house and spend their summer here. In spite of all, it is not my favourite of the southern cities – it is so shallow and stranded on its sandy shore. But yesterday and today we have been inland, trying to see the inside of the Manavgat river gorge. I have wanted to do this for years, as one sees the split of its rocks from the coast – and so yesterday we took our jeep and tried to work by the map which led by what it called a main road into a high tangle of forest and limestone ridges too narrow to turn on. On the very height we came upon a camp of the woodcutters who live in the forests and never mix with any other Turks – Tahtajis. Their women wear a headdress and costume peculiar to the tribe and we were surrounded by old viragos with not a smile on their face and the ornaments of their youth still worn across their foreheads. They speak a different language, and evidently had no welcome for strangers though the men, when they came up, were normal and friendly. We found ourselves far from our way, the gorges inaccessible below us and the river hidden, and the only village in sight leading away into roadless heights of Taurus. So we drove down again, with the whole of Pamphylia laid out in the sunset below, and today got up at 5.30 and tried the right bank of the river – and there had wonderful luck, as the ancient Greek aqueduct of Side is being explored for a new 'Centrale'. We followed it over winding little pine-hills, a few splendid arches standing here and there in little valleys: fifteen miles or so, all cut in stone, until the ancient masons met the rock and the ancient and modern start more or less together. The river pours deep and green out of sheer rock, and high plane, poplar, or pine grow above it wherever there is room. It felt like something out of Wordsworth. It was a perfect day apart from the shock of being stung by a hornet. We got back in time for a bathe in this shallow sea, quite warm. Liz is not a bit meant to be anything more of a traveller than Mayfair on holiday, and neither of them care a hoot about ruins – but I am not doing anything in particular anyway and it seems to be an idea that one can do one's courting better in Asia. I feel it will be a great pity for Mark to marry too soon, before he knows what sort of a life he wants – but it would be waste of time to tell him. It is such a razor's edge, and he so unconscious of it. How glad I am to be safely out of all those shoals.

Must go off now. My book seems to read very stodgily. I hope it will not be too much pulled to pieces.

Much love dear Jock,

FREYA

JOHN GREY MURRAY   Montoria
                                                  12 October 1966
Dearest Jock,

I feel like the cook who had so much work to do that she gave up and went to bed. I came back yesterday to what looks like two and a half months' accumulated letters – so instead of coping am writing to you instead! I am so happy, dear Jock, to read of your proper rest in Ireland; I only hope it was long enough – I was very worried about you. One can go safely up to the edge, but once over, even by a very little, it is the most devilish business to get back. (I found that twice after Hadhramaut.)

Rome on the Euphrates seems to be getting every sort of review. I have just got Raymond Mortimer (and sent him a card to say I regret he doesn't like me as a historian but am pleased with the record of our meetings): his review will get lots of readers, I feel, on quite false pretences. My noble effort to destroy a 2,000-year-old cliché is probably doomed to failure, but I get such comforting

106

private letters. Anyway I am like Montaigne in writing 'for myself' and am delighted to have some faint glimmer of all those references still alive inside me.

The Guardian Angel in a white cloud and blue dress is in his shrine and Maxwell Armfield who has painted him is here till Sunday. Now let me tell you what has happened. I said, in my mind, some months ago to the Angel that I ought really not to build the shrine till he had found me my jewel case again. Nothing happened, the shrine was built before I left, and the Angel himself was finished about a week ago. Four days ago the jewel box was discovered behind the kitchen sink in Asolo where Emma had hidden it and forgotten. What a lesson to pay one's debts!

The idea is to spend Xmas with Mooreheads and get to London soon after – and a long spring here: but it hasn't yet crystallised.

Love and thanks, dearest Jock, for the Romans and for all,

FREYA

DEREK COOPER
Standon,
Ockley
20 November 1966

Dearest Derek,

I am so glad to get your letter and to hear the good news that I may hope to see you in January or February. Either should find me at Montoria – and ready to take your ski kit. I had hoped to be full of zest after my cure, but it seems to be making me feel very ill, so that I don't think I can manage Ireland – and am comforted for this disappointment by the thought of seeing you soon. We had not suffered on the hill, apart from one or two tiny landslides on the road – but the whole tragedy is very miserable and the Po is the crowning disaster.[84]

I haven't had a word from Grey or Bingo[85] since early last summer as far as I can remember – and am rather shocked.

Lovely to think of seeing you and Pam. Thanks for her letter. I got one when I was at Amorgos and wrote at once suggesting a meeting in Athens, but the Greek islands must be *thick* with lost letters. Mine was rather sad because I could have joined your camp if only I had known in time. What a relief it will be, when Time no longer exists.

Love,
FREYA

[84] There had been disastrous floods in Italy.
[85] Lady Gowrie (Xandra Bingley).

107

Paris
22 December 1966

Darling Dulcie,

I spend much time thinking of you, and of Alan,[86] and all around you, and in two days hope to find news at Montoria. If my heart were not so occupied nor my body very tired I would be thinking myself very gay — lunch or dinner parties every day and the new suit quite enchanting. Perhaps you may bring it if you pass through Paris; otherwise some other victim, as the fittings are all over but it can't be finished in time. What a labour of perfection! In the next cubicle they were fitting the actress in the new Pirandello and it was a sort of scene from Molière or Mozart.

Talking of theatres, Nuri took me to *The Three Sisters* yesterday, beautifully acted by three Russian women of great charm and beauty; devitalising women they are, but what a poignantly vivid picture of the passing by of life and all its chances. Even more tragic a general view of life is Picasso whose whole history is on show now in his works. From exquisite things about 1901–6, they go through cubism and all the phases, many incomprehensible to me but in none there is not some sudden blossoming.

Dearest love,

FREYA

MR. AND MRS. T. DEUCHAR

Montoria
30 December 1966

Darling Dulcie and Tommy,

Assuming no news is good news, I have sent him a greeting today and hope to hear soon that he is sitting up, talking, and on the way to convalesce, and poor Lucy recovering from the strain.

I lay very low Xmas day and only let out that I was here on 27th, and we spent a pleasant quiet time. I am more and more pleased with the double-house; it means that one can see just as much or as little of one's tenants as one chooses.

It is quite lovely here, only one day with bits of rain and otherwise warm enough for even me to go without a hat, the mountains powdered with light snow and melting in sunlight, the bleached grassy hills and meadows all wakening already to green along the edges of their streams. I have already a little bouquet of stylosa iris, Christmas roses, and the sweet-scented

---

[86] Alan Moorehead had suffered a stroke.

camamenthes, and the six little winter prunus trees are full of blossom. No doubt the cold will come, but meanwhile the days lengthen. I take walks for circulation, and lie up for heart, and that leaves very little time over.

When, when will you come?

Love,
FREYA

Montoria
30 December 1966

JOHN GREY MURRAY

Dearest Jock,

I meant to write as soon as I got here but the whole Nemesis of an unprepared Xmas was upon me and I have only just cleared my table of cards belatedly answered. This is what always happens: one decides not to send, and then feels that a greeting can't be allowed to drop into a void.

The days are glorious, shining on Grappa snow – only a little at the top; and the poor little towns and villages are just like cats that have been thrown into the water, lying in the warmth and licking themselves clean. We went yesterday to look at Bassano bridge which is boarded up with a notice to say that the citizens and the 'Alpini', proud of their memories, intend to build it as it was before. We then drove up to the first town in the valley where all seemed normal except the river walls which had been breached and just tossed aside: it was only when one got to the houses that one saw them all empty, still smelling of water and mud.

I lay low on Xmas Day, so glad to receive your telegram. So many thanks – it made England come near again. Mr. Wilson, or perhaps just the loss of our poor Empire, has managed to turn it back very much into an island, and the Victorian image abroad (which was not a bad image after all) seems at last to have faded: this at least is what I felt in Paris amid all the NATO gossip. Nuri amused me with the tale of a friend of his who was delegate to the U.N. at Geneva and when someone there got up to say it was their United Christian duty to do something or other, he got up and said 'But we're *not* all Christians: I'm a Moslem Turk.' Applause and pattings on the back all round. Nuri gave me a fascinating description of what the NATO problems are for a nuclear war. It fortifies me very much in my conviction that America alone should deal with these weapons: nobody else can afford to make anything really useful. I must stop, dearest Jock, with love and wishes for 1967 – better I hope than this sad year which is closing at last.

Your loving
FREYA

Montoria

4 January 1967

Dearest Jock,

I am sitting between my three views in the sun and thanking friends for cards which still come in, and am so glad to get your little note among them: it is rather nice not to send Xmas cards and then to write thanks for those received, and makes Xmas more of a communication, and I like to feel all messages converging on my hill. It must please the Angel at the bottom of the rise.

I would like to write essays and will do so when I can – *must*, as you know, get one done on Palmyra; but I am not yet able to do any work worth while, and it is not *themes* that are wanting: I think I could easily fill three lives with what I would like to write. What has happened to English Literature to make it appear necessary to hunt about or to provide authors with themes? It is the moulding of manageable forms out of this reservoir that is the problem and the strain.

I am reading Montaigne. What enchanting and sprightly wisdom!

The Karmels leave in a few days. They seem very happy and I am becoming attached to them. I think this place is good for their 'immortal longings' or anyway for hers: she says she hopes to be here much more now, and they have come back from a jaunt of three days with a strong feeling for the economy of a house as against hotels. If the Gowries never write for the next six years, I might sell it to them for a huge sum!

Love,

FREYA

Montoria

5 January 1967

Dearest Dulcie,

Here things go happily uneventful and I have just finished dealing with one hundred and fifty cards I found waiting. The Karmels are still here and leave on Saturday, and have now really become attached to the magic little hill and hope to come more often and for longer. I like having them here, because anyway I have a great deal of the time alone and it makes me happy to feel that someone beside myself is enjoying it. I watch them walking about in the sun, as happy as two little elderly pigeons, and sometimes wonder if the fate of the place will be Karmel rather than my own plans for the people I love. It is what happens: one builds, but the end goes beyond one, though the building remains.

Two beautiful presents have come to me and help me through the hours I lie with my feet high up; one is the Bach Christmas Oratorio, wonderfully executed, and the other an Italian synopsis of the *Divina Commedia*. It has a musical background and I would have preferred that cut shorter and more passages read; but it is lovely to hear the immortal words in their great arch of meaning, from the easiest whisper to the terrible nobility or ferocity of the damned. I will never make up my mind between Shakespeare and Dante: they took different directions with equal power and there is no comparing, and luckily we have both.

Francesca is trying bravely to run both her houses, with a sort of storm-flicker constantly on the horizon. Marriage, she says, is not quite what she thought it and Franco now has a temporary job as night watchman, which upsets her a lot. She has a wonderful brightness in her eyes, like a force of Nature released, a torrent of shining irresistible water, not human but terrific, the force not of love but of the primitive goddess. Franco, on the other hand, looks a bit worn.

Dear love, darling Dulcie, to Tommy also. I do so long for some news and good news. Have so missed you all through this fortnight of glorious sun.

FREYA

JOHN GREY MURRAY Montoria
20 January 1967

Dearest Jock,

Polizzi is keeping me horizontal all the day (or at least sitting in an Etruscan way) except for a let-up and walk in the afternoon, so I remain in bed till lunch and — apart from really making the legs better — it does let me work a bit. I shall hope to do the essay on Security which has been haunting me for over a year — how one is frustrated by this slowness! You needn't complain of being tired, dear Jock: all you need do, and would if you were wise, is to take a holiday — preferably at Montoria. You have another twenty years to go before you need realise that the downhills don't go up again: there is nothing for the fifth act except catastrophe or release! Not that it depresses me; and I shall try to get to Samarkand before the Finis.

I have knocked off my Russian while trying to write these articles and began browsing my way through the old novels (they are all in Dulcie and Tommy's room and I am sleeping there now). I began with *Trilby* which came out two years after I was born and is the world my parents knew in Paris and often told me of. That charming atmosphere suddenly revealed

III

itself as *home* to me. Then browsing along, through the Twenties and the aridity of Aldous Huxley etc., it suddenly struck me that this is the way, through its novels, to get at the picture of an age – and when did that cleft appear which cuts off my happy *Trilby* climate from today? I have now read quite a lot and the notes which make me feel an alien in their world become dominant in the Twenties: it is there I believe and not among the poor young of today that the destruction started (with the generation before them, my generation, to all intents wiped out). It appears in these books so clearly – a generation blossoming between two wars, its values so shaken as almost to be destroyed, its courage quite inadequate to see that two and two make four – quite inadequate even to see that some careful arithmetic is needed. It is these, now in their influential middle ages, who offer nothing but mediocrity to the young – and who shall blame the latter for turning away from their parents? With mediocrity as an aim, decadence is the result: I believe it is as simple as that – and it breaks my heart, for we were not mediocre in our day. Let us hope that the godchildren will pull the world round again. I feel sure they will – somewhere: possibly not in England.

Now this is what comes of sitting for an afternoon writing letters in bed!

Love,

FREYA

MRS. DAVID PAWSON   Montoria
                                                  21 January 1967

My dearest Pam,

I make lovely summer plans to sail from Venice at the beginning of August. Is there a chance of your being free for ten days or so? And should we go to an island, Thasos, and across to Samothrace? I am writing so early in the hope that you can keep clear. I have a longing to see Boudonitsa and Thermopylae (have never been to) and we might cut across from there? If you think this feasible, do fix two rooms right away and let us stake the precious time. It does so melt away in one's hands! After mid-August I must go on East, from Istanbul to Samarkand if I am fit; if not, to potter about Anatolia as I have a book in mind. I thought of following Ibn Batuta's journey among the later Seljuks and writing a modern version?

I am glad you like the book, but what makes you think I don't like the Byzantines? On the contrary, they seem to me to have brought the Empire back to sanity. The Romans and Britons are not *really* alike, you know; whatever else we have been, it is not venal and that was the worst Roman defect. Also we have an unobtrusive but perennial fountain of imagination which they singularly lacked (their poetry stopped and ours does go on, even now, from age to age). I think this British-Roman similarity is another of those historical clichés.

What fun, dear Pam, if we could have another of our little holidays together. Surely David too can get away *some* time? Do let me know, and I will immediately start getting well for it!

Ever so much love to you both,

FREYA

JOSEPH ALSOP   Montoria

21 January 1967

Dear Mr. Alsop,

It is a very long time since we met, and you may have forgotten me, but I remember with pleasure conversations at Ronnie Tree's house in Barbados, and have always hoped that we might run across each other again. I have now just finished reading your *Silent Earth*, and must tell you how *very* much I have enjoyed it. I was led to it by your article on the palace of the south-east coast, and already felt a wish to write and tell you how a godson and I went to Siteia (about ten years ago) and, bathing from the little cape of Paleocastro, saw it to be full of shards of red pottery embedded in the rock. The bathe was forgotten and we worked for the rest of our time with penknives and finally dug out a tiny but complete Mycenaean pot. These lovely moments, how one remembers them!

I am so encouraged by what both you and Maurice Bowra say in defence of the amateur historian that I have asked Harcourt Brace to send you my book on the Euphrates frontier through the Roman age (it is called *Rome on the Euphrates* in the London edition, but they do sometimes change the title in the States). It is due out early in the spring. It tries to destroy what I consider to be a cliché 2,000 years old, and has had much kinder treatment than I expected from the historians and a blessing from Steven Runciman. But I doubt if I have got the excellent *clearness* with which you line up the evidence.

How lucky we still are in this ominous world to be able to find still swathed in their original atmosphere, their hard gaiety of rock and sea and sky, those secrets which you love! Last summer I spent a month in an un-contaminated little Cyclade and was invited to the Panagya (15th August) a couple of hours inland by mule, and there found the Homeric feast in full operation. The church invited all who came to lunch, and when we arrived, two men were busy skinning the last of thirty sheep, suspended from olive trees. The church was a small whitewash affair, in a solitude of rocky hills like fossil sponges, but flowering in their austere way with scented thyme. And there were about a thousand people, swaying on their mules or walking, and the white and turquoise flag was just going up and the little cracked bell tinkling for Mass. When that was over, and the coffee-man had been busy with all our drinks for a long time, the sheep in huge copper cauldrons were at last cooked and the crowd moved in relays to long stone tables in the shade of boughs. The rough earthenware red bowls from which we ate might easily have been Cretan or anything you like, and so might the amphorae from which the girls poured our rezzina. The most Homeric touch, unfortunately, was the smell, that 'sweet savour' which the Gods so enjoyed, for the thirty sheep had butchered and cooked not more than twenty yards away and the sweet sticky blood-smell very nearly made me faint. But it was Homeric all right.

Forgive this long meandering letter, and thank you again for the excellent book (Michael Stewart now in Washington told me about it).

If you happen to reach Venice, do come up and spend a day on my hill.

Yours sincerely,

FREYA STARK

LADY CHOLMONDELEY   Montoria
                                              24 January 1967
Dearest Sybil,

I am so happy to have your letter and cheering news about Rock. The spring is round the corner and may you both enjoy it with no shocks after the awful year. How lovely Houghton must be when all the beech buds begin, 'like flocks to feed in air'.

I am going through a rather dreary patch, not so much bothered by my legs which can be laid along a sofa, but my head: the circulation trouble seems to affect it and I can make myself concentrate less and less. If I get senile quite soon I hope you will still love me for old time's sake (you would, you are the truest friend); but what I think and hope more likely is that I may have to do less and write easy things and not too many.

I am absorbed at the moment in Moran's book[87] and rather shaken to

---

[87] Lord Moran, Churchill's doctor, had published his diaries under the title *Churchill, The Struggle for Survival*.

see his symptoms so like my own (but of course I do *drink* less). It is a tremendously valuable book, not great because no great talent in the interpretation. Was he so tiresome? Or did Moran not really feel sympathy? I think he does come out a bit diminished; the same intimacy with Wavell or Smuts would have required nobler words. I would like to know what you and Rock think.

I have written, with ever so much effort, an article on Palmyra for Paul Hamlyn's *Picture Book of Ancient Cities* (rather amusing, my husband is doing Jerash in the same volume, rather better than mine I fear). Having done that I now have only one thing I care about in hand and that is an essay on 'Our Second-Rate Security'. It has nothing to do with armaments, but life and death and time. I will send it you when done.

Oh poor England: it gives me more pain at the heart than doctors can cure.

Dear love to you both, dear, dear Sybil.

FREYA

JOHN GREY MURRAY Montoria

3 February 1967

Dearest Jock,

I am so glad to get your letter, and also the telegram for the birthday that is rather better forgotten; it is gloomy to be near, if not in, the time when one exists rather than lives. I have been looking through old essays and think one could make a book, part old and part new, on 'Thoughts and Places' or 'Thoughts and Journeys' (some such title) – half on travel and half on this and that? Only it would need about a week to select and then I could see what is missing and add a few essays. Could you find any time to come out? I have time now (too much time but not enough energy) and nothing to interfere except the David Cecils if they come for the Easter vacation – but nothing can get an answer out of them.

Meanwhile so many thanks for replenishing the bank account – just in time to save an overdraft which seems to upset their computers. History, apart from infuriating the true-blue expert (two vitriolic reviews so far), doesn't pay very well does it? Three and a half years to write, one and a half to publish the Romans – it works out at an income of about £200 a year and all that sweat! But I am very glad to have done it and even the worst review hasn't *contradicted* the theory. Some proper historian will take it up, as they will the Xenophon-Alexander thread, and will insert it into the

115

stream of history and nobody will think that it was me in first place; and that is what I really care about – that and the fact that the books may be read for *pleasure*:

> from my base metal may be forged a key
> that shall unlock the door they howl without.

Steven[88] did me a true service by liking my book and saying so, as it has made me immune to the others – and also Arnold Toynbee who wrote the *Literary Supplement* review. Do you think I might write to him or would it be indelicate as he is supposed to be anonymous? I would love to visit him when next in England.

The Montoria news is slightly perturbed by the fact that it looks as if Francesca is started on twins. Emma has renounced the motor bicycle, but went completely temperamental (female frustration over Francesca etc.) – and I now must find someone who can run this house without more than average drama. Anyway, having told Emma that next time she gives notice I will accept it, all is now peace.

I am also hovering on the edge of a Mini-Moke. They make them here and say they needn't be paid till after August when I hope to be solvent, and they are sending one for me to see. It is open with a canvas roof and doors than can be put in in winter, and as far as I can find out is the only *small* open car – lovely for summer excursions. It would be fun if you could get out to inaugurate it. (I am open to any other car suggestions if you know of anything that will *open easily* and not with just a square hole in the roof.)

Much love and do try and come,

FREYA

MRS. T. DEUCHAR   Montoria
                                                    4 March 1967

Darling Dulcie,

The Derek Coopers have just left and looked quite different and resuscitated; and no sooner had they left than four young things came from the Hodgkin house, just up from Florence where they have been washing down books.[89] They all came to dinner in jeans (haven't brought anything else) but rather enjoyed our antiquated world and we had Bach after dinner as *background* music (that rather hurts) and then discussed war and peace and such. There is much too much feeling and too little thought and it isn't their

[88] sc. Runciman.
[89] After the flood in Florence the previous November.

116

fault. The one young aesthete fascinated me as he had long flaxen curls to his shoulders and it took me about twenty minutes to decide that it was a boy after all. But I liked them and feel a warmth of pity, they have such a huge job and are neither equipped nor helped. I do blame the parents.

Dearest love,

FREYA

LADY CHOLMONDELEY   Montoria
                                                   7 March 1967

Dearest Sybil,

I hope all is well but am anxious when a long stretch goes by without news; the last came quite a time ago and Rock was recovering from pneumonia and I would be happy to know that he is quite over it and no complications. All seemed so well before, but these two years have wrecked one's nerve – *everybody* I care about seems to have been or to be in grief or sickness. The worst is Alan Moorehead, who after over two months is still scarcely able to speak. They are hopeful but I am haunted by fears.

I am very quiet here with the pleasantest sort of visitors now and then who let me work in the morning and are pleasant in the afternoons. I manage to amuse myself with essays and Jock is getting a book ready (I hope late '68) of essays and oddments from the beginning of my writing in 1932 onward – *The Zodiac Arch* I thought of calling it, to go with *Perseus*? It makes me wonder, as I play with this filigree work, what makes one want to write at all? Not money, even when I was desperately poor, and not success in its public form. The pleasure of my friends certainly, and the hope to do something however small not unworthy of our great stream. I remember when the atom bomb was so much in mind how I thought how one could not bear to write if no one were to read in coming generations. But chiefly I suppose it is the endless pleasure of wreathing words and meanings, as if one were playing with beads.

If I possibly can I hope to go to Bukhara in the autumn – mid-September I suppose. Have you any idea to whom and how one writes to ask? My Russian is fairly good for asking the way, etc. I have Archie Wavell's books which he once gave me and his little notes scribbled at the side.

Very dear love, dear Sybil. Please send news.

FREYA

Montoria
                                                                29 March 1967
Dearest Jock,

Yesterday was full of tragedy: the Madonna on her hill had her *festa* and Henry's little hill was crawling with young girls supervised by two nuns; and Emma and I – alone in the house – came out to see them taking half my white narcissi up the opposite hill (there was a beautiful *lake* of them between the ilex, about 700 all in flower). I rushed up but it takes twenty minutes. However, I found those two monster nuns ready to lie themselves black as their robes: they hadn't *seen* a narcissus, and only later was I told of the whole bus filled with armfuls. I came down the hill and saw the remaining flowers being feverishly gathered (Emma left to guard was *sewing* indoors) and when I got back not one was left. Franco and Francesca returned from their day off and he was just in time to get the last culprits – a band of about six whom he brought up to me after a hand to hand show. They were frightened by then and said they would all *kneel* to me if I forgave what they called 'una distrazione' (absent-mindedness). They came from Castelfranco so we sent them off uncomforted but are not pursuing either them or the nuns, but the three smallest culprits from S. Zenone were recognised and are being visited (but not further damaged) by the police tomorrow. I wept over my narcissi and the general depressingness of mankind – and am making a fence though I can't afford it.

                                                                   Love,
                                                                   FREYA

Montoria
                                                                10 April 1967
Dulcie Darling,

I felt so sad as your little waving figure disappeared in the distance, and now I go on missing you and thinking how happy it would be to have you and how you would enjoy it. We have had beastly weather since you left, all the rain saved up since New Year, but managed two little tours to Padova and Possagno, and hope for better luck in Siena; and meanwhile it is such fun to have the wonderful Cecil talk, the real *art* of conversation, taking up any idea that comes, discussing the characters of Hamlet, Desdemona, not the boring gossip about acquaintances but about these whose *real* characters after all one knows so much better. David is just finishing reading the essays and doesn't want to chuck out any more; but he has found a few bits over-lapping to take away and suggests a few sentences between each essay to bind them together as they are so diverse. It seems to me that this is a good idea.

Otherwise no news. A lovely time in spite of rain looking at the Giottos; and then three Titians tucked away in a guild hall; and another look at two beautiful Veroneses; and a magnificent Tintoretto Crucifixion and small head by Bellini. It is fun to go just now and then for a day in these towns of which Italy is so full. We think of stopping in Mantova on the way back.

Darling Dulcie, thank you for coming,

FREYA

MRS. T. DEUCHAR   Siena
                                                              15 April 1967
Darling Dulcie,

We are having such a happy time, all wanting to do the same things, all able to say what we think just as it comes into our heads, the weather just variable enough to be exciting, the time of year perfect, the scenery the most beautiful in Italy, the Cecils never saying anything that isn't a pleasure and stimulus to hear, and all of us filled with that pleasant curiosity which makes life in general worthwhile.

Yesterday we gave up to Piero della Francesca, Arezzo, the great Fran-ciscan walls, and then up a quiet little Tiber valley to a cemetery beside a small old hamlet on a hill where the wonderful pregnant Madonna is all alone in a small chapel and on to Borgo San Sepolcro to see the great *Resurrection*. There can be no greater picture in the world for majesty, and a depth of something so sorrowful, a sorrow beyond sorrow. It is twenty-one years since I was here.

It is all very easy: six and a half hours' drive from Montoria, and half the days here in what B.B. calls the 'best of the Italian cities'. It has kept its atmosphere practically intact so that even the motor cars whizzing up its paved hill-streets seem part of the Renaissance. I am going now to join the party and we go to Pienza, built by Aeneas Silvius for a resting place on his way to Rome.

FREYA

Montoria
                                                    8 May 1967
Dearest Jock,

I have a houseful of guests just now and too much to do and that awful feeling of being swamped in paper – especially as my very basic rule of not thinking of more than one book at a time has been shattered by a letter suggesting a picture book of my travels. I would be delighted to offer this and of course it is not really more than getting the travel essays typed so that they can be *seen*, but even the grasshopper is a burden.

I have a charming little crowd coming and going, Simon, Alice, Charlotte, Benjamin,[90] old Lord Iveagh (ninety-three) and three nurses at Asolo (but the younger lot here at swimming pool every afternoon); Mark in the Folly working for his exam next week; Hugh Honour and John Fleming here for two days – all perfect guests who go their own ways. When they leave I shall have twelve days or so and then go to Florence for my one committee and on to the Mooreheads – a sad pilgrimage.

You will have heard that Michael[91] is appointed to Athens – fine and near and just as difficult as he enjoys! Their house has its roof on and looks nice and big, but who am I to use that adjective?

We had a little birthday party for my Angel on May 4th and asked the peasants around for a drink by the shrine – about seventy came, and sang songs: they were so easy and pleased and pleasant. Last night they had an open-air Mass with the Madonna under a canopy with a gold crown outside her red church on the hill: wonderfully Babylonian! The Bishop of Treviso with crook and mitre talked to us all from the steps. He said she paid a dividend of 1,000 to 1; no wonder religion is popular. But it was a simple and touching ceremony, going back to something long before history I should say.

Much love, dear Jock,

                                                    FREYA

Montoria
                                                    13 May 1967
Darling Dulcie,

You are going to have quite a shock, for I have bought an elegant little car called Spider! It is a beautiful bright sky-blue little object with white wheels and most luxurious inside, heating, wireless, three sorts of hooter

90 Simon and Alice Lennox-Boyd, and their children.
91 sc. Stewart.

(rather unnecessary), and two very comfortable leather seats, a Fiat 800 engine (whatever that means) and a luggage rack fixed behind. I felt I would have had to turn away from this little siren if only two people could get in, but both Mark and I found ourselves very comfortable in the space behind the seats. There is a hood for rain that takes only two minutes to button down or take off. And I am so intrigued by it that I propose to take some lessons and drive to meet you next time in Vicenza! I ought to wait till next year to buy it, but the poor Topolino, beloved as it is, looks almost beyond the point of dilapidation when it ventures among the handsome cars of Treviso. It will be kept for Francesca to do her worst. She has battered down the lights so that they only illuminate about three yards of road and Mark had great trouble in getting me back from Venice the other night.

He leaves today and has his exam on Monday. Another charming young man, Francis Witt, is here till tomorrow, and next day all the Simon family are off. They gave us a picnic on Grappa yesterday, in the style of my youth with only the waiters missing. It was a heavenly day and the whole hillside like a Botticelli meadow, a carpet of grape hyacinths, cowslips, and here and there a narcissus beginning. And the delicious mountain air. If you come in August we will go off for two days in Spider every week.

Dearest love,

FREYA

JOHN GREY MURRAY   Porto Ercole
                                                    24 May 1967
Dearest Jock,
    I was so afraid of the sadness of coming here where there have been so many happy visits, but it is all very touching and gentle. Alan so *good*, all his generous loving qualities helping him, and Lucy worn to a thread but happy in sheer devotion. Caroline to be married on Saturday[92] (the *one* day in the year on which I have my one engagement in Florence I can't break!) – and that youth and hope comes so happily into the stream. Alan can manage a few short phrases that come without reflection: anything more breaks down and one gets at it like those yes and no games; but he understands perfectly and they always bring him into the talk, and very slowly a new word here and there is acquired. They say he will get back to everyday talk: writing very doubtful and he himself does not think it will come back – but who knows. He is only fifty-five after all. The great blessing is that

92 Caroline Moorehead was marrying Jeremy Swift.

his mind is all right *inside* and he is in his own home and surrounded by love and understanding, so that it is a prison with vistas. I am so glad I came. It has lain like a black cloud over the spring and now, like so many sorrows, it shows a kinder side.

I left my little sports car at Mestre in Sandro's hands – delighted he was to get the steering back under his control. 'I tremble as I sit beside you,' he says, and I feel a bit nervous myself as it makes sudden bounds like the Ancient Mariner's ship and I am still a bit uncertain over clutch or brake and did rather crumple the beautiful new mudguard which is about as fragile as cardboard against the pillar of the *tessoria*. I am getting Sandro to give me lessons for a month and by then *ought* to learn if ever I can. With Francesca having a baby started and Topolino really pretty well finished, it is necessary to have *someone* mobile, and it has as a matter of fact given me a fine dose of *joie de vivre* again, however brief it may be. One of the silliest fallacies seems to me to be that old age should be prudent. Why, for goodness sake? Simon is so sensible with old Lord Iveagh who can't remember his own grandsons: he lets him do whatever he wants and says what does it matter?

Thanks for a strange little U.S.A. paper saying I am elected a 'daughter of Mark Twain'. What does one do about that?

I am sitting in lovely quiet sun and sea is shining. Dulcie tomorrow: Florence next day. Home on 1st – nice card from John.

Love,

FREYA

JOHN GREY MURRAY

Florence

29 May 1967

Dearest Jock,

I lunched with Nicky[93] yesterday and walked over the dear Tatti with her, its memories still very warm and undisturbed; and heard Harold Acton give a lecture on 'English Florentines' in a hall of the Signoria hung with sixteenth-century tapestries, the speeches opened by six trumpeters in scarlet with Dantesque caps and parti-coloured suits standing behind the chairman.

It seems unbelievable to have to be thinking for the third time what to do in case of war.[94] I hoped to stay quietly at home, but I am not quite old

---

[93] sc. Mariano. She had been Bernard Berenson's companion and amanuensis at I Tatti.

[94] Because of the war between Israel and Egypt. (This was the 'Six Day War'.)

enough and will have to go if it comes. But have done nothing because I still feel it may not come – it would be *mad* of Russia to allow a war and to defeat her allies of the future. As for Nasser, there must be wheels within wheels – probably an internal rivalry among Arab states? I wonder if poor Husain will come alive out of it all? It makes one feel sadly like Cassandra: all the Arabists of my generation have been foretelling this for about forty years – thirty-eight from when I first saw the Zionists at Haifa. People are now talking of the *status quo*: but one can't break into another person's house and settle there and *then* say the *status quo* is to be kept! I felt so strongly about this that I almost sat down and wrote to *The Times*, but then felt 'old and grey and full of sleep' and it is the young people's world after all. Let us hope they may not tell open lies in Parliament!

Love, dear Jock,

FREYA

MRS. T. DEUCHAR   Florence
                                                  30 May 1967

Darling Dulcie,

Here is this ghastly cloud of war. I am reduced to buying the papers! I thought, if another war came, I would be old enough to keep out and bury myself and try not to feel in it; but of course that is not so, and though Arabic will be no use with the *whole Arab world* so stupidly against us, there will be some use in Turkish or Persian. And the end who knows?

To think of happier things, the meeting was very pleasant and the chairman was Evelyn Shuckburgh[95] whose father gave me my first letter of introduction to the East. The son has the same nice rugged long-nosed face and is so nice and has invited me to Rome and promises to come up to us. He is the only person so far I have met to approve of Nutting's revelations:[96] most people seem to think that it is better to let sleeping lies lie, even if the honour of England is involved. I sat next him at dinner and had a long talk with a young M.P. whose mother is Italian and lives near Treviso. He has just travelled in the Arab East and is very keen, anxious we should give a guarantee to Aden and pained when I said it was just like giving a death warrant. I feel sure that our only policy is to keep out and wait till we can have some friends again in that world.

[95] Sir Evelyn Shuckburgh was Ambassador in Rome 1966–69.
[96] Anthony Nutting, Minister of State for Foreign Affairs at the time of the Suez crisis, had just published his account of the affair, *No End of a Lesson*.

Florence full of tourists, not the buying sort they say sadly. The shops more alluring than you can imagine. I had to use superhuman control not to buy anything at all except shoes! A lovely few hours for Uffizi and Bargello, and this morning walk round Fort Belvedere with the town spread in its cup below. The books of the flood are still being taken in van-loads to the fort where the cleaning and repairing goes on.

Will write from Montoria and hope to give a date for July for just a week. Lovely thought, darling Dulcie.

FREYA

JOHN GREY MURRAY   Montoria
                                                      4 June 1967
Dearest Jock,

No sooner had I sent my wail of annoyance than a pleasantly human (first for a long time) letter came from you wiping away these clouds – and I am so pleased to hear the news, especially of John's royal progress. Will he have time to see Expo I wonder?[97] I would fly over to look at it if I were rich in time and money: the sight of the modern world, as it looks to those who are now making it, is a very exciting thing. Did I tell you that a noble old man, Vincent Massey,[98] was here lunching and told me what a feat of enthusiasm it has been. Another old man (my age too), Osbert Sitwell, gave me lunch at Cipriani, very pathetic except that he is also very gallant, talking amusingly and almost inaudibly with his head down and his hands shaking, and a little smile. He comes to lunch tomorrow with his Maltese secretary, a vulgar man who must be a trial and one hopes is kind.

The event today was my venture into Asolo in that gay little car alone – and of course meeting a bus, but it was kind and slowed down. The Spider terrifies me as it responds with such enthusiasm to the slightest feather of a foot on the accelerator, but I can now get out of the garage backwards and go up and down my hill.

The stupidity of this war hanging over us one simply can't get over. Never has any one been more predictable over a longer time – and when we had just had a world war over the Danzig corridor – you wouldn't think another corridor would instantly be made. I wish they could fight it out and

---

[97] John Murray was on a publishing tour in the Far East. Expo 67 was the world exhibition in Mexico.
[98] High Commissioner for Canada in the United Kingdom 1935–46 and Governor-General of Canada 1952–59.

leave us neutral. I rather think this particular alarm will pass by – and when the next comes, I really *might* be too old: but now I would still have to go –and where? Turkey perhaps. I long to hear of the book assembled and might then get time for the essay to end it.

Very much love, dear Jock,

FREYA

MRS. T. DEUCHAR   Montoria
                                                   17 June 1967
Darling Dulcie,

Another postal strike is announced for July 10th; we may as well face it that we are sliding back into the Dark Ages. The poor idiotic Arabs I have always felt should never be allowed to *touch* their own affairs, but the mistake was originally ours and anyone who knew that world could foresee the reaping of a whirlwind for the last forty years. It *could* be settled now and Israel could make herself safe if she were magnanimous in victory and left it to the big powers to settle. But she won't. I would bet ninety-nine to one that the Shylock complex holds: whether Portia is around is another matter. Emma and I wearily went back to our old food lists and were about to buy half a million lire of stores, as there is no relying on Italian rations. However, we didn't!

I have had a house full: old Cairo friends, Harry Luke[99] still with me, and Lanning Roper,[100] who has been looking at the garden with a most creative eye. You will find all sorts of wonderful new ideas germinating and the little garden at the back will be a small Victorian paradise with four arches of roses and all the pinks, herbs, and scented flowers.

As for my little blue Spider, it has all the attributes of Love: fear and delight. Sandro gives me lessons but refuses to take me into Bassano yet, but I went by myself yesterday very gingerly and got Harry, who is blissfully ignorant, safe to the café in the *piazza* and out again. I *think* I could now meet you at the airport. Certainly hope to in August. Don't let us lose that month, darling Dulcie, because life is short!

Your loving

FREYA

[99] Colonial administrator and author.
[100] The horticultural expert and landscape gardener.

125

Montoria

21 June 1967

Dearest Jock,

So pleased to get a nice happy letter from your holiday. My ms. is now complete as far as I am concerned and I am delighted (but surprised) that you have no little pencil marks to make along its edges. I am very relieved to get rid of it and can now settle to the last article: I can do so little now that two things can't be done simultaneously especially with (a) domestic upheaval, Francesca leaving, awful drama but Emma *radiant*; (b) Lanning Roper, charming man, revolutionising garden and making me do a stone border along the lily path and four rose arches in the little wooded circle at the end; (c) Russian to be read before getting up in the morning or in any odd wakefulness at night; (d) Samarkand taking shape including smallpox, cholera, and typhoid injections; (e) daily exercise with brave guests in the Spider; (f) three guests in the house and all changing: Pawsons, Jardine, Caroline Swift, Waughs, and Nuri Birgi all before 15th July. I hope for a quiet fortnight then to finish the article, which is a very difficult one to write.

The car is great fun and I take it now as far as Asolo one way and Bassano the other and one of these days will try Venice. I am still a very erratic starter, especially up a hill. It is such an elegant little car and gets warm looks that make me remember the day when I and not my car were looked at like that!

We have all been reading Osbert.[101] Thank you so much for it. The drawings are superb – the text seems to me strangely un-adult, the Oxford chapter very much the best (and people always like a book that mentions their school or university memories). But he makes his mother definitely unlikeable and I wonder if he meant that? Or whether he was unable to deal with parental foibles like Gosse or Sitwell and make them lovable in spite of all?

Do come out, dearest Jock, before I leave for Samarkand. All the clouds would pass if you took even a weekend here instead of in Burgundy or Devon or Ireland. We have a very deep divergence, for it is on who finally arbitrates on a work of art – artist or introducer; and as I feel that the present misery of our literature is largely due to this outside management, it is a point on which I would never compromise. But it has nothing to do with affection and it would be nice if you came out so as to realise this at Montoria.

Dear love, FREYA

[101] Osbert Lancaster's autobiographical *With an Eye to the Future* (1967).

Montoria
                                                                7 July 1967

Darling Dulcie,

I go on 2nd September in a Turkish ship and on by air to Tashkent, etc.
That is to say if one travels at all, as the Middle East is apt to close on one
like a clam in these times of crisis. Pam and Derek Cooper have been sent
for in first aeroplane to fly to Jordan and will probably not be back in time
to come here end of August as they hoped. They have been seeing a number
of friends from Jerusalem (all pretty badly treated and in a poor state).

I am getting Nutting's book after reading bits in the *Sunday Times*. I
don't believe a lie like that would have been told in Parliament before 1914.
What *happened* in those Twenties? It all fills one with sorrow, and some
envy for de Gaulle who has his oil safe in Sahara and is on the more decent
side (eventually) as well. It has a sombre fascination meanwhile to see a new
pattern forming on the map of the world, with quite other forces developing, the end perhaps of the supremacy of naval power and with that a swing
back to the land countries, i.e. the supremacy of Asia? Who can tell and
who is interested to peer so far? It is almost certain that Israel will cling to
all she can and so either lose or corrupt her friends. Alas, Dulcie, I see
nothing but squalor ahead.

My little car now takes me alone in and out of Asolo even in the dark.
It has been the real pleasure of this rather sad summer.

Dearest love,

                                                                FREYA

Montoria
                                                                16 July 1967

Dearest Dulcie,

Michael arrives tomorrow and will I hope bring lots of English news, and
I will keep this letter to add to. I have no news here, a week of quiet with
no one staying and, as we haven't enough water to wash in, that is just as
well. The heat steams up from the plain, the mountains show through their
steamy veils as if they had eyes, and one hopes at least that what is shrivelling
all my poor little plants may be drying up the dampness of the floods. The
pool has so much chlorine in it that I daren't use it for watering (does
Tommy know if it is harmful?), so I go down there instead of to a bathroom. It would be heavenly summer weather if there were water.

By the time you come out I hope to be ready to drive up into the mountains. I have been twice up Grappa, twice to Bassano, twice to Treviso, and

quite often to Asolo, and hope to take Michael into Venice. All seems to go well unless I panic (though I was rather shaken when a woman couldn't reach me yesterday for tea because she was run into on the Bassano road).

Did I describe Osbert Sitwell's lunch here and tell you about his secretary? I wrote to Sybil and commiserated on poor Osbert tied to such a brash sort of companion and she writes that she laughed, as Osbert is *devoted* to him and making him his literary executor. Let us hope he is a hero to his valet, as that is what the young man was, but what a fate. He does look after him very well. One would so much rather die, however.

Michael has come and gone with an armful of mss. for me to deal with but little news, except all the very interesting bits from U.S.A. Pam writes that England has gone quite hysterical over Israel and Nutting almost pilloried for letting out the truth. What a sad world! It was lovely to get the little glimpse of Michael, so sane, explicit, and strong.

Dear love,

FREYA

P.S. I have to make a pipeline for water from the stream or lose all my little trees! No end to things is there?

MRS. DEREK COOPER   Montoria
                                                              21 July 1967

Darling Pam,

I wish I were with you, doing something useful. How good you and Derek are – getting down to the job in hand. I am sure there is nothing for the moment but just to help and let them feel there still are friends. The time will come. Nasser will sink – the Arabs have little use for failures – and I think Brown[102] has the right line and the Saudis may come along in a year or two and be our friends if we are wise now: they should have the whole of the South and we keep out of it all. The Jews will lose as they always do on the Shylock-line of wanting every last ounce, and this *should* bring America and all of us more into line with Russia. I thought it would, but there must be thousands of cross-currents and I am so out of it all.

But Pam, we can do nothing in the world until we have cured ourselves. What awful decline has come over us? Nutting is an honest man (though his defence of Nasser was poor I thought – I mean it had no punch behind it). But the facts are that we went behind our own agreements in secret and then denied having done so. If we had succeeded, this might have been

[102] George Brown, Secretary of State for Foreign Affairs.

slurred over just as one forgets that the Parthenon was built with misappro-
priated funds; but it failed and we are disgraced and uselessly so. Perfectly
normal English people seem to think that it is the failure and not the deceit
that matters. If any extenuating circumstance can be found for the betraying
of one's word, surely it should be given? And one does exist – and one only,
as far as I can see – and this is the fact that neither England nor most of her
government knew what was being done. This fact *does* exonerate England,
whose good name now seems to be held so cheap: and it is worth clearing at
the expense of any Prime Minister, however much one may personally like
him and be sorry.

My Russian journey seems to show no impediment so far. I fly from
Kabul to Tashkent. Can now talk enough Russian to get about. I should get
back late October. If you think I can be of any use then I will go anywhere.

I long to see Skimper and hear all about it and would love to see what he
says in his bulletins. Oh Pam – bulletins! – do you remember that little
office? How happy it was in spite of Germans at the door!

Dear dear love. Do come if you can, and send me anyone you like.

FREYA

MRS. T. DEUCHAR
British Embassy,
Vienna
23 July 1967

Darling Dulcie,

Your letter came just before I left yesterday, warming my heart because
of the affection which is the pure gold of this world. I have as you say been
rich in my friends, both giving and receiving, and have cared more for this
than for anything else, always. May it continue, even as one gets blind and
deaf and all the rest with this creeping illness of *age*.

As I had that free week I felt it was too bad to have kept it for nothing
and took the Pilchers'[103] invitation to come here for the weekend, especially
as Montoria is a disaster, everything dying. Not a drop of water anywhere
and I have to spend vast sums to get a lorry with a little tank every day.

It was hot spending yesterday in the train, from eight to six, up across
Carinthia and over the Semmering, all grass and wooded hills, peaceful and
soothing, though to me dull to live in as I like *something* rugged in a landscape. Like the pretty Austrian girls, there is a want of style and even the
endearing castles on their small hills don't look as if they had grown there

103 Sir John Pilcher was Ambassador to Austria 1965–67.

through their stresses and terrors. This is a fine Embassy built as such, with five great rooms opening out of each other. I stayed here when the Caccias were doing it up after the war, and later with the Bowkers. It is delicious to enjoy *two* baths, morning and evening, after my three weeks washing in about four pints!

We are off today to lunch in a *schloss* with a granddaughter of Franz Joseph who fell in love with a young man, aristocratic but not royal. The marriage couldn't be allowed, but she took a train to a suburb here, and telling her lady-in-waiting that she was going across the platform for a paper, stepped into a train going in the opposite direction, where the young man was waiting. We are going by the Danube and the castle where Coeur de Lion languished in prison.

Dearest love,

FREYA

MRS. T. DEUCHAR
British Embassy,
Vienna
24 July 1967

Darling Dulcie,

I told you all wrong about our hosts in their *schloss* yesterday and, as it is History, must put it right. It was not the wife, who is a charming blonde Celt with four tall children, but her husband's mother who was the old Emperor's favourite granddaughter and ran off with her young Lochinvar. The little great-grandchild is there in a painting sitting on the Imperial knees in a white sailor suit, and is now a tough blue-eyed and gay old boy with a passion for stalking and shooting animals of every sort. They live in a fifteenth-century castle tarted up in the eighteenth (nineteenth?) century to receive another Emperor and peacefully enclosed like all this part of Austria in the greenest of trees and meadows, so sheltered and peaceful that I think it would be boring and one would look around for any rocky ridge to cut the view. It was a large amusing pure Austrian party in a dining-room with walls ten feet thick, and the whole available space upstairs and down covered with antlers, with their teeth hung round them on little chains to show their age (I can't imagine why *one* specimen of each isn't enough for anyone). I sat next our host and enjoyed his talk of hunting in Africa and Vietnam, and felt sympathy when he said it is the lovely desert and jungle days he loves and shooting all those animals is just an excuse (though unnecessary, I couldn't help feeling).

Two young men were on my left, panting too to get out into wild places, one of them carrying around the rather difficult name of Hapsburg; there are twelve brothers and sisters and they too live in a *schloss* on the Danube we passed on our way, and are grandchildren of the Archduke murdered at Sarajevo (the father killed by the Nazis in one of their camps). The house is full of old bric-à-brac, an 1850–70 air about it, with pale frescoed patterns on the walls, all with a comfort of solidity and many servants. The feeding of the fine great maiolica stoves in every room must take a woodsman all his day. As I went up the whitewashed stairs (between white pillars and black antlers and a tigerskin and black Vietnam buffalo head torn from his forests) for a siesta, I was shown a collection of tiny bright birds under little glass domes, collected by the Archduke when he was touring the world and had not yet started 1914 and all our troubles by his murder.

Tonight we are going to Schönbrunn to hear the earlier *Barber of Seville* by Paisiello; and tomorrow more music, Haydn and Dvorak in the fine court of the Hof-burg, and then this little jaunt will be over. I hope I may not find everything reduced to cinders at Montoria.

With love, dear Dulcie, and thanks for your dear words.

FREYA

P.S. You would have loved the opera last night in the tiny enchanting private theatre of Schönbrunn, *huge* Imperial box and everything all round, balustrades, coats-of-arms, eagles, etc., all reddish gold. The opera fascinating because one sees Rossini's whole reactions all taken with a turn away from sentiment to gaiety and just the immortal touch added.

JOHN GREY MURRAY

Montoria
16 August 1967

Dearest Jock,

The water-knot is cut in a Gordian way and a deep shaft already fills with twenty-five gallons a day and we hope for more. The people are very good – all ready to wait a year to be paid. We evidently have a good reputation!

The hurly-burly has been added to by our Sindaco who asked if the San Zenone choir could come and sing us mountain songs: so twenty-two are coming tomorrow night and we will give them wine and sandwiches. A *social* secretary is what I need!

The Spider is so much admired, even the petrol stations pay compliments, though one of them yesterday told me they never had known a motorist unable to tell them whether the engine is before or behind (I always forget).

I took Gavronsky[104] up to the Marostica castle to dinner with Damaris' brother and all of us, and came back at night – very pleased with myself on the evening of the Assumption, with every town in Italy emptied of its inhabitants and whizzing around in cars. They have police everywhere and give a list of all the deaths every morning with the news.

Love, dear Jock,

FREYA

JOHN GREY MURRAY

S.S. *Truva*,
in Marmara
6 September 1967

Dearest Jock,

A very smooth voyage on a rather nice ship ferrying cars and all one class: one can have refined meals in the *salon* or buy what one wants on trays in the cafeteria, and this seems to work very well. A splash of London was produced by the Osberts, Ashley Clarkes,[105] and Jock Jardine (though he already Levantinised). I liked Anne[106] and Osbert was in fine form – 'just like my Papa' the barman said, smoothing out imaginary moustaches! They went off at Smyrna and I waited till the ship had emptied and then found Eddie Wilkinson in his office – all the old people there (seventeen years from my first visit), all of us a bit fatter and possibly wiser.

We strolled over the museum: beautiful things there, Hellenistic marble girls and delicate jewellery and most lovely sixth-century B.C. pottery painted in the dull little suburb (today) of Clazomenae. Lovely, vanished Ionian world: we just catch the hem of its garment as it disappears. We went to the old museum where marble lies about round an old Greek church under trees; and then up the hill with its long flights of steps and little houses, where the theatre and stadium lie invisible, to the walls of the acropolis where the bad people used to stroll seventeen years ago but now there are just a few aimless loungers like ourselves. The houses have grown thick but not offensively, and the magically delicate Ionian outlines spread away, cape beyond cape, coloured like the sky, a landscape for angels!

Thrace is coming in sight – and I will post this with the proofs and write later.

Love,
FREYA

[104] Jan Gavronsky, a Polish friend.
[105] Sir Ashley Clarke, ex-Ambassador in Rome, and his (second) wife, Frances.
[106] Osbert Lancaster had married Anne Scott-James.

                                        10 September 1967

Dearest Jock,

I have got here. It doesn't seem true yet, but I washed and slept through the afternoon and have now been walking in the evening light, like everyone else in Kabul it seems. It is all as I remember my first Damascus days – the incredible squalor and the strength of life pouring through it. A feeling of freedom which has suffered too much ever to tolerate the loss of this one thing that remains to it – itself. There is a complete absence of subservience here which I remember finding good in Iraq and Syria so long ago.

I had two Bosphorus days of idleness and went Pan American to Teheran: quite hateful, like being part of the animation of a huge cigar – 120 passengers, I should say, in rows of six, tightly packed and fed by the stewards as if for pâté de foie! With all this there is a revolting *satisfaction* both in Britain and U.S.A. air travel, as if one were being so privileged to all that efficient squalor. Such relief to get to Teheran where I was allowed to sleep on a red velvet sofa meant for diplomats in the waiting room, and as I hadn't enough change to pay my excess luggage in Iranian money, the nice little official said that what I had would do. It was a wearing night with tourists breaking about one and drawn away like waves. We left at 5.30 – the sun hitting Damavand, all yellow, splendid in a yellow sky and everything else outdazzled, till shark-fin ridges began to emerge and then a chaos of desolation, a Picasso cubism all tiny or big triangles of erosion, small ones and great, and neither tree nor water nor, I imagine, grass. Not a road or house to be seen, until the poor streams began to trickle and here is Kabul with trees here and there (within walls mostly) and the great passes all around but some way off.

The Ewanses[107] sent to meet me and their police head brought me to this hotel so reminiscent of the England that was – but different: all young people lunching and mixed languages, and Punjabi ladies in their satin trousers drinking tea. I go to the Ewanses to lunch and meet everyone tomorrow and will keep this till I can tell you more definite plans. I am anyway going to be sent in a lorry to Peshawar over the Khyber, perhaps in a fortnight's time.

                                        13 September 1967

This has been waiting for news of my starting for Samarkand, but I am still held up by the fact that either the Italians or the Russians failed to book me on the aeroplane. I hope for a seat on Sunday, and meanwhile have

107 M. K. Ewans was then First Secretary in Kabul.

driven up – eight hours on a Turkish sort of road – to Bamian, where I am writing now. No picture can give the peacefulness of this valley. One comes down to it through the wildest most contorted gorges with the river beside one; the cliffs take on vague Gothic shapes as if a great procession were forming; then the valley opens to lovely cultivation, the river winding bright silver. The mountains have been with one all day, but veiled in light and dust, so that they are more *presences* than real hills, but here they stand in rising tiers, range behind range, behind the cliffs where the two Buddhas stand in their niches and all the small niches around them. I made an inadequate sketch, but nothing can give the serenity which no doubt brought the Buddhas in the first place. The vague shapes of the Gods still seem to gather above them in the natural faces of the rocks. It is all a peaceful harmony of earth and man together, for the earth is in everything – in the colour of the mud-walled houses and the peasants' clothes whose white loses itself to old ivory in no time. I am so very glad to have come, though suffering agonies from sinus in dust; but who would not pay for such days?

Two very pleasant Frenchmen joined in my car and as we all like to photograph the same things all is well. This is still the East as I first saw it, the people in their turbans and fine coats, tall and with long walking legs, and a great mixture of faces from Persian to Arab or Mongol. I must stop and send this and hope you may next hear from Samarkand.

Love dear Jock,

FREYA

JOHN GREY MURRAY   Samarkand
                                                19 September 1967

Dearest Jock,

It seems strange, but here I am. We got into a very excellent aeroplane yesterday and breathed again as we got out in the Oriental atmosphere, the desert-ringed, earth-brick-built oasis, full of trees and waters, surrounded by heaped mounds of Samarkands destroyed and forgotten – the citadel of Alexander's Maracanda, the desperate heaps of misery left by Genghis and Tamerlane. It has been a wonderful day. The artisans who were separated and survived the awful depopulations were kept to rebuild Samarkand and here are their lovely works, the oldest the most beautiful, most delicate fancies, more perfect even than Isfahan. There is a street of tombs, daughter and wife of Tamerlane and others unknown, a sort of Via Appia between sun-baked walls, melting with turquoise domes and walls, traceries cut deep in the earth-baked medium, every device and pattern of delightful fancy worked by these people whose homes and generations were destroyed. With what sad hearts they must have done these lovely things for the usurper, the last sunset of their civilisation. The oldest of these tombs are the most beautiful – but when one comes to the other wonder, the great centre of Samarkand called the Registan, there are three great façades of colleges on a rectangle, and Tamerlane's grandson built the earliest of them, and the next –soon after – is even more beautiful, with two of the loveliest ridged turquoise domes imaginable. The whole square is one of the world's wonders and a reward for all pains of travel. It comes like the cry of a civilisation across these wastes of space and time and I keep on thinking of Flecker's poem of the Saracens and the statue that survived.

The Russians are doing very careful restoration and preserving and the museum here is beautifully shown. The whole of their achievement is prodigious and Tashkent is coming along to be another in the chain of these great Central Asian civilisations. It is already a comfortable, clean, tidy town spread with many trees and gardens over a huge space, and will soon be a town of gardens too. Here, with fewer earthquakes to contend with, the old character has kept itself. The Uzbeks have charming peaceful faces, quite resolute but friendly. My little bits of Russian are welcomed in the flood of foreigners they have to deal with.

Love,

FREYA

JOHN GREY MURRAY

Bukhara

21 September 1967

Dearest Jock,

I flew up from Samarkand this morning and here I am for four days now, the old city a fifteen minutes' walk away and this *gastinitza* full of East German tourists half way between old and new. I spent two hours in the familiar East – the streets between mud walls and sudden openings, a dome with a stork's nest, a main road running into covered cross-ways where the silk shops still sell, to a few green squares of trees, and a pool, an oblong of masonry with kebabs cooking round it and crowds, including women (a few), sitting on the wooden platforms that were made for sitting cross-legged. It seems to me that the Russians are being very wise down here, interweaving East and West gently so that the people adopt their new ways not only without shock but with enthusiasm. There will be changes, but meanwhile they have a drive and enthusiasm which we lack. This will surely remain, when the over-centralising fails and gives way to an easier discipline. It really seems to me to be a very great achievement.

They are also very good at restoring and keeping the historic things unspoilt and separating old from new. And though the structure of the town is unchanged, it is kept clean, and this of course makes it very different, and the one-storeyed house on the main street, with a canal and gardens full of melons in front and thin trees and road, I should like to live in myself. There are lots of old schools, mosques, mausoleums, but nothing supreme like Samarkand.

23 September 1967

This is my third day and I begin to watch the Intourists come and go and feel different. It is such a mistake to think that the tourist traffic makes one *liked*: this horde staying two days only, without a word of the language – one can feel the repulsion they produce. My few Russian words are like magic – they turn the people into charming friendly human beings. Now that travel is becoming unmanageable, I would make an elementary knowledge of the language compulsory in every country for travelling. I drove out this morning to a sort of monastery, sixteenth century, among the cotton fields and was taken by a woman driver who told me how awful she found it never to be able to speak a word with her customers. The intelligentsia are evidently hostile, but the local Uzbeks and Tajiks and Russians from Ukraine whom I have been meeting are most friendly though much too busy with Progress of their own to care about us in the West. The air here is fine: fresh in the morning and evening and dry and hot by day – and orange sunsets over the horizon where the Red Desert, the Kizil Kum, must stretch away.

I go back to Kabul in a week and hope for letters.

Love,
FREYA

JOHN GREY MURRAY   Tashkent
30 September 1967

Dearest Jock,

I wonder how many of my letters arrive? You must let me know. I have just sent off a p.c. from Khiva made to welcome the future tourists (I believe I am the fifth foreigner) and it seemed too much to expect the post to function from the Oxus.

Khiva was a great experience altogether, mostly because of Oxus. They

136

told me here that I couldn't reach it, but the landing ground is seventy kilometres from Khiva and only sixteen from Oxus so I went with the tourist hotel head and we were lucky enough to find a local ferry steamer just setting off. Getting on and off by a plank laid to the river bed is not what one is meant for at seventy-four – but several old Methuselahs were doing it and friendship established itself on the basis of our similar ages. This gave me some marvellous photos if only they come out – the old men peering out from the huge sheepskin hats one now sees nowhere else (a man can only get one, they say, by marrying an old wife who inherited from her first husband). We started out in a little creek and took nearly an hour to get across the enormous river rolling in the sun. No stones, but several matted rushy isles – I wrote out Matthew Arnold from memory for the head of the tourist bureau, a charming man with almost Chinese face who longs for English books. I will send you two addresses to send *Alexander's Path* to, from Kabul.

In the p.m. of this eventful day we drove to Khiva and that was a mixed experience because it is quite poor in its buildings – all nineteenth century – and they have practically emptied it of inhabitants so that it has none of the living atmosphere of Bukhara, but its massive earth walls are there and from them one can look at the crowd of minarets, schools, tombs, etc., and feel what an Oriental city looked like. It is unbelievably rich country all round, once 'the garden of Asia' and now third in the world for cotton – white dazzling mountains of it shining in the sun, or spread on the asphalt of roads (to the distress of cars). One of the most exciting things of this expedition was flying over the Kizil Kum, the Red Sands: even from the air with a softening sunset its grimness holds, not a streak below that is not rock and death and thousands must have died there. The few thin paths meet in spider-web tangle where many must have taken the wrong one.

Love,
FREYA

LADY HUXLEY[108]

Spinzar Hotel,
Kabul
1 October 1967

Dearest Juliette,

Are you surprised to see where your letter finds me? Just arrived from Samarkand. I spent a fortnight in that part of Russia and it has opened such

[108] Wife of Sir Julian Huxley, the distinguished biologist.

a window: the Timurid buildings beautiful beyond dreams; and Bukhara still a pleasant Oriental town. But I don't want to go again and was glad to fly away this morning. It is the knowledge of *fear* always round the corner: one feels it so strongly. And the people look full of purpose, and never loiter about, but don't look happy – no *radiance* as in our untidy Mediterranean lands.

Darling Juliette, what a good person you are, and what an uphill it is. I am seventy-four, and what I feel is that I too would be drowned in depression if I thought of old age as an end and not a beginning. As it is, I find myself wondering with a feeling of timidity but also delight as to what is round the corner. Julian has not got this happiness. Don't you think that is enough to explain everything? How can one feel happy if one is riding downhill with a blank wall at the end? An old woman in the hotel near the Oxus came to my room and said, 'We have everything but we have not God'; and it must have been a comfort to her to say it for she disappeared and came back with a pot of tea and two precious chocolates to give me. Over and over one finds it – this Goodness which doesn't live by bread alone. It is said that it will inherit the earth, and I believe this in spite of all the babels we build.

Dear love to you both,

FREYA

MRS. DEREK COOPER   Kabul
                                            2 October 1967

Darling Pam,

This is where I found your p.c. yesterday on emerging from Russia. So glad to get it and also to feel myself in the free wild air of this splendid country – still the East I knew forty years ago in spite of motor cars and tourists. The same tough sort of business men of varied nations out for no good, the same casual friendly servants (one wandered into my room and offered to massage my poor swollen legs, and did it with great relief). All this very unlike Russia where the Uzbeks and Tajiks would be charming and the Russians too, if only not so harnessed. But though we were herded – and what else can one do with a daily horde that speak no language but their own? – the actual places were strange and lovely as dreams.

I went to another, modern, town just opened and took a silly photograph of a refinery in the distance: within three hours the poor Director of Tourism had been reprimanded and my film was asked for and kept overnight to be developed. I got I think the worst fright of my life thinking of what my

Polish friends had warned me and realising that nothing could be done if they wanted to hold me. All night I lay in waves of panic, only soothed by a complete acceptance: if it has to be, I thought, I will accept it and think of the past and its happiness and hope to die soon. Then in the morning, at six o'clock, there was my little film, luckily producing a hideous picture of new workmen's dwellings as well as old touristy ruins – and the refinery cut out. I have never I think been afraid of a human being – but this cold machine terrified me as it does the people who work for it.

Love,

FREYA

MRS. T. DEUCHAR   As from Kabul
                                                        6 October 1967
Dearest Dulcie,

I am now for two days in Peshawar, over the Khyber, and going to look at Akbar's fortress on the Indus before going back tomorrow. There is still a Kipling glamour over this pass and the ring of mountains that half encircles the great plain; and the old ramshackle city streets, not beautiful but chaotically grown like a bees' nest, and the 'cantonments' with a certain discreet splendour still lingering under their trees. Only two years ago all the old city gates were shut at night, except one, and people were liable to be robbed, and undressed, quite near the suburbs. And Steven Runciman it appears was run at by a man with a bayonet as he was trying to photograph a Buddhist stupa on the pass.

The descent from Kabul is fantastic for steep wildness, the road winding and river leaping down its crags. The ancient way taken by Alexander was north of this and presumably a little easier. I came down anyway with our little army in its hot red coats marching up those merciless defiles in my mind's eye.

Dearest love,

FREYA

JOHN GREY MURRAY   Kabul
                                                     9 October 1967
Dearest Jock,

Back, over the Khyber and up the terrific Kabul gorge. What a citadel this country is between the northern high road (Russia) and the southern (U.S.A. – Kandahar); inside those it is mountains as close folded as a concertina. I found, being brought up on Kipling, that the whole of Khyber was Romance, with the names of its regiments and their dates – Sikhs, Khyber Rifles, Punjabis – sculptured and coloured on the rocks and the little forts still sitting on every hill, and a notice to tell travellers they must be out of the pass before sunset. No camels, because there is a disease on this side, but the road is double and the asphalt was made about ten years ago; and where the pass widens at the top, the mud villages in their walls and towers are thickly scattered, with a few trees and even fields, all inhabited, they told me in Peshawar, by fugitives from law.

I made this excursion in the Embassy Land Rover which goes once a fortnight for mail etc., and lunched *en route* with the driver at a ramshackle little tea-house; suddenly realised that it must be well over twenty years since I had eaten my meal 'by hand'.

I take a day off in between trips and clean up and read in my room and have just finished Evelyn Waugh's *Officers and Gentlemen*: it is a true picture, it seems to me, and makes me like Waugh better. If I were dealing in criticism I would put him in the family of Petronius – a voice of decadence but, here and there one feels it, a regretful voice. He will live no doubt but I think, like *Euphues* or other passing fashions, appealing to a small sealed company in their time: it isn't like Hardy (whom I was also reading), the *English* voice along its major stream. Here and there, almost unnoticeable, one can tell that he heard and felt that major voice, but he only lets it be inferred and is explicit only for failure – (same as Osbert really) the inferior alone is to be spoken. Ever so long ago W.P. wrote to me when we did not yet know each other well, and signed 'Yours affectionately'; then he added a P.S. – 'No! Affection is a poor word, and love is strong.' It was an equally reserved, but a more manly generation? This here is a manly people too: one feels happy and free among them though almost certainly it cannot last. My Persian is beginning to come back – words dropping from nowhere – and I would like to return among them. The months given to Russian were not wasted; I was able to talk and quite a number reverted to human beings – but I shall let it drop now: it isn't the air one wants to breathe in one's last years. It will be, if anything, my early loves, Persian and Arabic, and Turkish, and the only Eastern journey I should still like to make beyond is Kashmir and Nepal. I have a feeling that a huge *geographic* change is taking place here, the return of supremacy to land transport as against sea – it would tilt the whole balance of civilisation East again.

I must go and shop for the five-day trip.

Love,
FREYA

140

Way from Balkh
                                                    14 October 1967

Dearest Jock,

Balkh was very fortunate. It is all ruin, but with such an atmosphere of
ruin, the earth walls crumbling, the long acropolis crumbled, the site of its
population filled with graves – and in the later Islamic circuit, far too big
for today. The trickle of today spreads under shady streets too broad for their
traffic, and the market crowd cluster with cloaks and turbans and spread
their wares on the ground round the one great Timurid monument left
them, where the fine blue tiles are dropping away too, and the white doves
nest. A little hotel without light or water but pleasant and solitary in its
garden has started and we spent the night there – and came away yesterday
over ten hours of ups and downs on a camel track: now half way back to
Kabul.

                                                    Love,
                                                    FREYA

P.S. If any victim can be found coming out would you press a little suitcase
of roses on them?

MRS. T. DEUCHAR   Montoria
                                                   14 November 1967

Darling Dulcie,

I had one day at Izmir seeing friends and then a smooth sunny voyage,
but arrived nine hours late in Venice which made it midnight. No one to
meet me, so I crept drearily back on board and next morning took a taxi. I
found the house like an ice box and Emma at the hairdresser; all because,
having given day and ship and all by letter long before, I had not repeated
it all in a telegram. One wonders how the human race ever got beyond the
stage of caterpillars moving nose to tail.

I have finished my Turkish *Macbeth* and am so pleased at discovering a
way to make language-learning attractive. One is learning the words and the
colloquial usage, while reading interesting stuff. I furnished myself with
Lear, Hamlet, Antony and Cleopatra and *Julius Caesar* in Istanbul, and if
you do send me a book do let it be Shakespeare done by some really good
editor. Dover Wilson I imagine is the best? When one struggles with a
translation, one notices so much that had escaped one. For instance, in
Macbeth the marvellous *gentleness* after the banquet climax: not a word of
reproach from Lady M. It is like one of those smooth places one suddenly
finds in an angry sea.

I have not yet got my water system, but there is an ugly little box-house for the pump at the bottom of the hill and it should all be done in a few days now. *Hundreds* of letters, etc., a two-month collection, and now Xmas cards to send. I long to write but can never get at it, and may have lost the gift. So much I would like to say, but exhaustion comes after about twenty minutes. If it goes on I shall be sleeping the clock round. If it were not for all this, I could have a lovely quiet month as I know of no arrivals except Stewarts and Morans, each for very few days. As for you and Tommy, when will that be? I feel it like Alice's jam, yesterday and tomorrow, but not today. But I hope to see you early in 1968, as I plan a month in London, mid-January or early February. The place for *meeting* one's friends is London, but for *seeing* them is Montoria. Little trees are being planted and it looks so beautiful. Yet I have been very lonely in it these last three years. The fact is that I am not really possessive: the feeling of owning something gives me no pleasure; what I enjoy is sharing and that seems almost impossible in this world, though I imagine the basis of the next. Sometimes I long and long to step across that narrow stream and feel *at home*. But then the beauty of this world pulls at one's heart, and often one meets Goodness and it is like a pool of clear water.

Dearest love to dear Tommy, too.

FREYA

LADY CHOLMONDELEY
Montoria
24 November 1967

Dearest Sybil,

It is lovely to get home again and a golden November has been given to comfort one in the greyness of the world. So many people must be very hard hit, and it really is miserable to see England slipping like a drunk without, apparently, a light to guide her. Perhaps it looks worse from 'abroad'? Nor is anyone I know giving much optimism for the future.

I know Mellaart[109] and all the extraordinary trouble he has been causing. It is an archaeological tragedy, as his dig near Konia is the most exciting thing in Turkey of that kind, I imagine: a vanished civilisation with the earliest known painting on human-built surfaces, vultures that could be done by Picasso and a stone torso that might be Michelangelo – of the seventh *millennium* B.C. All this excavation is stopped (as far as I know) – and therefore God knows what is happening to it – because of his idiocy in

[109] The archaeologist James Mellaart.

publishing an article in which he described a meeting with a girl wearing a priceless antique bracelet, then a visit of several days to her house in Smyrna, making drawings of the treasure. The Turks read this and naturally made enquiries and Mellaart gave a name and address which proved to be non-existent. The wretched British Archaeological Institute and all the archaeologists have had a very hard time, and Mellaart is, I believe, sitting in his Turkish wife's beautiful old house on the Bosphorus, drinking far too much and very frustrated! That is the story as far as I know it. The general idea is that he is not, as one might imagine, implicated in treasure-smuggling, but the insanity of not *either* telling the Beaux-Arts of Turkey about the treasure, *or* keeping quiet, seems unbelievable. I have twice heard of, but not actually seen, pieces of such treasures, once in Persia and once in Turkey: the whole country except the authorities knows and nobody tells. In Turkey this happened about twelve years ago, and I tried to get the local governor interested, as all the historic value of the finds is lost if their place of origin is unknown. Nobody would take the slightest interest, and only this year I see that a beautiful basin, of the age of Justinian I imagine, is published in a book called *Trésors de Turquie*, which says that most of that find has not been recovered.

I hope to see you, as I plan to be in England roughly for a month from the last week in January. Let me know when and where in good time, because it is all going to be very short. Life *crumbles* in our hands, doesn't it?

Dear love,

FREYA

JOHN GREY MURRAY   Montoria
                                            31 December 1967

Dearest Jock,

Have got home and and here is the year closing white and still and sunny under snow. May all go well with you dear Jock in 1968 and onward. It has been a sad year: like the end of *Alice in Wonderland* with the cards shuffling down all round, and one doesn't wake to find it a dream. Your uncle's loss too must make the great room feel empty,[110] though his is one of those among all I know whose death gives least cause for sadness.

It will be lovely to see you all soon – and so nice to be sheltered in the

[110] Sir John Murray, Jock Murray's uncle and senior director of the publishing firm, had died.

143

kind Moorehead flat. I will ask friends to look in there and move as little as I can except at weekends.

Love and *au revoir* in three weeks!

FREYA

MRS. DEREK COOPER Montoria
4 January 1968

Darling Pam,

So glad of a letter, but a bit distressed by a feeling that that old Tartar the body is letting you both down? You are no doubt doing far too much; it is like Lincoln, adapted, 'You can go all out for part of the time, and you can go a little out for the whole time, but you can't be at full stretch for the *whole* time.' Do make sure to get away in spring and come and rest here, and don't go into the summer heat, please, please.

I am horrified about poor Grey, saddled with these awful financial dilemmas. Does he want to keep the huge white elephant to *live* in? Oh dear! The trouble is, Pam dear, that it is the countries of *centripetal* and not *centrifugal* families that keep strong and invincibly prosperous. Italy, France, Greece, Lebanon: their families *build* them. We are scatterers, and nothing can be more wastefully expensive than commitments all over the place. Do get rid of Dunlewy and have that milestone settled, for it really does lead you down a road with no outlet. As for me, the Karmel lease looks like ending, though they will have to pay up to April next I hope.

But my financial dilemma is one of age. I have been counting up the requirements for the next ten years if I live so long, and they do demand a lot of things that one could very well do without before. You and Derek have another twenty years to go before this remorseless arithmetic faces you. But then, if you want an active and rewarding old age, you too will have to: (1) travel in greater comfort: no more of those happy trips third class in steamers; (2) provide for illness; (3) eventually, in my case, probably pay for someone to travel with me (poor thing); (4) be able to afford short jaunts for fun; at present I save up for years for Samarkand but can never afford a fortnight in mountains, or Rome, etc., which all my most broke friends are able to do; (5) most of all, be able to have friends rather than tenants in the bottom flat, especially as I get less mobile. The time of earning one's living goes by.

Now I have calculated very carefully, and I feel I could do all this if I get half of what I spent on this property. The other half would be my

144

present and I would love more than I can say that you or one of the boys should get it. It is quite a nice present of £25,000 – and I believe you would be very happy if you could make the sacrifice to get it when Dunlewy is sold. You could have the bottom flat, and that and cook and gardener and upkeep of garden (quite a lot, alas!) would be the interest on your outlay for my few years, and you would still be young to enjoy it all when I slip on.

This year has been a fearful strain because I had to fence the whole thing, and put five lovely gates, and dig a well, and we now have our own plentiful water all over everywhere. It is really a fine and valuable property now and the oak trees begin to throw a shadow. The whole of this landscape is now, they tell me, secure from overbuilding as the Italians are at last awakening to the danger.

Love,

FREYA

MRS. T. DEUCHAR Brussels[111]

3 March 1968

Darling Dulcie,

All went beautifully according to plan and here I am in the most charming house, rather like a fairy tale, in the midst of the Brussels suburbs. Trees and patches of snow all round it, and other houses faintly visible, but no sound of cars anywhere near and inside full of all Nuri's engaging trinkets arranged with Ottoman devotion to detail so that the effect is like a labyrinth of exquisite little objects which make one feel as if one had become quite small oneself and could be lost among them.

I had a good crossing, the pursers recognised and welcomed me on board (so often have I been to and fro) and no one took any interest in roses. I had time that evening for two elegant hats (summer and winter!) and turned my eyes resolutely from all else, and caught a crowded train which got me here in time for a bath and dinner of twelve, Burrowses,[112] Peter Coats, and all else Belgian. A great-grandson of de Lesseps[113] beside me with whom I condoled on all the damage caused by his family inventing Suez (though it did produce *Aida*). We are now off to look at castles so I will write more from Montoria next week.

[111] F.S. was staying with Nuri Birgi on the way home after a month in London.
[112] Sir Bernard Burrows, Under-Secretary of State at the Foreign Office, had been Ambassador in Turkey 1958–62.
[113] The Frenchman Ferdinand de Lesseps was the principal engineer of the Suez Canal.

Dearest Tommy, how good of him to see me off. It gives me a warm feeling whenever I think of it, and so does Standon altogether. Dear, dear Dulcie, so much love and thanks for *cherishing*.

FREYA

JOHN GREY MURRAY   Montoria
                                                            14 March 1968

Dearest Jock,

I am nearly through all the dramas that welcome one's homecomings and am hoping for a quiet stretch before guests begin to come in April. A whole spate of lovely garden work is in the offing, as I have spent the equivalent of a winter suit on shrubs from Mr. Hillier, and they *should* be here soon. Lanning is an angelic man: I hope he will have a vast garden of his own in Paradise. He has sent me my list back with careful details so that the plants may find appropriate places. Meanwhile tulips are blossoming on one side while the daffodils hesitate on the other – and the grape hyacinths planted last year are all out like wild flowers in the grass. White crocuses too are pretending to be wild. If I am spared, I believe this will be the nicest garden in Venetia, all full of surprises. It is still very cold with a thin wind that has brought the field-mice indoors. One of them bit my finger while I lay asleep in bed; this was too much and Signora Polizzi is bringing me a cat. Hares too are taking to eating the bark off my quinces; they choose the rarest, as I do carpets.

I ended my social life with an agreeable evening in Paris with a French doctor who married a Hungarian *artiste* – charming people with whom I spent a dream-day on an uninhabited islet off Amorgos. Then I got here by the easy train leaving Paris 8 a.m. and in time for supper here. I found Harold's second volume[114] – *deeply* interesting but I had to give up reading 1939–41, as it produced floods of tears – almost unbearable to think we are sliding down the same slope for the third time. Few people realise that if one continues to go downhill one must hit the bottom eventually. 1942 onwards I could read and was fascinated by the light thrown on de Gaulle: the explanation seems adequate but not the excuse – as Pope Leo said to Bismarck when he introduced himself unasked into his Council. It is terrifying to think what must have passed through that mean mind while Churchill at his side was being deliriously welcomed by the Paris crowd.

[114] Sir Harold Nicolson's *Diaries and Letters 1939–45*.

I can't work more than twenty minutes at a time and am taking it easy, mostly getting the Turkish photographs into shape. There is an idea of an Afghan picture book: nothing may come of it, but I think anyway that I might go to Afghanistan this summer to see Herat and the West which I missed. I have a warm invitation for little expeditions in Persia on the way by Denis Wright.[115] It will all get spoilt so soon, even if it keeps clear of wars.

Love to all at Cannon Lodge,

FREYA

MRS. DEREK COOPER   Montoria
                                                          14 March 1968

Darling Pam,

It is always a tremendous stirring-up to go to England: friends with such *various* periods of one's life attached to them, all coming with the old memories. I saw quite a number of our Middle Eastern friends and I stayed my last week with Joanie,[116] Mrs. Collard gave a little party to meet the pro-Arab M.P.s, etc., . . . Arnold Toynbee I was so glad to meet (he wrote me a marvellous two-page review in the *Times Lit. Sup.*). I lured Skimper to lunch which Dulcie gave to get my *young* Arabists to meet – two such charming ones, Francis Witt (wintered in Hadhramaut) and Colin Thubron (wrote a first-rate book on Damascus). When I talk to them, I feel life has not been quite wasted, and they are great dears and come to see me. Mark is coming out too – now working at law after the Yemen. He too met Skimper: it is all a little band and the Middle East will be their affair!

The swing back towards the Arab is I believe on its way. One has to give Israel a bit of time to damn herself – not a *glimmer* of generosity or under-standing. I will try and write, but not just yet. My feeling is that before we can do any good we have to outlive the colonial-imperialist reputation. Then the young can begin in a free field, and as individuals and not parts of a government; but till the prejudice has gone, it shackles every effort and spoils it. Anyway it is on its way out. When that chapter is sealed, the Empire will show for what it was – a stupendous miracle of an adventure which held the world in the hands of a tiny nation, in comparative peace and genuine freedom. We were part of it and we need not forget it. Like the

---

[115] Sir Denis Wright, Ambassador to Iran 1963–71.
[116] Princess Joan Aly Khan.

snow on the hills it has gone, and feeds unexpected rivers in unknown lands. What a pattern it is, our poor little overloaded planet.

I love you dearly,

FREYA

MRS. T. DEUCHAR   Montoria
                                                  20 May 1968

Darling Dulcie,

Tomorrow the Gowries arrive, and meanwhile here are the Huxleys. He is eighty-two and with an old, old trace of brilliance like one of those musical boxes that make cracked tunes – not wisdom nor goodness which are the only vintages that last. Poor Juliette continues to be bright, devoted and unreconciled inside. Sad beyond words.

It fits into that awful world of Lytton Strachey I have nearly finished.[117] I will keep the book for you to take, as I shall not want to read it again. All through those years while that little group were trying to be clever (and succeeding one must say), I kept on thinking of the long lines of steel helmets plodding here up to the mountain passes to keep the world for them intact. There might have been no war as one reads, except for the inconvenience of a board meeting now and then to see whether the future of the world could be saved without Lytton's help! Rather surprisingly, I seem to have met most of those people – Virginia Woolf, Duncan Grant, Vanessa and Clive Bell, Lady Ottoline, James Stephens, etc. . . . The book has strengthened my feeling that the Twenties was the time of our decay though it has taken that seed another two generations to develop fully. Lytton has the blindness to pity Keats for dying 'without copulating', a man whose horizon went beyond the universe and had all beauty in his heart. Miserable people!

Bless you and Tommy, dear Dulcie.

Your
FREYA

JOHN GREY MURRAY   Montoria
                                                  26 June 1968

Dearest Jock,

I had three clear days between visitors and went off to Venice, feeling that I needed to come up for air – i.e. a little time with nobody's problems

[117] In Michael Holroyd's biography.

in the offing. Found a charming retreat in the Casa Frollo I had heard of for years but never been to – a vast seventeenth-century *palazzo* on the Guidecca, the whole of Venice (and rather ugly back of the Salute) spread across the water, and a pleasantly nostalgic feeling of the *pension* of my youth, quiet dim women sitting at little tables making inaudible conversation, and a brave effort to make the coloured tablecloths look gayer than the *pensionnaires*. The hall was so huge that its seventeenth century managed to enwrap one, and so did the low halls and passages upstairs, with shiny brick floors and austere little bedrooms (only cold water) breaking out from them. This medieval atmosphere won the day and made the tourist Venice just non-existent.

Tomorrow is the sale of my Lear at Sotheby's. I hope will help with the travelling.

Love,
FREYA

JOHN GREY MURRAY Montoria
1 July 1968

Dearest Jock,

Tickets are here since yesterday. What a relief – thanks ever so much for all that promptness.

There is still a hiatus between Athens and Teheran as the aeroplane was full up, but I hope it may settle itself today. Anyway I leave here on 16th: will write again. Am now going to dentist and then Nuri who arrives with all the latest vitriol of de Gaulle to tell.

I think of lovely peace in Afghanistan though they say about 120 in the shade. My Guardian Angel never did a better job than when he nerved me to launch into debt again for water: we have just filled our pool and can water everything and no one else has had any for a week. The whole little hill would be *dead* if I hadn't got the well: what a sound it is, splashing in the moonlight, with a nightingale or two still singing – the voice of life in the thirst.

Love,
FREYA

Kabul

20 July 1968

Dearest Jock,

I feel as if I had gone back some thirty years – sitting here in shade while the gardener in his yellow skull-cap and loose green clothes waters the zinnias of the border: the sort of life built up with many precautions and exclusions so as to make itself tolerable for the Englishman abroad (fast-disappearing species!). I came out safely and easily with a bit of chaos and loss of one bag by either Italian or Olympic Airways. A nice day in Athens with the Michael Stewarts, though there is a definite loss of affection for the British – one notices the coolness even among the customs officers.

Here I am kindly adopted by the nice Pearsons till Francis Witt arrives. We then have a choice of a Land Rover through the middle of the country with a party who are going – but possibly too late – or a trek of our own round the north which can be done in a strong ordinary car but is less interesting and *very* hot. By the time Francis comes, his fate will have been settled one way or the other. A Land Rover for ourselves would cost 120 dollars a day – rather too much for us for a fortnight. It is a country that should be done on horseback and the centre route would be fine to do; but it measures out at 500 miles!

My Persian turns to Turkish as it comes out of my mouth, but should improve.

Love,

FREYA

Kabul

21 July 1968

Dearest Dulcie,

Yesterday we dressed up and spent the night (till 3 a.m.) on the terraces of the Embassy, all illuminated and circulating drinks, with dancing in the ballroom, *the* English entertainment of the year with a cosmopolitan crowd of all that in Afghanistan is learning to be Western. Other evenings are agreeably spent watching the rehearsals for *Twelfth Night*, to be given on August 15th. Meanwhile my own programme is getting into shape too gently. When Francis comes in six days I will take him north as he *must* see Balkh. Then I think we shall join quite a caravan of Land Rovers to get across the centre of the country to Herat.

Just as I was leaving Montoria the Gowries wrote to say that they can't manage Montoria *and* the new house inherited in Ireland and say, very nicely, that it isn't fair to ask me to wait longer. They might sell the new house in a year's time, but that is all too vague and I shall have to bring it to some conclusion this winter. I won't do anything till you come out for you know that it is yours at any moment for half its cost if you want it. But that would no doubt mean selling a picture. W.P. used to tell me to consider Browning's poem of the Statue and the Bust. How much I owe him! Every thought I have ever thought, worth the thinking.

I think of you often, darling Dulcie, glad for you, in spite of all, that your first meeting with death was in someone not *too* near. Mine was a little niece, my sister's first child, whom I helped nurse and who died with a little spasm in my arms, and I can still feel the sorrow and the greatness of awe and the beginning of that feeling that life and death are one. One cannot keep them apart. Perhaps it is that we forget this that we are no longer so finely tempered a people as we were. I think of this, watching this wild nation with its noble old faces, their whole lives spent in the presence of calamity of one sort or another, through which their tiny boats are steered. To such times too of trouble and sorrow the serenity of Plato or Shakespeare or Dante belongs.

Love to you both,

FREYA

MRS. T. DEUCHAR   Kabul
21 August 1968

Darling Dulcie,

I got back day before yesterday after a fortnight crossing Afghanistan from east to west, right through the middle. Wonderful week: two nice people offered Francis and me seats in their Land Rover, otherwise this best Afghan journey would have been beyond us. As it was, it was all enchantment, every night a different camp by some river or little high-pitched valley where the green sheep-nibbled turf showed water. Only the nomads about there, or the print of their journeys in hundreds of lines of small steps of goat along the hill slopes or broader steps of cows.

We came here to the tents of Central Asia, the *yurts* with round roofs and painted screens. Lower down, the walled and towered villages live in their small basins of corn and mulberry or apricot trees; and lower still the streams gather. One night we slept where the Hari Rud that feeds Herat is broad enough to ford, and in the dawn were wakened by over one hundred camels

151

crossing, the little gipsy girls sitting on those high saddles, the voices and the splash of water all mingling in the first shaft of the sun. Hard and beautiful world. It has not changed here in the last one thousand years, but every year now will change it; and they talk of the Asian highway coming through.

I am so glad still to have been able to do these long days, 6 a.m. to 4 or 5 p.m., and end with two sizzling days round the deserty edge of the country, Herat, Kandahar, to Kabul, 1,100 kilometres along the Russian-American highway.

Dearest love,

FREYA

MRS. T. DEUCHAR

c/o Leigh Fermor,
Kardamyli
1 September 1968

Darling Dulcie,

Here have I been for three days, and two days more, just breathing air and sea. The mountains are dove-grey in the sky and red like foxes as they run along the shore. They push and shoulder each other till the sea wraps them in light and here, among their cypresses and olives, Paddy and Joan have built themselves a house of the hillside stone, quite unimaginably solid and beautiful. Arcades and a great roomful of books and steps down to their little pebbly bay. They are very happy and there is a lovely atmosphere of leisure with space and sunlight running all through it.

I go back for a day to Athens and then to Patmos for a week with Teddy Millington-Drake, and then to Euboea; by the 26th I should be at Montoria in the throes of that horrid crisis,[118] but comforted by the thought of your coming.

I found a little mountain of letters waiting for me, and such kind reviews of my book; have answered all and would like to write on my journey, but seem unable to do so and wonder if I shall ever write again. On my way I spent a night in Teheran, at the summer Embassy where I stayed in 1931! The great tent where one dined under the *chinar* trees was still in use. It felt like going back into my youth.

Your loving
FREYA

[118] Emma had left after thirty years.

MRS. T. DEUCHAR Euboea

16 September 1968

Darling Dulcie,

I got back from my week on Patmos and just had time to pick up mail in Athens, be driven to lunch at a luxury club that now spoils the lovely approaches of Sunium, and get into a bus for Euboea. It took me nearly five hours over the island, rising to forest one would never expect in these naked-outlined hills, and got me to this charming little sea-town. Austen Harrison, with a poet (Philip Sherrard) on one side, and a rich Lord on the other, has a little house that sees Parnassus and Helicon across pale blue hills and sea.

Meanwhile I must tell you about my Patmos week, which turned out to be an Edwardian sort of houseparty, with the island as a background to conversation, but of the kind that I am very bad at, all about people's family affairs and characters, the sort of party I remember before the war. The centre of it was Mrs. Wyndham, whose mother was Ada Leverson. She *made* the party and I liked her, though it all seemed something seen very small, like a telescope turned its other way round into the past. Instead of Galsworthy they talked of modern novels, which also left me high and dry. Teddy painted his abstract pictures and sometimes joined us on a beach – lovely beaches, calm even when wind blows beyond the headlands; and the battlements of the eleventh-century monastery showed grey above the white-washed houses that stretch along the highest island hill.

Much, much love, darling Dulcie,

FREYA

JOHN GREY MURRAY Montoria

4 October 1968

Dearest Jock,

I am glad to get your note and had been wishing to write every day for the celebrations.[119] Rather sad that your Manifesto (just sent me by a book-seller) puts Mlles Sagan and Murphy cosily with Lord Byron and leaves me under the surely rather strange 'general and educational' heading. Paddy and Osbert share these adjectives and exclusions, so I can bear it, only wonder how the choice was made.

I am in the midst of this domestic crisis and rather pleased to have managed to feed the Eustons and Simon's two brothers without a cook. We have taught Francesca eight dishes and she has the makings of an *excellent* cook

[119] The 200th anniversary of the publishing house of John Murray.

and is getting very keen, but not very clever with her husband whose dinner she completely forgot – with the result that he reverses the Victorian tradition and retires to his mother. I am hoping that the present of half an acre of land for a house may soothe him. Even so, and with all this drama about, it is an immense relief to be without Emma: to get old in an angry way is a terrible infliction and it was like a sort of scorpion tail waving over every domestic who began to look happy. It is borne in on me that this is the first servant in my life I have ever *sent* away – and I do hope the last. They are very hard to get now and most people put up with anything and let life get drearier and drearier.

5 October 1968

We are off for a night to Ravenna and then the Eustons leave. So pleasant to have them and such genuine true friends. Stewarts arrive 9th or 10th. Thank goodness Franco back; the enormous cookery book I bought for Francesca a great success – all well in the kitchen!

Love,
FREYA

JOHN GREY MURRAY

Montoria
13 October 1968

Dearest Jock,

Simon and in fact about twelve Guinnesses have just come and gone and lunched us three at Cipriani. Simon then came up and we spent two hours over the book which is to be called either 'Landscape Albums' or 'Time, Movement and Space in Landscape'[120] and will be only 500 copies, all signed and *very* expensive – but rather beautiful with brown wavy endpapers and box, a brown leather back. The printers seem very optimistic and Simon has shown it to various people and they like it. It seems strange to me that 500 people would spend twelve guineas or more, but I expect that it is a good idea to turn it into a luxury product. Although it is not your book – and this I never cease to regret, dearest Jock – would you be ready to give it a helping hand for distribution and tell that nice man who goes around to add it to his list? Simon is bringing out a prospectus with sample illustration to distribute.

It is a great relief to me to have it lifted off my shoulders and with one thing and another about a hundred copies are already bespoke. It makes me

---

[120] It was in fact called *Space, Time and Movement in Landscape*.

feel a bit more energetic about my Afghan travel diary of which I have got three pages down. The absence of a cook makes writing much more difficult, but the domestic climate is clearing and the new maid due on Wednesday. The resuscitated Topolino, with new engine and painted yellow, is re-bought and due tomorrow to convey her to and fro every day: Francesca and I will do this till she learns to drive!

All love,

FREYA

JOHN GREY MURRAY   Montoria
30 October 1968

Dearest Jock,

The latest drama is a message by telephone from the police to say would we look out, as all the villas around are being robbed of their silver – three in Asolo, two in San Zenone, another near Castelfranco. So we are shutting ourselves up every night, letting down the iron shutter, etc., and have hidden even the silver teapot; and Franco has brought up his three guns and he and Francesca are sleeping in the house with baby Stefania. It is all quite strangely familiar after two wars, but gloomy: the police say it will subside after Xmas as these things happen 'per le feste'. They seem quite hopeless about ever getting any clue: 'There are only three of us,' the *brigadiere* explained rather pathetically over the telephone.

Something very depressing is happening to me – I am just *perpetually* tired, *so* tired that I fall around, asleep: it can't even be old age merely and has been growing on me these last few *years* but now is really burdensome. Quite a lot of cooking is going on however and there is a golden sort of gay peace these last October days.

Love,
FREYA

SYBIL, LADY CHOLMONDELEY[121]   Montoria
20 November 1968

Dearest Sybil,

What a dream! And perhaps either going or returning, you could stay over a day or so to see my little hill?

Persia would be at its best in spring and with luck we might find the

---

121 Her husband, the 5th Marquess, had died in September.

tribes moving to their summer pastures. I should think Isfahan, Shiraz, Persepolis first as it is warmer, and then north to Meshed, and Nishapur and some of those less known northern places?

I am not strictly limited except by my roses in May, and by two considerations: one is that, if you remember, I was asked (much to my surprise) to the Windsor state dinner for the Italians, which was then *postponed*. The other is a squalid preoccupation with finance, as I have had to hand £1,000 to my departing cook (after thirty years) and must somehow repay this as soon as possible, so that I can do very little this year. I could do a little however, but not nearly enough. The matter now is, dearest Sybil (I am so *happy* to to think of such a trip), that if you are rich at the moment you will have to bear most of the brunt, and if you are poor (quite possible with things as they are) we would have to do a Spartan sort of journey. I would so love to see the pastures with you when all their flowers come out. And it is not a precipitous country like Greece for motoring.

I am tied in domestic tangles, but getting through and I hope it was all for the best. I think of you, so often: it would be *lovely* to have a little time together.

Your loving

FREYA

P.S. I am reading the *Vita Nuova* again after many years. It has I think the greatest love sonnet in the world, even counting Shakespeare! One can see the faint wraith of the *Divine Comedy* coming.

JOHN GREY MURRAY   Montoria

2 December 1968

Dearest Jock,

I am so glad to get your fine long letter, and to see you emerging from your orgy – a very splendid one however, and must have made you feel very proud and happy: to be at the summit of 200 years is not after all everyone's achievement. And I have been getting extracts – the *T.L.S.*, etc. – and happy to see the *warmth* of all the writing.

I will write properly at the weekend when Michael arrives and I have heard all the news. At the moment I have the nice Pearsons with whom I stayed in Kabul, and took them to lunch at Belluno and look at all those erratic mountain peaks, surprisingly clear of snow. Here it is frosty at night, but so warm by day that the solanum still dangles its little flowers and roses come out at my window. Any day we expect Hillier's plants to arrive, and great activity when they do. And inside the house we go from one crisis to another, but I hope subsiding, like the waves settling after a storm. Emma has got her £1,000 and I feel poor but honest.

Two chapters of *The Minaret of Djam* are written and I may have one more by New Year and will try to send. Not much hope of getting it done till near the end of next year. The brain is still very ineffectual and it gives me an actual pain to *think* – I can't keep it up for more than a minute; but now and then ideas come pleasantly dropping by themselves.

6 December 1968

Michael got here last night after a gruelling drive from Val d'Aosta to Bassano in thick fog. Here we sit in the sun and look down on it all. Such a Xmas feeling about his arrival – roses, pearls, shoes, marvellous tea, polish, letters, and most of all the book,[122] and Osbert, and *Cornhill*. The shelf of my books has no more room – and yet I hope to squeeze one more! It looks so beautiful in its best dress, the *Zodiac* I mean. Great fun to hear the news here, and to be generally amused by Michael's conversation.

Love, dear Jock,

FREYA

SYBIL, LADY CHOLMONDELEY   Montoria
                                                        4 January 1969
Dearest Sybil,

I have just got back from the Mooreheads and find your letter: it is so *good* to get something that switches so happily away from all that is troubling at the moment. What fun it is to turn plans over and play with them so that one can enjoy future, present, and past; the people who say proudly that they never make plans miss all this pleasure.

The Shuckburghs in Rome told me that the Italian State Visit is now fixed for April 22nd. I have no idea whether the ceremonies are to be the same or whether the same invitations will be sent, and it will not make the slightest difference to my happiness if I miss it altogether, but if it happens that I could include it by leaving with you from London on April 24th or so and coming back for a few days later in May – would this make any difference to you? The Meshed country would be better I rather think in May than in April – and May 15th would be time enough for me to see my roses here.

[122] *The Zodiac Arch.*

157

I have written to ask about hotels from friends and also to get the name of the Museum director, who is one of my many friends whose name I never can remember. He pleased me by telling me that my book is still the best guide to the Luristan bronzes. He will show us the gold cups in his strong room.

Dearest love,

FREYA

SIR MICHAEL STEWART   Montoria
4 January 1969

Dearest Michael,

A happy New Year. I am just back from Porto Ercole and find your good letter, a comfort in a desert, as (a) all my plants have been mislaid for eight weeks between Rotterdam and the Italian border; (b) both kitchen stove and boiler broke, but Francesca got them mended just in time for me but not to save Stefania from bronchitis; and (c) Bertilla's mother *died* on eve of my arrival and I am just back from the funeral. Otherwise Mme La Marquise is as well as Age allows. All your plants look O.K., the whole landscape bleached with ice at its heart. I feel like a marmot at home and am now settling down to tackle all my Xmas letters waiting here, a pleasant job with thoughts of and from friends.

Plotinus is almost convincing me that Time, non-existent, doesn't matter. He is more satisfactory to me than the Bible and I read him every day. Also a beautiful second book by my disciple Colin Thubron. He does, more perfectly, what I have tried to do. He is a direct descendant of Dryden and that probably helps. But do read *The Hills of Adonis*.

I agree about Carpaccio, full of charming sentiment but mediocre? But I think Tintoretto should be *graziato*. When they took down the San Rocco canvases some years ago they found a tiny scrap turned in that had not faded: brilliant, lavish, unexpected, unrecognisable colour!

With love to Damaris and Olivia,

FREYA

SIR MICHAEL STEWART   Montoria
26 January 1969

Dearest Michael,

The plain is white with frost every morning but we live in glorious sun and only freeze at night. Your plants against the wall seem happy anyway and I am now anxiously watching mine to see if they sprout in spite of all their hardships. The trees seem quite happy thanks to Hillier's marvellous (but expensive) packing.

Awful troubles with Francesca, who has gone primitive completely, and Franco, like many another husband in general, says kindness is wasted on her. All else seems quiet. I took the Gibsons on their one spare day to see the most beautiful early eighteenth-century villa, beautifully stuccoed and furnished, belonging to the Conte Marcello.

My book now has four chapters. *Awfully* heavy going.

Love to you all,

FREYA

P.S. I am quoting in my book a nice epigram from Epictetus: 'Man cannot make progress if he is facing both ways.'

JOHN GREY MURRAY   Montoria

2 February 1969

Dearest Jock,

Your letter came beautifully timed for my birthday, which I was happily forgetting over a lazy morning in bed, and I was so glad to get it and have all good news – the best that you are off for a proper holiday at last.

I think you are quite right about a straight mortgage being better. I do hope that may be done this year and let me stop thinking of finance in my last years. Michael tells me I can get large sums for my chaotic mss. and to write to Anthony Hobson.[123] I did and he wants a lot of details but says one can make quite a lot, and I am delighted at any thought of getting rid of *paper*. Could you let me know what is in those vaults of yours? Anthony says the Americans are only interested if they have *all* the mss., and it remains to be seen if they like the typescript, though it seems all right if sufficiently scribbled over. In view of this source of income I am trying to write my first draft by hand, which makes it illegible even to myself.

The Karmels have been winkled out into the open to say fair and square that they do not intend to pay any arrears ever; so Mr. Punchard is I hope ending the lease. I have agreed to buy the furniture at a valuation so long as the proceeds go to what they owe already, which will be nearly £2,000 in April. The furniture is hideous but convenient as it is all ready for letting – but I bet there will be trouble over that too. All this does not harass me; I am so thankful when it isn't one's nearest and dearest that let one down.

123 Friend, bibliophile and a director of Sotheby's.

The whole of Lombardy is swathed in mist, and even here it comes boiling up, but doesn't stop the first crocus, out yesterday. I am sorry not to be on the Riviera, but going in June, and will keep to the last week of my plan for this month, in Portugal with Dorothea Landsberg. It has been on the *tapis* for years, even while dear Bertie was alive, and it should be very carefree – I am not even taking my camera!

I have been away for a day only and that was to lunch in Venice with the Cinis who wanted to know me and gave a sumptuous lunch-party with well-chosen guests – Fosco Maraini (Sikkim and Tibet); Branca, head of the St. Giorgio; a photographer who has been publishing Turkey – very well too I believe; and the head of the Accademia. It was gay and pleasant and Cini a Renaissance mixture of charm and tycoon and culture; and his wife a very nice ardent indiscriminate traveller. Travel without background seems nonsense to me – but what a subject to start at the end of a letter.

Love, dear Jock, and do have a glorious time in Morocco (probably cold: take overcoats).

FREYA

MRS. T. DEUCHAR   Sintra
21 February 1969

Darling Dulcie,

I am here till March 1st and am still with that transplanted feeling which air travel gives, no *transition*, although it took quite a time, as I left in the heaviest snowstorm of the winter. I finally reached Lisbon at night, poor Dorothea patiently waiting. My idea (and clothes) for a quiet country visit shaken by the news that King Umberto was invited to lunch next day (yesterday) with twelve other people, and two more luncheon parties coming – my pleading that landscape is what I like best in a new country quite useless. But it was very enjoyable, and I sat next to the King and found him wonderfully easy, charming and sincere to talk to, with something unspoilt and rather wistful about him, and happy I think to talk Italian. He complained that his travels are so often interrupted because he is bundled away from any country as soon as it shows signs of revolution and this now happens nearly everywhere.

The rest of the party were an unusually cosmopolitan mixture, hardly any couple the same nationality, mostly settled in villas on these wooded slopes of Sintra and must spend their whole time seeing each other, and have nearly all asked me to luncheons. But I am promised a drive or two. It is *romantic* landscape – Bertie once told me it is to landscape what Titian is to painting and that I think is so. The stony peaks stand out of wood that goes from pine to rich varied forest and then broadens and opens to plain and the Tagus estuary and sea. I long to roam about and also to see the strange ornate sixteenth-century architecture.

This sudden plunge into the social world makes me wonder how other authors manage. I couldn't possibly write at all if it were not for the semi-solitude of Montoria.

Dear love,

FREYA

MRS. T. DEUCHAR   Sintra
28 February 1969

Dearest Dulcie,

I leave tomorrow morning, and as I expect to find a little mountain of letters to attend to, thought I would write this here in Portuguese leisure and add a word when I reach your news – as I hope I may, and hope so much to find it good. Also a date of arrival at Montoria? I have been reading a book on food and discover that we not only eat wrongly but *too little* and are all under-nourished to deal with illness when it comes. A film star called Gloria Swanson aged seventy and with the figure of a sylph is making me a list of the essentials for being like her (as to figure, not stardom). It sounds delightful to be encouraged to eat *more* and she swears that my absurd tiredness will roll away with my tummy, and you will convalesce in half the time and things like heart and liver and all those poor little overworked machines will become as frisky as they once used to be in times one can't even remember. As you know, I am ready to try anything and felt this is better than faith-healing!

A touching lunch with King Umberto yesterday in his ugly seaside house of exile. It was built for him by devoted followers so that he had no hand in the designing, and its small garden looks across a boulevard, hidden by trees, to the grey discouraging Atlantic. There he lives with the portraits of his ancestors all round him, and one devoted follower, a nice Neapolitan who walks about as if he were still wearing court dress. A Walter Scott atmosphere about it all and the King walks among his guests with a mixture of dignity and charm that is very moving. His wife lives away from him in Switzerland and his children are awful and he looks delicate and has been ill lately.

I leave tomorrow early by air, and hope all may be well. At four this a.m.

161

we were awakened by an earthquake. I thought it was an aeroplane, which slowly grew louder and louder till I thought, 'If it *is* an aeroplane it is going to crash on this roof', and got out of bed, found the light not working, and all the household gathering with candles. The centre seems to have been in the north of Portugal and in Spain.

Love,

FREYA

JOHN GREY MURRAY

Montoria

7 March 1969

Dearest Jock,

It is too late at night to begin a letter, but it seems a long time since you travelled in Morocco and I long to hear about it and how it feels to be back. Did John fall on his feet? I am sure he did, and so very good for him; one should be given just as much as one can carry – that anyway seems to be the philosophy of the Almighty.

I am hoping my six chapters arrived safely and soon to hear that you or John or both have read them. There is a curious impediment when one has sent mss. away that prevents any more writing till one gets news – a sort of block.

We had a sadly stormy parting from Francesca, who went for Beppi with a *broom* (a poor sort of weapon) and poor exasperated Franco, who came begging pardon all round, said to me as he went: 'You are so lucky, Signora, not to be married to Francesca.' She couldn't bear to have anyone else anywhere near. I am sorry as I liked her, but we are very peaceful now. Long may it last.

You will be going to the Huxley golden wedding? Fifty years of looking after Julian! Juliette should appear with a palm branch in her hand like one of those Byzantine martyrs.

Much love dear Jock,

FREYA

JOHN GREY MURRAY

Teheran

2 May 1969

Dearest Jock,

This is where we return tomorrow but are really in Isfahan and all has been lovely so far.[124] Shiraz a whole city blossoming with roses, the kinds we

[124] F.S. was travelling with Sybil Cholmondeley.

have in our gardens but huge bushes filled with flowers: 5,000,000 were bought for the Shah's coronation, and they are massed along five miles of avenue from airport to town. The sights of Shiraz are the tombs of Hafiz and Saadi, both smothered in roses and every sort of flower. The whole town atmosphere is given by its two poets – and here in Isfahan also I am told that every social gathering breaks into verse. We have lunched with the old aristocrat I knew nine years ago, in his country house with blue-washed court and oval pool and *trees* of white roses.

Apart from this we have done our sightseeing: Persepolis and Pasargadae, and the site of the old and very barbarous Islamic capital at Istakhr; have called on old Professor Upham Pope whom I met in New York in the war, and have now been seeing all the mosques of Isfahan. An old guide took us round the Friday mosque after hours, when the women in their brown veils were standing here and there and all the strident contrasts of the day seemed to subside. The Isfahanis still love their town and have made a hotel to show all the traditions of their skill: not an inch of undecorated space – all beautiful, only *too* lavish: the only failures are the customers who look very dowdy in their travelling groups. The least ornamental are shepherded to the back – but we got compliments and attention because of my hat!

Love,

FREYA

JOHN GREY MURRAY Montoria
19 May 1969

Dearest Jock,

I have just got back and still don't feel de-Orientalised. It is extraordinary how easily I slip into the way of life of Greece and anything east of it – until, that is to say, one reaches the borders of India and feels outside and not inside the window pane. We flew to Meshed with Damavand an immaculate snowy triangle on our left – and found a clean white hotel meant for the well-to-do Persian pilgrims, and spent three days seeing ruins and the tombs of poets; Nishapur for Omar; an agreeable morning with the curator, who is a retired civil servant and sips his tea and plants lilies under his shady trees; with an eighteen-year-old daughter whose face is that of the best miniatures, a beautiful oval, and has learnt about a hundred words of English in four years (the elder sister married in New Jersey!). The old man manages to combine these separate worlds in perfect harmony and I wondered as always how these people manage their old age with such peaceful mastery. Having dismissed

New Jersey in a sentence, he took us to see the tomb (a mosaic lacework of tiles and all geometric in honour of Khayyam's mathematics) – and the mosque beside it, where women wrapped in their *chaduri* were creeping about the coffin of one of their imams; and so drove back to Meshed through a long open valley whose waters are held in by small foothills – all open in dusty freedom.

Sybil came out with all sorts of superstitions about the dangers of Meshed, having been told that one was always insulted in the bazaar unless veiled. We however walked unveiled and were not insulted, and looked at turquoises and Korans, and more at the people who were from all far places for the month of the pilgrimage. One is not allowed inside the outer gate of the long open spaces where the souvenir sellers have their booths, and the arched tiled doorways lead in. We had to enter this space to see the Museum, but had to veil, and two nice passers-by helped me with mine, holding their own modestly in their teeth while they did so. It is the clumsiest garment, that instantly drops off if hand or teeth let go.

Firdausi's grave was on another day and also finely built and well tended with poplars and visited by a group of students who insisted on our being included in their photograph. There is just the marble mausoleum and a pool and garden of pansies and geraniums, a gay mixture, and a tiny squalid mud village, and long stretch of walls eaten away almost to the ground and now enclosing nothing – after Tamerlane.

A great ruin of a khan lies off the road to the Russian border, and we found a policeman who refused to let us go without a pass and sent us with a soldier to get one from the frontier garrison. It all seemed strangely familiar! Both Sybil and I had left our passports behind at the Meshed hotel, and we spent two and a half hours in the captain's office while two of them investigated, and finally got us vouched for by the British Council. By this time we had also made ourselves as much of a burden as we could by asking for lunch, which the garrison sent in; and they finally released us and sent us to see our ruin, which by then the afternoon light was making most beautiful, shining on poppies on long slopes around it and catching all the delicate brick ornament still unspoiled.

Let me have news dear Jock – I seem to have been a long time without.

Love,

FREYA

P.S. I hear vaguely that dear old Harry Luke has died. He was eighty-four or even eighty-five, and I found a letter here saying that he hoped to get out of doctors' hands and come out; I shall miss him.

Florence
                                                                    27 May 1969

Dearest Mark,

My plan has more or less got settled for Istanbul about September 3rd and
then three or four weeks into October in the South. It will make no difference if you suddenly find yourself free and send a telegram and join – except
to make it much pleasanter.

What, however, would be even more exciting (though possibly just as
difficult) is if you could think of spending part of *February next* in Nepal.
Such an amusing thing has happened. I heard of an ex-Colonel of Ghurkas
who continues to live in his adored mountains and organises expeditions for
people who want to walk about there. He takes them right in among the
giants, round the skirts of Everest or Annapurna. I am no good for walking
(thinking of the wind on Taurus) but I wrote and asked if he could arrange
a fortnight's riding, although I am six years beyond his age limit. He sounds
quite pleased and has written an excellent letter of suggestions, and says that
though walking is the only way of getting near Everest, there is an even
more beautiful bit of wandering round Annapurna, the most impressive of
all these ranges, that can be done on ponies. He suggests about three weeks,
half getting acclimatised or resting (lovely lakes), and half actual trekking.
Very few people I would ask to join on such a jaunt so I hope you feel it as
a traveller's tribute as well as love and affection, dear Mark. I shall try and
do it myself just to 'raise my eyes to the hills'.

                                                                    Love,
                                                                    FREYA

MRS. T. DEUCHAR   c/o Colahan,
                                                        Mortola Superiore,
                                                                Ventimiglia
                                                             6 July 1969

Dearest Dulcie,

I do nothing here but draw, all day long, copying Rembrandt or Holbein
as the case may be and delighted with this new window. It is marvellous to
have something so absorbing and not too tiring, as I can draw for three
hours as against one hour's writing! The house is perched on a cliff with the
glittering coast below looking west beyond Monte Carlo, cape beyond cape,
and inland to a most beautiful mountain outline which I try in vain to get
on to paper.

Why not learn to draw or paint, Dulcie? I have been thinking all these days how happy it would make you. All the creative things inside you would suddenly find something to feed on, and the actual world in itself would give a new delight. I am only copying as yet, but even that gives as it were a lot of new eyes as one sees what the great painters saw, following their minds stroke by stroke.

I will write from Montoria when my tenants are in and I find a mountain retreat to finish the book. Do write to your loving

FREYA

JOHN GREY MURRAY   Mortola Superiore

13 July 1969

Dearest Jock,

Now I am off, in an hour, to spend the night with Hilda Besse[125] and tomorrow spend a very long day in trains on the way to Vicenza and Sandro and home – and hope to find a little batch of news. I have three days before the tenants are due, and when they are installed hope to leave in my little car with all the Afghan mss. and my typewriter for the hotel on Grappa and to finish the book for you. It will do it a lot of good to have had this interval before being looked at again. Somehow or other I must try and include an hour a day for drawing in my rather crowded life. The three weeks' work have gone very well and Colin Colahan says it is well worth going on. It has even so given me great delight; when I get a chance I will send along the collection.

I have been too hard at it to walk much about these hills, but went twice along the little paths I used to know with W.P. and felt he was there quite near me looking at those old familiar views. Went down to L'Arma to dine with Costanza, but that feels sad now, full of ghosts – all its sunlight now overgrown with trees that I planted, and the old pieces of furniture, the chairs and wardrobes that my mother painted for my wedding, looking too full of memories to be comfortable. Costanza herself is well and busy with her plantations, and the motors are whizzing along the new Corniche road above.

Must send this, and write next from Montoria.

With love, dear Jock,

FREYA

[125] Widow of the Red Sea shipping magnate and philanthropist, Anton Besse. F.S. had stayed in the past at Le Paradou, the Besses' house in France.

Montoria
16 July 1969

Dearest Jock,

You will be glad to hear that I have found a very quiet little hotel on Grappa and go there Monday and hope to come back with *The Minaret of Djam* almost complete. I can descend now and then if necessary for references, etc.

I am buying a new dress – the first for years – and a mowing machine, and it would help me a lot in my financial vagueness to know what Stark Researches can put into my bank: very helpful if they could put it in anyway. Also what my own little store has? I should be rather affluent this year, and how pleasant that would be!

I got to Paradou for one night and was glad to see it and Hilda again: Hilda very spry but getting terrifically talkative. This seems to happen with age though I believe I am getting the other way. Such a stupid woman had us all to dine at Mortola and said 'What do you *do* with your Arabic?'

'I talk to Arabs when I am with them,' said I.

'Why don't you try to get a job on the B.B.C.?'

'Because I don't want one,' said I.

'Well, that's arrogant: but I like it,' said she.

Now why should the simple truth be arrogant? I could have found a much more cogent adjective for her.

Love,
FREYA

Montoria
18 July 1969

Dearest Jock,

Your letter just come and nearly knocks me over by what you tell me of Sybil's generosity. How *wonderful*! She said vaguely that she didn't intend to wait till she died but I had no idea this was really to come about. It is lovely, warm and touching to think of, and how delightful that a way to spend it all has been prepared by Providence as it were – otherwise I might have bought another little hill! It will cover Nepal, and a little shopping in Delhi on the way, and should make 1970 a nice easy year and that will be rather a blessing. What blessed wonderful friends I have – mostly you, dear Jock, loaded with my unending little troubles.

My tenants are settling in quite happily and are sizzling in Venice today.

On Monday I leave them and have got a quiet little pub waiting on Grappa and will drive myself up – very carefully, as it would be awful to die with all that money unspent.

Love,

FREYA

MRS. T. DEUCHAR   Montoria

1 August 1969

Darling Dulcie,

My unknown Highlander is the most charming young man you ever met, and *so* good-looking.[126] I would be head over heels in love if fifty-six years were taken off my shoulders! He has fought two and a half years in Malay and on his leave goes walking in some country in the hills. I asked him what made him so persevering in coming to see me, and he said it was the introduction to *Perseus*, the mountain pass and the constellation above it. How happy when one's words fall in the right place! I took him to the Stewarts' house last night where there are his dear and charming sister and two young daughters and an intellectual young man, all knocked of a heap that anyone should be a soldier and asking him why. And he was the only (apart from the mother who gets up early to read a little poetry and do all the work) human being complete and satisfactory there. He carries a volume of poetry in his knapsack and has beautiful sensitive hands. Oh dear, I hope he finds the right wife. He loves his profession. We were looking at some Afghan photographs where a limestone precipice surrounds a smooth white slope. 'A splendid defence,' I said. 'I was just thinking it,' said he, 'one could slip down and get away.' What a comfort, Dulcie, to have people about who want to live and not just talk about living.

Dear love to you and Tommy.

FREYA

JOHN GREY MURRAY   Grappa

12 August 1969

Dearest Jock,

This is to tell you that the *Minaret* is packed and ready to be taken to you by one of the Stewart guests on the 20th: it is a wonderful opening of prison

---

[126] Major Colin Mackenzie had been writing to F.S. for six years and had now paid her a visit.

doors when a book finally gets off. This one is very small, but it has taken a lot of writing with rather feeble powers. When Ernest Barker produced a historical volume at eighty-one I remember thinking it strange that his wife made such a fuss over it – but I now understand perfectly. The remarkable thing is what Dr. Johnson said of the dog standing on two legs (was it?) – that he should do it at all. If it isn't good, I will stop writing; but I hope it *is* good.

As for title, I think just (Afghanistan) in brackets would be best? One only wants to give the information and not to take the accent off the Minaret. Also I don't think this deserves to be called a *journey*; if anything an excursion, but I think just Afghanistan either added or under the title would sound best. There is also an uncertainty in my mind about the chapter headings. I feel that I want to emphasise the abstract bits of philosophy (if that is what it is) and not to add more emphasis to the travel, which will already have the pictures and anyway is more obvious. With this in mind, will you give the headings a thought as you go? The little book is in your hands, dear Jock – may it not disgrace its foster-parents!

This has been a very good experiment for work: no other temptation except walking, and that has been an excellent combination. Three various parties have come up to lunch with me: it is a Babel at meal times, but in between one can step away into woods or grassy slopes, all dotted with peasant houses whence the cows are pastured – all to be spoilt soon but not just yet.

A huge pile of prospectuses to send out for *Landscape* which comes out on September 15th. Do drink its health after all its vicissitudes dear Jock. I hope you can afford a copy, as I feel Simon is going to lose heavily so I *can't* ask him for any!

The travel book is at least a year away, but I have been wondering if you would like it dedicated to you? John has *Perseus*, but I don't believe you have one (though I may have forgotten) and surely that is wrong. A nice book of travel essays, with the portrait as frontispiece and little bits of poetry between?

Love,

FREYA

P.S. (from Montoria). Driving down with the klaxon not working and suddenly clouds of steam because the tube from the water tank had bust. I found a garage in nice open country which said 'open' and was locked, but had left a *chaise-longue* in the shade; so I waited there for one and a half hours reading the wonderful poetry of Hölderlin, who is a new discovery, and looking with pleasure at the wall of Grappa overcome. When the man came along I suggested he might turn round the 'open' and make it 'closed' when he went off. 'Such a trouble to do that every time,' said he. One feels rather like that down here in the heat.

JOHN GREY MURRAY Montoria

27 August 1969

Dearest Jock,

These days are a hurly-burly: Gowrie family just left; old friends to tea; goodbyes all round to neighbours; John Sparrow and his philosopher and Reynolds Stones arriving tomorrow, and all the Jellicoes following; I escape for two last days in Venice to collect myself and fly to Istanbul on September 5th.

Miss Foyle has asked me to be guest of honour at a dinner on October 1st for Charles Lambe (the life which has just appeared):[127] I could do this on the way back from Turkey I think without much expense or delay. I could manage five days in London and just see you and Simon and Sybil and fly off again? What troubles me is the awful fear that a speech would be required and that is something I hope to have cut out of my life!

It was lovely having Grey and Xandra and their wild little boy. I asked John Sparrow what time he reached Padua to send Sandro to meet him, and he answered 'Some time in the afternoon.'

Love,

FREYA

JOHN GREY MURRAY Istanbul

9 September 1969

Dearest Jock,

It seems strangely natural to be on the Bosphorus again, in this friendly old house which one of these days will tumble right in. It is now I think the fourth time I have stayed here, and I fall into all its easy grooves. The babies have grown into children, the children are young men and women; the visitors find it a little more difficult to go up and down the sea-washed steps; the unpainted wooden walls are a little more bleached by their winters and

[127] *Admiral of the Fleet: The Life of Sir Charles Lambe* by Oliver Warner.

summers. This Asiatic side still keeps its quiet cobbled streets and plane-tree shadows, chiefly because one is liable to a waiting of several hours to get a car ferry to cross. In about two years they say the bridge will be there: already the plans are drawn and financiers have been buying up the lands – motor cars will smother the little villages that still climb steeply up their hills. How lucky to have seen it still scarcely changed.

It is wonderfully restful here in my big empty room: five tall arched windows and the Pontic Sea flowing by.

Love,
FREYA

SIR MICHAEL STEWART

Montoria
3 October 1969

Dearest Michael,

I had been thinking that it was a long time since I had news of you or had written, and sure enough here was a nice letter waiting for me. I got back yesterday, not from Turkey but London, where I ended up so as to go to Charles Lambe's commemoratory (nice word?) luncheon. Mountbatten made a speech, not inspired, and rather disintegrated like that beautiful profile of his, *ahimé*. But I had a very happy time sitting next to Sir Francis Chichester.[128] We *both* exclaimed joyfully at sitting next to each other and had a splendid talk of deserts and seas, like tumbling suddenly into the Elizabethan Age. He has a charming face with that delicate, clean-cut *neatness* of the Elizabethans, those little wisps over the ears looking clean-cut and close-shaven and grey.

I got to Ani at last, without a permit, but Providence sent an officer along just as the sentry was saying 'Yok'. Lovely great downs and hills, like water-colours of Scotland one hundred years ago. But I am not enthusiastic about the Armenian architecture. We went afterwards to Edirne, and that is the most beautiful mosque in the world I think, a *dream* of grace and lightness. And it was pleasant in between to relax in the old Bosphorus house with the good friends.

Did I tell you how glad I was about Ditchley?[129] It was arranged by Nancy Lancaster with exquisite taste and fine bits of Kent's original furniture, I do hope still there. I stayed a weekend with the Ronnie Trees, and

---

[128] The well-known yachtsman. He had made his solo one-stop circumnavigation of the world at record speed in 1966–67.

[129] Sir Michael Stewart had been appointed Warden of the Ditchley Foundation.

hope to spend more. A lovely job, dear Michael, and will let you come here, too.

The David Cecils are coming here for a fortnight tomorrow.

Lots of love to you both,

FREYA

MRS. T. DEUCHAR   Montoria

12 October 1969

Darling Dulcie,

I came back to a mountain of letters and am still not quite through, kept busy too in a pleasant way by the Cecils. They like to look at villas, so that we have been lunching and dining at Malcontenta, Fanzolo, Maser, De Lord. In between we made a little two-day expedition to Aquileia, Grado, Udine, and Cividale where, tucked away in a chapel, rather badly built by the barbarians, is a Lombard bas-relief of the ninth century which B.B. used to tell me was the most interesting monument in Northern Italy. It is long straight figures, what ancestry? Greek, Byzantine, Gothic, strangely modern, by some artist unknown of those dark ages, most strangely moving. Udine was a discovery, with an entrancing seventeenth-century *piazza* and a whole gallery entirely decorated by Tiepolo, and a very good hotel behind its old unretouched façade. David and Rachel are the pleasantest travelling companions and I thought so often of you and how you would have liked it. We are now going to Mantova, Sabbioneta and back by Parma or Verona. I think Italy is *the* country to be old in, the most lovely things in the world within easy reach and in such variety, and it is very restful to have to think of journeys of three *days* instead of months.

I am getting my ticket for January 27th or 29th straight from Rome to Nepal and back and as soon as the Cecils have gone am going to tackle the problem of *boots*. No one now faces those hard things studded with metal ridges that took me up Monte Rosa fifty years ago. I think with such pleasure of the anorak and those soft pyjamas like a nest to shelter in the folds of Annapurna, and will think of you whenever I put them on! If you can still add to your burdens with a Brigg Sunshade, it can only be got at 185 Piccadilly. They are the only people who produce 'Explorer's Umbrellas', and I was too late to go to them by the time I found out. The things you get here break by the second day, but Mr. Brigg will go on through anything. A hook handle is essential, and the colour does not really matter though black seems rather sad. They used to have green with a sort of grey

172

outside but now, they told them at Albemarle Street, they have only green and yellow.

I must go, darling Dulcie. Do please come soon. We have never had a more beautiful October, every day a miracle of blue and gold, and the windows wide open.

Dear love,

FREYA

MRS. T. DEUCHAR   Montoria
29 October 1969

MRS. T. DEUCHAR

Darling Dulcie,

I am struggling with too many problems and if it were not for Caroly would *sink*. But the Bertilla situation looks very good if it is permanent, and the cook, although a cold little fish, is all right (except that they loathe each other), and I hope to have an elderly help for Beppi who has wrecked the garden by not watering. He says that watering brings moles.

What is far more worrying is a return of my excessive tiredness, and I have to write as Thames and Hudson are in a hurry.[130] When one has to write seven chapters on different periods and has only specialised in *one*, it means a lot of reading as well as writing. I am, however, bolstering my morale with a spring suit, a plum-coloured one for Katmandu in February. They tell me I must book my room now as there is very little accommodation and only two 'suitable' hotels.

A Texan family [131] has bought a huge villa near Vicenza with beautifully planted garden or rather park of rare trees, so beautiful. They took me to lunch there in a car I long to possess, bed, frigidaire, washbasin, all inside it. But I don't think I could drive it. They also promise to sell my house. This reminds me, dearest Dulcie, to thank you for buying two of my expensive books. Simon writes that 120 are sold. I don't believe he will make it, poor darling. But it will have been so good for him to have done something not for money, and lovely to look back on in his old age.

Must send this and get back to the book. I know what the man felt to whom 'the grasshopper was a burden'!

Dear love to you and Tommy,

FREYA

[130] They had commissioned F.S. to write *Turkey: A Sketch of Turkish History* (1971).
[131] The Lamberts.

Dearest Pam,

Little thoughts fly out to you, and especially when the Eastern Mediterranean comes in sight; but it has been a patchwork year and one thing after another and next year not much better as I hope for a summer in England. But just in time for *dinner* in Athens on January 29th on the way to spend my birthday in Nepal. And then I hope for a few days on the way back in early March, but Nepal is such a big Unknown to me that I am not making any definite plans till I see how it goes. Sherpas and pony and ticket are fixed. What do you say to that for optimism in this uncertain world?

I feel sure you will settle on England, and then, like all of us Levantines, will be consumed by nostalgia after the second year, and be very happy if you have that little *pied-à-terre* in Greece. By then I hope I shall have fixed this house so as to have a few months a year free *with an income*; and we can see each other much more easily than now, so you must keep room for a camp bed in the *pied-à-terre*.

At any moment I expect a colonel or two here. It is so like 1920–22: strikes every day, holding up letters, medicines, *roses*. The strikes are against the rise in prices, too idiotic as they are what makes them rise!

I am not going to do anything about Xmas, but will send a loving wish, dear Pam and David,

FREYA

Darling Dulcie,

I have still boots to find here, but meanwhile have been dealing with *feet* and found a good pedicure in Venice. I find it tiring to go and come and shop, etc., so spent the night with Genette Venini and was so *moved* by this gaunt vision of Venice in winter, the water lying in pools on the *piazza*, the low plank bridges to the door of St. Mark's with Chinese-looking processions passing in single file, the old warm coats pulled out to wade about in above the high rubber boots in which Venice now lives in winter. Few foreigners, and at four in the afternoon the great church inside was all shadow, and 'Silence' written on placards everywhere (and not needed for the whole place was the embodiment of silence). The water was lapping about the steps outside over the lovely pavement, and the great arches glimmered pale gold as if the Past were supreme here with no future, lifting its sad and beautiful crown. On the dry places of the *piazza* the pigeons were strutting as if it were their own.

Dear love,   FREYA

SYBIL, LADY CHOLMONDELEY   Montoria

11 December 1969

Dearest Sybil,

They say that half the inhabitants of Italy are down with influenza and I am one of them and have just cancelled my committee meeting in Florence and have four days to lie in bed and recover. So glad to get your letter meanwhile; I wish you were here, dear Sybil. There is so much *comfort* in the landscape from my windows: it is so wide, and so many people are living in it, their little houses and clumps of trees stretching away to the far edge of the plain, their crooked rows of vines and patches of maize so touching in their poverty and care – and one feels as if all these works and lives were one great river so swift and sure and safe. Meanwhile however we have a new strike every day and I am sending this to be posted in England.

You ask how I am. Chiefly anxious at the moment about my feet: I bought a fine pair of boots for Himalaya and they produced a horrid rub the first day – only just healing. I hope now to have found a very soft sealskin that will fit and am longing to try it out as soon as the rub has healed. Otherwise things are not too bad, and may be wonderfully improved by sitting on a mountain pony. The room, ticket, and all is fixed and I am keeping my fingers permanently crossed.

I read nothing except Byzantine history for my little text for Thames and Hudson: there are five chapters and I have done modern Istanbul, the Prehistoric Turkey, and the Classical: Byzantine, Crusader and Ottoman still to come.

This will be for Xmas and I shall think of you, darling Sybil, wishing that the warm little thoughts could bring you comfort.

Dear love,   FREYA

HON. SIMON LENNOX-BOYD   Montoria

8 January 1970

Dearest Simon,

I am feeling rather depressed as this 'flu-bronchitis isn't leaving me soon enough to get off to Katmandu on the 29th and because of the climate there

I have to postpone till the autumn. So I shall be sitting here quietly through the spring and hope for England in July and August and you and Alice and four children in September. Anyway the month is being kept clear in my little book and you can have all the lower flat for a nursery.

I am also very anxious for news of how the book goes. Sybil Cholmondeley says she has done some good propaganda but that it is a very economical Xmas. I do hope, dear Simon, that we reach 300: I hate to think of you really losing on that splendid venture. Everyone writes warmly about it and I am so happy to think of it in print – you will go down in history as a Patron.

Love,
FREYA

JOHN GREY MURRAY Montoria
28 January 1970

Dearest Jock,

Why should you fear reality? If ever I meant anything it is what I write about death in *this* book, and I can't think of it as anything but union and not separation. This is no morbid feeling but an acceptance that has been with me ever since I faced death consciously in my bed under the trees in Persia in 1931. I think it has been a strength and comfort, and hope it may continue. But as for all these dear *objects*, I should hate to leave them indiscriminately and my little list of nearly 200 people is now very carefully chosen and my poor executor will have to get it packed. It would please me and be a great honour if Albemarle Street would make a little niche somewhere, but it would mean a little space and that may not be available, and I would like the things to be kept at No. 50 and together. You must consult John too – and we will look at it all when you come.

The heart continues to beat too fast and the temperature to slip right down out of the thermometers, and no one really knows the anatomy of this virus. But I got out in my car as far as the bank today – and had a letter from Katmandu suggesting November 8th: hope this may come. The heart is good, if erratic: the doctor looked at the X-ray of the chest and just said 'A very ancient lung'; ungallant no doubt but true. Good enough to sit on a pony anyway and the poor old thing seems to have tossed off the bronchitis.

Longing to see you,

Love,
FREYA

Montoria
                                                        19 February 1970

Darling Dulcie,

Jock has come and gone, a lovely visit but so hard-working that we never had time to look from our books. *Yours* is now out of my hands. I shall see only the page proof and then the finished copy. I think it will look nice with sixty-two pictures and hope you will like it. Then we put together a collection of travel-essays on which I have a few weeks' work, and then looked sadly at the *mountain* of my letters which need two months of a typist to sort them and I have a feeling will only be useful to my biographer. But apart from this we did a good deal of post-mortem, i.e. settling on what to do with what. You will be pleased I think to hear that Jock is quite willing to devote a room at No. 50 Albemarle Street to my parents' portraits, sketches and bronzes, with a little vitrine for an embroidery, and note book, a sort of memorial room. This idea pleases me, and it will be kept for people who want to sit and do research.

This letter is continued after a day's interval entirely taken up with a hell-of-a-row between Bertilla and Beppi who have now *both* given notice and are thinking it over. Angelic Caroly rushes up to the rescue. If it were not for her I would sell out here I think. The thing is that they need someone always pottering about and if I do that I can't do even the small amount of writing that I do do (what a sentence!).

                                                        Love,
                                                        FREYA

Montoria
                                                        9 March 1970

Dearest Dulcie,

I was so glad to get your letter about my television interview. Of course I haven't the vaguest idea of what I said, so it was a relief to hear that all went well. I am amused by one or two friends who have written and told me they liked my technique in pausing before a reply. Of course it wasn't technique at all, but if one is suddenly asked what one thinks of the modern women, or the future life, or such, one does need a second or two to think it out!

I am now trying to finish the Thames and Hudson. It has been much more work than I bargained for and is really a bird's-eye-view of the whole panorama of Turkish history, no joke to squeeze into 28,000 words. The last centuries are unfamiliar to me, and it is a sort of Cyclopean struggle against odds, and the miracle of human character and tenacity winning at last.

I have an invitation to stay at Marmaris in May, and I have decided to go for a fortnight from May 13th and come back by way of my Florence Committee. I asked the doctor if swimming wouldn't be the best thing for the lung and he gave it up and said he isn't used to being asked by Signoras near eighty whether swimming is good for their lungs. I only hope it may be warm enough by May, but Marmaris is fairly far south.

Love,
FREYA

Montoria
12 March 1970

MRS. DEREK COOPER

Dearest Pam,

I was just saying to myself really those Ruthvens are hopeless: not a word from anyone except a little card from Bingo saying they were both happy which cheered and comforted me no end but was after all only a *crumb*. And now here is your letter and good news all round, all as it were *developing* and Allah grant it goes on doing so in the right direction.

It is very vexing to see the French being so much more wide awake about the Arabs than we are. Do you really think Jewry will be divided? Not on your life! Why should a nation suddenly do something it has never done for 3,000 years? Their one strength is that they don't divide. What they will do one fine day is just to go too far.

I would love to have a long talk and hear about it all. And would love Derek too to see the little trees: an olive *grove* now and all growing, and cascades of roses down the hill. It is becoming not a garden, but a 'landscape with flowers'.

Nepal, alas! is off till November, and I hope to get fit for it by then. That lovely journey is a present and I should hate to have to decline into spending it on something useful.

Dear Pam, what long years you let flow by! It is seven years since this house was built and in three years – or rather less indeed – I will be eighty: the world seems tipping over the edge of space away from me, but happily.

Dear love to you and Derek and any of the children,

FREYA

Montoria
                                                                  19 April 1970

Darling Pam,

So good to get a letter and the news from Dunlewy, and especially that
Derek is well. I am glad you are not off to Jordan just yet. I sometimes feel
I ought to have gone, but I think I would have crocked up at once and been
a nuisance – and now I look at all the propaganda which comes pouring in
and feel that I can add nothing useful. Every generation must change the
dream in its own way, and ours was imperial and brotherly too: I never
remember explaining to an Arab that *an elder brother could lead them*
without being listened to by those who were so eager to be led. Perhaps all
leading would have failed, but ours certainly did: yet it was a noble dream
and great men in it. Someone will climb on those unknown stepping stones
– perhaps some unsuspecting leader of another race: the pattern weaves itself
in many colours.

My Highland Fusilier major is helping in Northern Ireland and writing
poems while he does so. He is pessimistic about a speedy end.

Dearest love,

FREYA

Montoria
                                                                  12 June 1970

Darling Dulcie,

I should love to hear Joan Sutherland, and both 7th and 8th are free
evenings. But I feel that two late nights running *before* the Houghton party
is too much, so you must choose whichever you prefer. If we go to *Norma*
I might go for the night of the 8th to the Eustons and on from there (as it
is on the way). I have never heard Joan Sutherland and that would be a
great treat. Sad about the *Merchant*! If we go to *Norma*, could we call on
Michael on the afternoon of the 7th and choose the beautiful Swan Song of
Tweeds? And will he make it by end of August so that I can take it to
Nepal? Such fun to do this with you, makes all the difference. I am taking
all my mss. to sell at Sotheby's so that I hope to see a clear little path for
some time ahead, full of pleasant Events.

I arrived here with no voice, an appalling state for a woman, but it is
coming back.

Dear love,

FREYA

179

Ardchattan Priory,[132]
Connel, Argyll
9 August 1970

Dearest Dulcie,

That rather crowded day was added to by an unexpected meeting in Jermyn Street with Mrs. Pawson from Athens. She saw me from her taxi, had to make it do a huge détour to come down the right way of the street and found me just recovered from having fallen on both knees, tripping in my country shoes on the pavement. The English are so *gently* polite on these occasions and rush to help. Anyway no harm was done and I emerged into the unexpected arms of Pam and squeezed out a last rendezvous, between tea with Diana Cooper and supper with Skimper.

Then lunch with Huxleys, all just like thirty-five years ago except that we have all got old; but Juliette keeps her youth inside her with angelic goodness shining through, typing for Julian while her own sculpture which she loves lies idle and untouched. I had a little sleep and then found Diana lovely as a rose among her pillows, with leg in plaster. She says she cultivates a limp anyway as it is the only way nowadays to cross a street or find a porter. I left to repack at Albemarle Street, meet Pam P., and reach Skimper's for dinner in Bingo's flat looking out on Primrose Hill. Two adorable baby daughters, and a long *listen* to all the reasons for going into television. I see the point and all is well if it is really what he wants to do. That after all is the trouble with most people: they haven't made sure of this important point beforehand. I am so glad to have managed to have this long talk and think they are glad, too.

Very easy journey to Glasgow and the friendly train on, everyone chatty and helpful, up along Loch Lomond and Loch Awe and here into the heart of the Highlands on Loch Etive which is a sea loch opening to Mull. I am staying in a thirteenth-century Cistercian priory with rough little bits of stone wall or arched doorway left in the more modern. The house a labyrinth of ups and downs with little Highland girls scurrying in the background and the odds and ends done by anyone handy. That lovely easy country-house feeling which also seems to me now to belong to my youth: people strolling in and out, doing what they please, in big shoes and shabby old clothes made for lasting. My/your beloved burberry coming into its own and the Kurdish skirt. They took me up the loch in an open motor-boat, about fifteen miles between the dark green slopes that sweep like waves from either shore. I find again all the remembered magic of these Highlands, their

[132] Home of Colonel Robert Campbell-Preston. His wife Angela was a twin sister of Lord Cowdray.

remoteness, and the feeling of life so continuous that its very roots seem visible and the beauty made, like that of Greece, from the mingling of land and sea. A squall came down between shafts of sunlight, and we hurried down avoiding the mid-current which can rise in a matter of minutes. I am so happy to be seeing all this once more, and finding it still here, and rather wonder why one need ever leave the shores one knows. Yet it will be fine to think of Loch Etive in the shadows of Annapurna; and the one helps the other.

Love and thanks,

FREYA

MRS. T. DEUCHAR   Montoria
                                                    12 September 1970

Dearest Dulcie,

There is lots of news here, some very gay and pleasant as my three guests (Simon, Alice, and friend), six children and two nannies left in great spirits. It was a great pleasure to have all those little legs scampering about (with no active part to be taken in their management).

Michael is arriving for five days, and the Gibsons on 15th, Nevills in October. The Lambert party gets more dashing and Texan every day. Evelyn[133] arrived for dinner here with quite a different set of guests from those we thought we had invited, a very nice but so slow-speaking American with two children whom he has taken round the world and now wants to put in an Italian school as they refuse to go to England because of their dog. The world belongs to the young!

I have had a case of conscience to deal with. My friend Peter Green has written and sent me his life of Alexander, all unsuspecting. I had agreed to review it for the *New York Times* (London), but find it monstrously prejudiced and unfair. What is one to do? I have had to write a review (as much softened as I could but it isn't much) and it will probably alienate Peter for ever.

Can you give me the joyous date of your arrival? My Nepal plans hold, D.V. Hope not to be hijacked in the desert of Sind!

Dearest love,

FREYA

[133] sc. Mrs. Lambert.

Montoria
24 September 1970

Dearest Dulcie,

My Guardian Angel has sent me what I hope may prove a godsend, a young secretary-couple who are typing out my letters from 1912 to now. It means reading them all and I have been all this time at it, 1912–27 so far. It is a strange labour, coming upon a stranger who is yet oneself and watching life hammering her out. It takes one's mind off present squalor and lets one see those of the past in a mild perspective. And even so I have nothing to complain of, and friends truly kind. What I should have done without Caroly through this lonely year I don't know. As it is I shall try to remain here when I get settled after Nepal, and pull the garden through the summer. When that ends I rather hope to have sold the house and then think again. I would not mind selling it outright and building *one room*, with small one for maid, and kitchen, close by with the same view. The view is the one thing that has given steadfast joy, ever changing and yet ever the same, and I should be sad to leave it.

It is most beautiful now and the woods just turning, and I hope to be soon able to walk and practise my sealskin boots. Hepatitis and hijacking seem to be the two dangers of my journey. The thought of Amman, to have watched it grow to be obliterated, lies heavy on one's heart.

Very dear love,

FREYA

Montoria
26 September 1970

My dear Lanning,

I couldn't bear to write to you before, because I was so upset about my poor garden: not a thing had been done to it during my two months' absence and it was *desiccated*. I have actually found a man now and have divided the little hill between him and Beppi who is (slightly) subdued. I told him how I had watched him looking quite inertly into space for twenty minutes at a time: 'That is when I am *thinking* about work,' says he without a quaver. There are no major disasters however, and now everything has been reviving with water, and I have sent a much larger order that I ought to Hillier, feeling that I haven't too much time to watch things grow! What I will get ready are the supports for roses, and so grateful if you will look at this inadequate sketch and tell if that is right (allowing for mistakes in perspective).

Gibsons leave today. We had some good days and lovely weather. Missed you – and Biddy.[134] I hope for news, and wish so much that you were here. Any time before 20th October or after Xmas – though I know the prospect is not very hopeful. Your roses are there to speak of you and are now putting out lots of green leaves and some blossom.

Ever so much grateful love, dear Lanning,

FREYA

MRS. DEREK COOPER   Montoria
                                                15 October 1970

Darling Pam,

A dear letter from you to thank for: glad to hear all safe – the bare bones of what one has now to be satisfied being glad for! There is a horrid feeling that the trappings of civilisation are being stripped.

I long for a good talk with you and Derek and to hear what you feel about the future of that poor Fertile Crescent. I have no certain feelings and would scarce know how to act if I could act at all. Have always felt the Arabs will eventually pull through even if everyone agrees their methods are mistaken: it is an age of violence and violence tells, and one of the saddest things is that these are the methods that succeed. The revolt against them slowly rises to a certain pitch and then the Dictator appears. It is a dreary outlook.

I leave on 30th and must be here on December 28th – all between rather vague. I am then going to sit quietly and read through my innumerable letters. The letters to my mother, anxious to please her by finding all the nice things I could about me, make me seem very conceited – but otherwise it is an interesting view of the Hardness of Life.

Bless you and yours, dear Pam, always.

FREYA

MRS. T. DEUCHAR   Katmandu
                                                6 November 1970

Dearest Dulcie,

Mark is due tomorrow and I am hoping for a letter – but write tonight because there may be little time after his arrival: we have only two days for

[134] sc. Hubbard, a close friend of both Lanning Roper and the Gibsons.

183

passports, shopping, arranging the return, and then are off to Pochara on the lake to camp that very night. I can still scarcely believe that this is true and not the dream of a good many years still going on. It is just *romance*, all the things Keats and Coleridge saw in their visions, here part of everyday with the patches of squalor (no sanitation, one imagines, for the human smell floats about everywhere) left out by them but very present. A poor people, but so gay, polite and charming; a climate that tastes like wine straight from the great northern wall – the mountains far more majestic than anyone I know has described them. I feel delirious at the thought of being among them and suddenly, the first time as far as I remember, wished myself younger to climb some lower ridge. The heart gave a bump as a matter of fact even in the aeroplane, and now after a week I thought I could try the 330 steps to a Buddhist stupa and found breath very short. But my walking will be level or downhill and our organisers seem quite happy about it. There is a sort of frontier between the tourist and those who come for the hills. The former, mostly American, getting very numerous. The Japs building a grand hotel with all the view at 13,000 feet, an oxygen mask to descend on anyone's bed who likes to press a button. A nice doctor tells me they are preparing an Everest expedition with parachutes to help them down over the glacier! The British have done two successful climbs on Annapurna, but two men killed on way down. We shall have it all in sight wandering round its contours along the old track to Tibet.

Dearest love, to Tommy too. It is sad to think of Christmas without you.

FREYA

MRS. T. DEUCHAR

At the crossing of the Himalayan range,
between Annapurna and Daulaghiri
17 November 1970

Darling Dulcie,

This letter will reach you after I do, but not many letters are sent from this apex of the world and I think it must please you to know that you are thought of as near Heaven as I am. *Warmly* thought of every night as I wrap myself in your woollies or wander out (boots and your burberry) to find some little privacy among rocks under the moon.

This is now my highest point. The others, Mark and a nice young man who has more or less joined us as our journeys are the same, have made one day farther north where the flat begins and our tumultuous river runs smooth, and the frontier of Tibet is near. But I have come to the end of my *breath* and nearly suffocated the night before last until I thought of opening the tent and the oxygen in that icy air revived me. The same last night: I keep it closed for a few hours for warmth and then open. So I am here in absolute quiet till I meet them again tomorrow. It is a wide gap with two of the great summits, one on either hand, a little to the south. It is the main chain and Everest a little to the east and nothing I can ever tell you will describe the awe and the majesty of this approach, the last terrestrial footsteps to infinity. I sit here and look for hours, the look of Ondine as she ages, do you remember? with all one has to give in one's eyes. The three visible peaks of Annapurna are melting in their snow into the sky, the shoulders of great brown hills support them, and then the rounder curves and spearheads of the pines. We are 9,000 feet up, but they are still 18,000 feet above us. But it is not height, which we somehow share, but the feeling of *amplitude*, the manifold ranges so rising that the whole world seems to be a part of their adoration. I cannot express it, dear Dulcie, but tears are in my eyes.

Luckily I had no idea of how difficult the Himalayas are for riding, because I would not have dared it and would have missed it all. But I have got here and the good Angel will take me back I hope; if not, one must not wait till asked, but *give*, and I will not grudge even the fall down a precipice (of which there is such a variety round about here), if it is required. But these little ponies are like cats, and wherever the paths are steep their immense ups and downs are managed by slabs of stone arranged in stairs; and we, pony and I, climbed 2,000 feet up stairs in one afternoon. We have been nine days, six or seven hours a day with one day's rest. Mark walks and is getting very tough. So am I, though with blue bruises all over my thighs from holding on.

Love to you both,

FREYA

COLIN THUBRON   Katmandu
                                                      29 November 1970
Dear Colin,

Mark is reading your book on Damascus (and liking it) and I am thinking of your novel and hoping to hear its latest news when I get to Montoria about 15th December. The great Himalayan adventure is over and we flew here yesterday from the last view of the hills that we lived with for eighteen days: every day more beautiful, different, and dangerous. So it should be and in fact *is*, life and death so very near together, one doesn't quite know which is which. The beauty and wonder were so great that I didn't much care. We reached the pass where the backbone of the Himalaya runs between two of its highest summits: the watershed runs north of this point, but the river turns smooth and scatters like veins of green marble over the wide flat valley, to its watershed of the plateau in Tibet. The winter trains of mules and horses and donkeys were coming down from these high and bitter places, with tufts of red wool standing high on their foreheads and the donkeys with necklaces of bronze bells, so that a deep and stirring sound came from the valley where they passed. Wonderful world.

Dear Colin, my love and wishes to all.

Love,
FREYA

MRS. T. DEUCHAR

Montoria
8 January 1971

Dearest Dulcie,

We have had a heavy snowfall now melting on all the southern slopes but so beautiful that one could spend all day looking out of the window. I have however been doing a lot of odd things – tidying all the books and deciding that life is too short ahead to accumulate any more. It has made me read a Henry James novel: I don't much care for the sort of world he pictures, but he has a faultless choice of words, individual and accurate, a constant pleasure. Then I read a novel about Roman Britain when the Wall was just being abandoned and felt comforted to think how something came through worse days than ours.

I have written a letter, for *The Times* or some other, about the threat to the Asolo landscape: and otherwise am busy with the immense job of getting my letters typed and keeping my two young Americans at it. I have promised a day in the mountains when 1931 is done (a long way to go before we reach yours!).

Darling Dulcie, do please get me some sort of news. Thank goodness Lucy said you were up and about. *Please* reassure your harrassed

FREYA

MRS. T. DEUCHAR

Montoria
8 February 1971

Darling Dulcie,

On 20th I go for a fortnight to the Colahans to draw (the only way, as it is hopeless at home). On my birthday I went to see duck-shooting for the first time: wonderfully restful sport for all except the ducks, whom it was our job to harry in a flat-bottomed boat (ancestor of gondolas?) from one end to the other of the pale lagoon that fringes the coast. We were entertained in a Hansel and Gretel house of carved wood brought from the Tyrol and wonderfully welcoming among its marshes. The party went off at 5 a.m. to sit in those uncomfortable butts; I however only joined at eight for the inferior task of chivvying those poor birds.

Send news back by Michael, dear Dulcie,

FREYA

HON. MARK LENNOX-BOYD   Montoria
                                      16 March 1971
Dearest Mark,

My news is that an unknown reader[135] has presented me with a camp car, a Volkswagen beautifully furnished, with tent attached, one comfortable and two rather more sketchy beds and all one needs to be independent of hotels. It is to come down from Switzerland in June. You *must* get away to come and try it out. The kind benefactress could not bear to think that my Afghan trip might have been defeated by the absence of a Land Rover.

Love always, dear Mark,

FREYA

LORD DAVID CECIL   Montoria
                                      6 April 1971
My dear David,

What sad news. All these little blossoming hills calling you in vain and the holiday chances of this world dropping away into Time. But I am hoping for a letter to tell me that there might possibly be another clear fortnight this year? If so, please seize it and prevent its flying away! I shall be here, as far as I can see, for all except a few days of early June (in Florence). Do, please, let me know well ahead, because everything seems to fill up more and more. No doubt because I am getting to be slower.

I am also busy with a task put off for years: tidying what letters I have, mostly written to my parents. The extraordinary thing is that my reading

[135] Mme Anita Forrer.

gives m*e no idea* of what the person (myself) is like. I suppose one is too much inside. Anyway, it seems to me to read more like a nineteenth-century novel than real life, the crowding promiscuous events and some sort of a character emerging. Most lives, I suppose, are like that; but it seems to me that my span, 1893 to today, is such a significant one in human history that any record covering an everyday existence must be interesting to a future generation? What I feel most strongly is that we lived in what was, after all, a heroic age: St. Crispin didn't find us in bed; and that is a deep happiness.

Love,

FREYA

MRS. T. DEUCHAR Montoria

2 May 1971

Dearest Dulcie,

The postal strike interlude seems to continue beyond the strike and Simon is the only one among my correspondents who truthfully admits that the habit of writing letters has *gone*. It is rather sad, as the post now brings hardly anything but bills to show that England is still there.

This year I am making no plans beyond one for mid-September to sit somewhere in Turkey and have a teacher to soak myself back into the language which I have nearly forgotten. Otherwise I am here with only a week or so away. No news of who is coming or going, but faithful friends look in on their way – Barclay and Theo came and gave news of you, very welcome; and now Alan[136] and Simon are in Venice, and Gibsons and Nevills here, and life is much less solitary with a coming and going of Stewarts. I lead a double life, half in my old letters and the warm, wonderful letters of friends to me: sad because most are dead, and I am old and grey (though not yet sitting by the fire), but also comforting in a more perennial way. I have a feeling that a book can be made which would not be forgotten, but it is not I who can choose or arrange the ingredients. Meanwhile I have to economise so as to pay for months and months of typing: no chance of England till 1972. And I wonder what will have happened by then?

The little hill is lovely as a dream, full of trouble with Beppi but otherwise vegetating in happy peace. What will happen to it I have no idea as a crisis is sure to develop as soon as I set about a sale; but the Dormobile

---

[136] sc. Lord Boyd.

gives me a wonderful feel of *freedom*. If we had a revolution, I could live in that quite well.

Dear love to you both,

FREYA

COLIN THUBRON Bodrum
14 May 1971

Dear Colin,

I am sorry about the novel. Do look at it again, but after quite a number of months when it can meet you like a stranger! You may find it is not nearly so bad as you think. On the other hand you may find that the novel is not your medium – you have the gift of writing, there is no doubt of that and that is the main thing, but you may be like me, who writes as a painter paints and couldn't do a novel. Is it the difference between Keats and Browning – the feeling oneself or watching other people feeling? I don't mean it so crudely, but I do believe there has to be a standing aside from oneself for a novel and that is never quite so *vibrant* as what comes direct from our own heart? Or am I talking nonsense? But I hate to think of the frustration it must have been and the disappointment. Have you discovered, as I think I have, that it is not only when one is at it that one is getting on with a work. When you sit down again to that blank sheet of paper you will find that quite a lot has been quietly going on inside you. And when you go to your island it might be quite an idea to have no plan to start with, the unconscious will be working away and find one in good time. Why Cyprus, with Lawrence Durrell and all, instead of a less known one – Samothrace and the firewalkers, or Kythera, or Naxos with all the Italian Renaissance behind it (I would like to do that myself if I had world enough and time)?

Best, best wishes dear Colin,

FREYA

MRS. T. DEUCHAR Montoria
13 June 1971

Darling Dulcie,

We came down yesterday with the Dormobile and I tried it very gingerly on the empty road below and it goes *beautifully*, except that the driving seat is too high and will have to be lowered for me. I shall however be very careful and not, or at any rate try not to, drive it alone. In a way it is easier than my little car, as one looks straight down on the road in front. And it is a paradise of gadgets inside: Tommy will love it. I do long for you both to see it.

I shall be very relieved when this tidying of letters is done. Your first ones are just about to be reached, so you see what a long way still to go; and my U.S.A. workers are not very assiduous – not in their own minds but just because they have no great idea of what work is. Perhaps they are right?

Mme Forrer is here for a few days and drove the Dormobile down, and is enraptured by Montoria. It is getting to have a sort of quality of magic, like an Ariosto garden – the roses nearly over and the wild grasses taking their place, and vines twining. I should so like to leave it for Bingo if only I could. It is rather consoling, Dulcie dear, to be near eighty with the port so near in sight.

Must go – do write.

Love,
FREYA

LORD GOWRIE   Montoria
                                              21 June 1971

Dearest Grey,

I am so glad about the poems.[137] How *sensible* of the Oxford Press, and they will be beautifully produced. I do hope they will encourage you to go on: it is hard to be a poet in these days – so few places quiet enough to sit and think in and let the poetry come through.

The news today says we are in the Common Market if we want it. At the end of the war I thought we should have built up a trade and possibly friendship with the Balkans and as far as possible with Russia, that is to say link up with that old trade route as our world empire slipped away; but I think we are not back in the saddle yet to look out on anything but a rather parochial horizon and we will be better as members of a confraternity than all out on our own. France will double-cross and Italy will cheat, but we may pull along as a family, and it would be a historic back-step if Wilson managed to throw his spanner in now. What an interesting time to be in the centre of things, dear Grey. I will love to have you here and have you tell me about it whenever you can come.

Love,
FREYA

[137] Published by Oxford University Press in 1972 under the title *A Postcard from Don Giovanni*.

Dearest Lanning,

I came back to find your letter and the wonderful list and, dear Lanning, I can't do what I ought and tell you not to because it makes me so happy to think of that yellow corner and the Stripes, and I shall think of the good days and of you whenever I pass by and cut little heads off, as I am busily doing now. But it is too much really – and now here is your letter with the notes and I am grateful all over again. I will do it all as the season comes round, and have begun by transplanting *Potentilla vilmoriniana* who looks quite happy in front of the house.

We have nothing but rain and storms so the watering seems to look after itself this year. It is such happiness to feel the little hill coming into its blossom and such fun, dear Lanning, that you should help this pleasure, as I have no garden friends to talk it over with out here. You must come and stay *very often*, it gives such pleasure.

And now the Dormo is here and functioning and with great anxiety of my friends I have driven it halfway down Grappa. 'It likes to *wander*,' a young lad remarked as we veered rather obliquely.

Love and thanks, dear Lanning,

FREYA

Dearest Lanning,

I ought to be doing a lot of things, but I have been out on those little terraces talking to my roses. What with rain, and not even a day's absence of mine to let Beppi omit the watering, quite a number have only just stopped flowering. New Dawn, beloved Fritz, Aloha and Cerise Bouquet went on and on; and now there are clusters of buds: Sarah Van Fleet, Frau Dagmar, Erfurt, Mrs. Oakley Fisher, Lady Waterlow, Mme Pierre Ogier, Iceberg, Pink Perpetue, Parade, and your little White Pet – they are all coming out again, and in fact there are more, such as Mutabile, and Blanche de Coubert. I am so happy to be among them. I don't think I can bear to move Casino, her great blooms are lovely now, shooting into the sky.

There have been a few casualties, due I think to last year's ill treatment and to black spot, which has been a pestilence in this strange, damp, misty summer made for unhealthy insects to flourish. As soon as we sprayed, the rains and dews washed all away. I now spray once a week and hope to have stopped it. The new roses have not felt it, and Munster and Holmhorst (what awful names!) are happily at home and blossoming. What a pleasure it is, dear Lanning, to walk about the little hill. The trees couldn't be happier and Koelrenteria is carrying sprays of blossom as if she were a Paris hat!

Are you coming out soon? I always send you a message when I go along the terraces, and hope to see you soon.

Much love,

FREYA

SIR MOORE CROSTHWAITE   Montoria
19 July 1971

Dearest Moore,

I have just got back from a little jaunt of three days along the coast of Istria with all those woolly islands that look like the backs of poodles, now largely decorated with nudists – and German at that. Here and there is a sort of fortification line of hotels of the pigeonhole kind invented by Mr. Hilton, strangely menacing and grim. But the sea is there, and shining in ribbons among them, and the little towns have Venetian corners with balconies up steps, where people live as far as one can see in their old way and look at us, who represent their income, with distaste, as well they may. We tried Italian, German and English on them, all equally unpopular. I had been once, before the hotels came, as far as Parenzo, and all the talk, even of the children at their games, was then Italian and it seems to me that this has now diminished. The summer gaiety is made by the small yachts etc. that line the quays where one walks up and down in the evening coolness and examines their variety.

Now I have come to the end of my paper without saying what I wanted – that, alas, I shall be away from 5 September to mid-October (in Turkey), but here before. So why not come on your way out?

Love,

FREYA

MRS. T. DEUCHAR   Montoria
27 July 1971

Darling Dulcie,

If only you were here you would be exercising the Dormobile with me. I hope to have a nice young Sicilian teacher who has set up a driving school in Fonte and sat by me yesterday telling me hundreds of things I was doing wrong: it was rather like one's first dancing lesson. I drove sedately out of garage, down hill, round by San Zenone, back by Fonte, off and on to main road and home: it feels rather like steering one of Columbus's caravels. Today we went to Treviso, and I hope soon to be able to make real expeditions and look at lovely little towns. What with this and the letters I am rather ruined, but one does feel that any day in a Dormo might be one's last and economy quite out of place.

I have written my little essay on Asolo for *Country Life*. Am now expecting a house *full*: four Grafton Eustons for ten days and tenants below on the 6th August. Garden shrivelling up in heat.

Dear love to dearest Tommy also,

FREYA

MRS. T. DEUCHAR Montoria
1 August 1971

Dearest Dulcie,

Just in haste to say that your letter has come. I am having trouble over dates and am taking a dislike to package tours however cheap – but with or without package am deciding on reaching London September 7th and going on four days later.

I am a bit harrassed as everyone seems to be collapsing all round – Mme Monnet acute arthritis, Dorothea heart attack, the owner of Rocca Pisana (I wanted to show the Graftons) ill in hospital; and the Dormobile went on strike in Asolo *piazza* Saturday *midnight*. That hard-worked Guardian Angel sent Jim Moon walking across out of nowhere to convey five of us home. We went to a ballet in Queen Cornaro's castle garden: that was lovely, with cypresses in groups like shadowy ghosts of towers, but the ballet *awful*, all very thin and ugly arms and legs and the ballerinas being tossed around like packages. A moral was I believe in the offing (as it is an American production) – but all I could find was an illustration of women being a burden!

I will let you know when I get to Lucy's on the 7th – and send all love meanwhile.

FREYA

Montoria
                                                    18 August 1971

Dearest Jock,

We had a pleasant Dormobilia up M. Grappa with the tenants (two archi-
tects, H. Wood and Anthony Mauduit) and wives and four children, and
we found mists on the top on the far views, but cool airs and flowers, hare-
bells and grass of Parnassus everywhere and autumn gentians beginning, and
sweet-smelling dianthus; and camped below the top and made a fire and
coffee — having brought cold meat also and eaten a precautionary *pasta
asciutta* at the top. I wonder if I shall be able to sleep in *my* bed on the
Dormo? There is always a couple or a pair to whom I elegantly cede it and
have to rough it suspended in the roof. However, we greatly improved on
our first organising with the patient Graftons, and made another fire for
breakfast and cooked eggs. My idea of camping is one with slaves to cook
and wash up, and I think my technique will be lunch and possibly breakfast
in a nearby pub for human intercourse and local colour, and a little concoc-
tion of Emma's, requiring nothing but fingers for its eating, ready in the
fridge.

                                                            Love,
                                                        FREYA

Montoria
                                                    26 August 1971

Dear Jac,

Alas! I shall be in Turkey on September 19th. This is very sad and I hate
to miss you — but there is nothing for it: I go on September 11th, and come
back in October. I go to *study*, as my Turkish is almost forgotten and I have
fixed a room at Halicarnassus and two hours a day from a teacher, and —
combined with bathing — hope to spend four good weeks. You might com-
pare a language to love, it slips away unless it is attended to; and my trouble
now with Eastern friends is that they all speak English and never will give
me a chance. So I am only looking in on them on the Bosphorus and going
by myself and am reading *Julius Caesar* (with a dictionary): he goes very
well into the strong manly language of the Turks.

                                                    Affectionately,
                                                        FREYA

Montoria

3 September 1971

Dearest Tom,

I am just leaving for a month in Turkey and here is your book on the
Crusades in the nick of time: I shall be so happy to have it with me and will
read it under the walls of Bodrum, and am so very glad to think that you have
completed this work so long and carefully prepared. It is good of you to send
it me. Whatever failures they were, the Crusades have thrown Romance
over the whole of the Eastern Mediterranean shores: one is never unaware of
them, the strangely compelling power of a *dream*.

Love and thanks, dear Tom,

FREYA

MRS. ALAN MOOREHEAD   London

1 September 1971

Dearest Lucy,

Here is a sheet of your own paper on which to thank you and Alan for
your dear hospitality – such a help, and making all easy, and I could not
have spent my three days more comfortably settled.

I have been able to settle the plan of the letters with Jock and David Cecil,
and we are going to publish the war years (1939–46 inclusive) as soon as we
conveniently can. Now there is a proposition we unanimously want to make
you: we need a *Selector*, to read all the letters and all the books (to avoid
too much repetition) and arrange them for publication and we all *very much*
hope that you would take on this job. It is quite a big job, but I hope you
might like to do it and Jock will add his persuasions to mine. I should be
most delighted to feel my possible immortality in your hands.

London is so gay and becoming *Continental*. I wish you were both here in
your flat.

Ever so much love and thanks dear Lucy,

FREYA

MRS. T. DEUCHAR   Montoria

2 November 1971

Dearest Dulcie,

Did I tell you that I have been ill (same as two years ago – only worse, as
it got my throat and made me feel strangled, just coming to life and collapsing again like Desdemona)? I haven't yet been out, but am feebly out of bed

---

[138] Tom Boase, an old friend of F.S. and ex-President of Magdalen College, Oxford,
had just published *Kingdoms and Strongholds of the Crusaders*.

and full of frustration at not having yet *seen* the garden. I cheer myself by thinking of the coast of Caria and hoping for a word soon to tell me about our happy dates. Things are like waves: you get over one and the next is coming; but I have, as you know, to look at waves ahead.

I was excited for once by the news of the vote for Europe, so much bigger than expected. The wonderful *reliability* of the British public! They talk nonsense like anyone else, but vote quite differently and sensibly. I think of Musso and the Hoare-Laval pact, or the election that turned Churchill out after the war, and this, which is a mighty step — the flash of our Empire ended and we are back in the pre-Cape-of-Good-Hope world. This heroic age that we have lived through will appear what it is: a glorious diversion, while the steady tramp of our history takes over again. I think this step will be a blessing for the young, who were at a loose end for a target to their thoughts and aims and devotion, and now they have Europe to build. It is very exciting to have lived long enough to see the beginning of this process.

Love,

FREYA

SYBIL, LADY CHOLMONDELEY

Montoria

25 November 1971

Dearest Sybil,

What lovely plans! Of course Hugh and Fortune[139] would be *perfect* and you must talk to them, and here is the letter to Peter Dibonas to send on if you approve. I have sketched out a tour to give him an idea of what we like, but of course can change whenever and as ever we like or adapt according to our feelings and the weather.

If Fortune wishes, one might take the two young ones as well? There would be cabin room, and they would both pay. And so I feel should I, dear Sybil, because I am going to sell a ruby pendant I have only once worn (at the Nevill ball); and it would pay for the trip as well as the Grès suit, and give me much more pleasure than it does now, sitting waiting for burglars in my secret drawer.

I think of this with true joy and feel you will enjoy it so. And all this coast, except possibly Rhodes, is not yet spoilt. One could go by car, but that misses all the coast south of Didyma altogether. But we could see the

---

[139] The Duke and Duchess of Grafton. Peter Dibonas was the captain of the *Bala Rama* on which it was hoped to sail down the Turkish coast the following April.

wonderful group of places, Miletus, Priene, Didyma, by car on our way back to Izmir.

Must send this, with love,

FREYA

MRS. DEREK COOPER Montoria

27 November 1971

Darling Pam,

Splendid news for March. I should be here and it seems very long since I saw you. And I hope for a little pottering up valleys in the Dormo, so don't cut me too short. Emma is back, and I haven't sold, but will do so and build a cottage, one huge room and three tiny bedrooms, on the north side of the hill (out of sight), for summer. I can't afford, but chiefly don't want, to be cluttered with possessions the last years. So am now looking for someone who wants this place in say five years' time, and will give me the run of the garden and no responsibilities, and pay meanwhile for my little retreat and some pottering in the Mediterranean. My little house will have a cold thin wind, but lovely in summer and three of the four great views. And I will be able just to lock and leave it (if one could do this with husband or wife how many marriages would be saved!).

Love, darling Pam, to you both.

FREYA

JOHN GREY MURRAY Montoria

8 December 1971

Dearest Jock,

I got into my little car for the first time today and took it to Fanzolo, the plain all frozen stiff with frost while we have been having our St. Martin's summer up here. Though *weak*, I hope to get off in ten days and over Simplon if feasible. We have new winter tyres studded with nails and if all goes well it will, I hope, establish my way of travel for Old Age: no time-tables, hustle, infection, noise, and the anxieties of luggage. But of course it may all fizzle out.

With any luck I should reach you about January 25th, and look forward to a quiet little birthday at Hampstead if you will have me. How exciting to be thinking of a month in England! But – Houghton, Plymouth, Oxford,

197

three in Sussex, Dulcie, Dorset, Hatfield: all weekends and there are only four in a month! I will tell you the exact date and time when I know a little more after Paris.

It is quite harrowing even to read over my letters of 1965 and the climax of Montoria; and looking back, I do think I made very little fuss over it at the time. I will have had nine years of the little hill this coming spring, and I think I shall have to sell it this year even if I find no buyer to accept the delay of a life-interest in it for me. But I will make my tiny cottage and keep the right to walk about the roses and swim in the pool; and spend the winters, if necessary, in Asolo hotel. This is Prudence with a vengeance, but it will let me get off to Turkey and Persia and Dormobile all over Italy, and even perhaps *write*?

Love,

FREYA

STEWART PEROWNE

Montoria

4 January 1972

Dear Stewart,

Thank you for the telegram, so pleased to get it.[140] 'Dame' is a rather austere title I think? I shall stick to 'Donna' in Italy! The people in Turkey call me 'Freya Khanum', which is the prettiest sound.

The Dormobile took me, the school guide and his fiancée very successfully to Paris and I was allowed to drive over the top of Simplon on a dazzling day. Three nights on the way and three to come back without *looking* at a hotel, and very comfortable and warm. But we had a hideous smash at Beaune (when I was *not* driving) along a road where fifty-two had been killed in the last two months – those dangerous straight flat French roads – by a madman on the wrong side, and poor Dormo has all its front shorn off but luckily no one hurt. They patched us up and I drove it back over Simplon, in an Ancient Mariner landscape of ice below and snow on top and snow falling, as near the mountaineer feeling as I can get at my age. I am rather broke with all this but pleased with the Dormo and trusting the Insurance may pay.

May all go well with you in 1972. I go to England till mid-March but then here except for the last fortnight of April till September.

Love,

FREYA

140 F.S. had been made D.B.E. in the New Year Honours.

MRS. ALAN MOOREHEAD   Montoria
                                                  16 January 1972
Dearest Lucy,

I hope this may catch you before you leave, in the hospitable flat where I hope to follow in little over a week now – though it doesn't yet feel possible. Jock has all my times in his hands and will tell you.

Don't worry over which letters come first till you have that whole vast lot in your mind. I am quite open to persuasion, only find it difficult to believe that my own life is more interesting than the war! The First World War surely was the climax for *my* generation; and the Second – a cry of protest broke from me when I read that 'so many issues have been overtaken by larger events': you might, you know, say the same of Thermopylae? The point of my generation was, I think, that we were pushed by fate into a form of life that was *heroic*, whatever the dimness may be that has come over this word; but this is the one fact, the piece of information, that I would like to leave behind me. I would like still to write some little thing about it, but I think that the letters should make it unobtrusively evident, for it was the *climate* of our time, and anyway it is I think the only 'message' that my generation can still leave behind it? I agree that it is not being consciously sought after today, but I think it will be very soon, and the fact remains, I most deeply believe, that true and conscious heroism is a necessary ingredient for happiness – not that it always provides it, but there can be no perfect content without it. I hope the letters will bring this out, and so will those written to me. Oh dear, poor Lucy, what an awful lot of reading lies before you! And the little typist, extremely slow, is nearly through 1967 here.

Dear love,

                                                         FREYA

MRS. T. DEUCHAR   Montoria
                                                  26 March 1972
Dearest Dulcie,

I came back[141] and found the spring here – tufts of pink or white blossom everywhere, the primroses touching each other in the grass and the roses *pruned* (Heaven be thanked).

I did manage a visit to the Louvre and to the two splendid exhibitions in Paris, but otherwise those five days were solely and delightfully devoted to clothes. Luckily Marie Clive shares this weakness; we saw the Dior show, not as imaginative as Grès except for furs that must be seen to be believed – panther and caracul worked into patterns and flaunting out round little tight

141 Via Paris, after six weeks in England.

skull-caps: the sort of thing angels could wear in winter and cheer up Paradise. But Grès had finer creations and I can't tell you what fun the fittings are now that they all know me, and refuse to do this or that, and study millimetres for the most advantageous line. The suit is admirable, and M. Jean the tailor full of admiration for the tweed; and as for my half-jewel, it couldn't have been better spent – an exquisitely simple dove-colour stuff that needs no ironing, and every detail carefully studied for slimming. As for next year and the other half, we have already discussed it and think of a 'little black', afternoon and evening and easy to pack. I hope I may be spared and you really *must* be there next time and share this little vice – though why a beautiful gown should be less moral than a good picture I don't know. They were all very pleased with me for comparing their clever touches to what I do on a piece of writing – infinite loving care of detail; and it is in fact the same.

All this euphoria came to a sudden end when I got home and Emma, with the cheerful face she keeps for disasters, told me that both Berto and Irma had gone off to Australia. They just got tired of the Belle Arti and its delays over their house and *went*. (It may just be bad luck but everyone fades away round Emma as soon as one leaves her!) The blessed Caroly has procured a simple rather dotty-looking man who, after much hesitation, said he must ask before deciding to come whether he could have two baths a week! I think he must have been badly treated and perhaps with kindness may turn into the treasure one is always looking for.

We are now with no one but Emma till Easter Tuesday, but no guests either – only a very ornamental and I think nice honeymoon couple who are hovering over this house. They seem just the right people – he doing films with Antonioni etc., and she an abstract painter. Keep your fingers crossed, Dulcie dear – I *must* get rid of a few of all the problems or they will crush me *flat*.

I am in the middle of my letters. Badly want you to read them, but you would need months – I don't envy poor Lucy her task of editing. When do you arrive? Please stay a long time.

FREYA

MRS. ALAN MOOREHEAD   Montoria
                                                    31 March 1972
Dearest Lucy,
    I must tell you that I have come round completely to your and Jock's advice that the natural sequence should be kept. The interest or main line

is not in the war, but in the almost Tolstoyan development of a human being in extraordinary family relationships. My mother came under the influence of Mario[142] (not sexual I am still firmly convinced but just as bad as if it had been). It drove my father to his Canadian solitude, and the whole struggle of my youth, after my own shock with my mother in 1917, was to get her to leave the house where her continuing was wrecking any chance of happiness for Vera's marriage; and then to get her to be firm in extracting her own and my father's money from that little cad's grip. This incidentally wrecked my health completely for many years and made a dreary stretch of exasperation in my correspondence; and it seems to me remarkable and a proof of decency on both sides that a warm and living affection was able to build itself up again. My journeys, and even my writing, are really the consequences and secondary to this grinding of my youth.

If one were a great novelist it were a subject made to one's hand; but even so it seems to me to come through in the letters, and all the better perhaps for being so imperfectly disclosed. The balance of the whole depends on shadow as well as light, even though it makes harder reading (especially the financial bits which yet are necessary for understanding). The desperate poverty of those years perhaps produces my pleasure in spending when I can!

What are you thinking about the length of the whole lot? Even if you delete the repetitions, there will be six volumes *at least* and as it is to be what is left of my life in this world, and as much of its value lies in the gradual emergence of a pattern through the apparently meaningless details of everyday, I am very much against a mere 'selection'. It must be 'life and letters' or else nothing.

I have doubts in fact whether it is not too intimate to publish at all? What do you think? If published, the bulk of it, all except repetitions, should be left, just because its interest is a private life's interest and the reticent biographies (of private lives) are not of much value. In a surprising way it seems to me that, as one reads, the life comes to *live* itself with a vitality of its own, built up, like ordinary living life, of all those irrelevant details.

Dear love to you and Alan.

Your loving

FREYA

[142] Mario di Roascio, who had married F.S.'s sister, Vera.

Montoria
                                                        14 April 1972

Dear Isaiah,

Thank you for that little window of the East you sent from Persepolis –
opening on to so vast a landscape. I don't believe the Persian civilisation has
been yet given nearly enough weight by historians – its enormous influence
on and through Byzantium, and its practical transforming of Islam?

What glimpses in *depth* you get with a sudden view! They make life a
thing that goes from point to point instead of a flowing stream; and I am
happy to discover that they go on into old age. I had one such in one of the
small Afghan aeroplanes that fly over the Hindu Kush – and there suddenly
was the Silk Road, an immense flat valley between those high ranges, winding into its misty distance of space and time.

                                                        Affectionately,
                                                        FREYA

Montoria
                                                        26 April 1972

Dearest Jock,

All those *books*; what a *waste* of effort when the plain and easy letters
seem to me to be so much better! I have now got as far as 1956.

What remains very clear is the record of our good and so long friendship,
dear Jock – how you *can* complain of the hitches, so few and far between
and chiefly due to publishers' illusions that they know more about Literature
than their authors! What I see in my writing more and more is the influence
of W.P., so deeply uncompromising and strong, so unhesitating in his
search for the best. I don't believe I could have found whatever I have found
without him. It is sad that my letters to him, that he kept so carefully,
should have been thrown away.

In a fortnight the election will be over on which every most trivial detail
in Italy, at the moment, depends. If it turns out Communist there will be
panic, though it would be a very weak government and the small *bourgeoisie*
here is so strong that I think it would weigh in against anything very extreme. But even as we are the prices are growing extreme and the wages are
making house-running so difficult that the Communists need hardly do anything more. All the big capitalists are no doubt well invested in foreign
currencies by now.

I wonder how much you have read of the Saga? Such a long way, dear

Jock, uphill and down — and a lot of it we have done as much together as a boy and his kite, which he holds by a string uphill and down to prevent its being too wind-tossed.

Love,

FREYA

MRS. DEREK COOPER Montoria

10 May 1972

Dearest Pam,

I always love to get your letters, because they are full of news of the godchildren, and yours has come and comforted me a little for this passing of my doorstep too often repeated. One day quite soon there will be no one at the door — in fact you may very soon see no door at all, as I don't want to quarrel with the Belle Arti, who object to my modest little house-plan. I am thinking of putting up a little group of three of the comfortable tents they now use — for Emma and kitchen, for guests, and for me, with a nice awning where one can sit and work or contemplate. If it can be managed without too many complications, I feel rather happy at the thought of getting rid of my possessions. I think of a beggar I once gave a lira to, in the porch of a mosque in Karaman. He had been sitting there in his rags for a long time, and what I gave him was evidently enough for his day, for he got up and strode away without a word of thanks in the Eastern way, but with such a conquering air of *freedom* that I have never forgotten him and sometimes think of him when my richer friends talk for hours about their stocks and shares.

Love,

FREYA

MRS. T. DEUCHAR Montoria

16 May 1972

Dearest Dulcie,

The house is very empty without you and I feel sad because I was harassed by too many things during your stay. Weather is *awful* and the poor roses can't come out. Diana Cooper is coming to lunch today with her so-nice granddaughter Artemis, and next Thursday I am by way of giving a tea-party to all the people I know in Asolo — while all we have are rows of little impatient buds instead of blossom.

I drove myself into Venice and back again next day to hear K. Clark's excellent lecture on Venice-Florence artistic relationships in the Renaissance. It was excellent, every word *considered* and right, such a restful thing in this world so full of *vague* feeling: and given in the austere naked splendour of S. Giorgio's Renaissance hall. Wish you had been there – I hope to have good news of you, dearest Dulcie.

FREYA

JOHN GREY MURRAY   Montoria

17 May 1972

Dearest Jock,

I have waited to finish the reading so as to see the whole picture, sixty years of life now drawing to its end and forty years of your good companionship. I have been looking at the 'monument' with all the detachment which W.P. taught me so long ago, when Literature was our daily food. And now that I have seen it all together I believe (with some surprise) that it is what we call a classic, that is to say not for today or tomorrow but for as long as the language lasts. This is not vanity, as you must know by now; the same by any other hand would have given me exactly the same feeling (feeling is not the word, conviction). It is not even my doing, as a conscious work of art would be, but is just a human story stamping itself on paper as directly as the stamp of a seal – there seems to be no process in the transfer. Other independent circumstances too have built the plot and brought the drama, and its personal mirror reflects a period of interest never to be surpassed in our world. By pure accident it *composes* extraordinarily well, with Lucy and I already agreed as to a minimum of footnotes; the lacunae make a sort of light and shadow play all through.

There it is, Jock, and I hope it may be a Murray classic in its day.

Dear love,

FREYA

JOHN GREY MURRAY   Montoria

20 May 1972

Dearest Jock,

Your little note comes just after my long letter went, and it upset me so much I was *sick*. Don't let us quarrel again over the same basic point; for better or worse, what I produce has to be mine. Your advice is welcome and precious, but it is only advice and leaves freedom of choice just as Heaven leaves it to mortals, and on this point (of practically total publication) I have quite definitely decided. I have given you the reasons so will not repeat, and all I can do is to offer the whole thing to you without asking any advantage for myself. But there is *no question* of more of a selection than I can agree to, and that is a *minimum*.

No synthesis on your life, dearest Jock, but much love,

FREYA

JOHN GREY MURRAY   Montoria
                                                                15 June 1972
Dearest Jock,

I still hope you may find a way to a full publication, but if you *don't* want to do it (I shouldn't say *want* to do because I know it is *force majeure* – I mean *can't*!), then a total publication must take precedence and it is I suppose possible that the people who buy the mss. might do it? I met a man from Texas two nights ago who said '*Don't* sell to Harvard: we will give you much more.' (I am anyway invited for a week in Texas in November.)

Not a word from David! You all seem to think me immortal physically if not literarily, and also these two years with all my young friends dying makes me more conscious than ever of passing time. Dear Dulcie is ill with a bad sort of leukemia and I don't believe there is much hope. She comes here in July if she can, but if not I will get over to her for a fortnight at the end of this month. Poor old Tommy. When I was so ill in Persia I remembered feeling the fear that it would hurt my father so much if I died before him, and Tommy is eighty-four and Dulcie sixty-two. It is no good thinking that Life is not hard. One longs sometimes to step over.

Such a lot of minor troubles too, the swimming pool not filling because water is *muddy*, and Checchi ill in Asolo so that Emma may have to go. Who wouldn't live in a garret!

Love through it all, dear Jock,

FREYA

MRS. T. DEUCHAR   Montoria
                                                                15 June 1972
Darling Dulcie,

I think of you all the time – three days ago went to Sirmione (to see about a cure), and into that lovely little church, and lit a candle for you with such

205

heartfelt prayer. Keep a good heart, darling Dulcie: you are so very brave, and so is dearest Tommy. I am sure your man is the best you could possibly have. Oh Dulcie, I would so gladly have this instead of you! Never mind; you will pull your dear little life through.

I have just listed 3,000 sheets of my mss. letters (hoping for a sale in U.S.A.): there must about the same number in Jock's, Cockerell's, your, etc., drawers. I hope something may come of it all, and with its ups and downs and good and bad not be unworthy of our day.

Pat Kinross is here, a perfect guest who wants to sit and work.

I am keeping June 26th–July 10th clear either for you here or I will go to England to you. Let me have news *all the time*: and tell me as soon as you can if you can come.

Dear love,

FREYA

COLIN THUBRON   Montoria
                                                       23 June 1972

My dear Colin,

There is something I would like to ask: and that is, whether – when this book is over – you might consider writing a biography, either as an introduction to the *enormous* mass of those letters (thanks so much for sending them by the way), or as a separate biography. This is all in the air because David Cecil is by way of doing it, but I think myself that he will never find 'the time and the place and the girl all together' and, if he doesn't do it, there is no one I should feel so happy with as you. We look out of the same window, dear Colin. It is all in the air, as I say, but I should like to know your feelings.

I am making a 'resistance' to J.M. about these letters. The more biographies or collections I read, the more I feel how the subject is massacred by its producer: it is always someone showing someone else, a three-cornered affair, and the impact of a *tête-à-tête*, with all its twists and inconsistencies, is lost. The trifles and the blank spaces don't matter, they are what you meet constantly in the living people with whom you deal. They give as it were the effect of light and shadow. I have been thinking of all this a long time and the result is that I am refusing to let poor Jock publish a 'selection' in the first place, but hope to succeed in finding someone brave enough to help finance the six volumes or whatever it may be. The selection I feel might come later, and the biography could be an introduction to either or a separate

206

thing on its own. Now you say you want me to write about myself, and here you have a 'mouthful', but it will put you in the picture of what you would be letting yourself in for with the eventual biography or sketch.

No painting and no writing meanwhile, but rather peculiar people coming to see the house; and I feel so glad when they go abortively away. This is quite dotty, as I must sell it. Meanwhile I am here all alone and enjoying it so much, with a visitor now and then moving as if against the living background of these little green hills.

Come when you like, dear Colin.

Affectionately,

FREYA

MRS. E. LAMBERT   Montoria
                                              6 August 1972
My dear Evelyn,

As soon as my telephone came to life again – maddening – I got out of bed (where I still am, but just leaving it) and rang you up only to hear that you had left that morning and were not to be back till September.

Now I am rather desperate being left without counsellor or friend for November. Mr. Turner has writen and I am faced with a twenty-minute speech in California.[143] Have suggested leadership as a subject which seemed suitable for Northwood and all those Distinguished Ladies, and it is a rather neglected quality just now. But am open to any suggestions and would like to know what sort of a speech they like.

Also *clothes*! What do I take? How do we go? And where do we start from? I shall go back to London from Turkey and could meet you there, or in U.S.A. if more convenient. They have kindly written that they pay the fare. Now I hope most ardently that I join up with you somewhere, so can you tell me if it is to be tourist or first class? It makes no odds to me! And where do we meet? I am very excited about it all but do wish you were *here*, dear Evelyn. Hope however that China is ravishing.

I am still in bed with gastro-liver-colitis, and only three kilos off my silhouette to comfort me.

Dear love,

FREYA

[143] F.S. had been invited to receive the Distinguished Women's Award of the North wood Institute (of which Arthur Turner was the President).

Hotel Europa,
Sirmione
3 September 1972

Dearest Dulcie,

What are you doing, I wonder? I wish you were here with me, *enjoying* laziness: a good little hotel kept by a Swiss on the edge of the lake with a garden, inexpensive, clean and not grand, and nice friendly visitors who come here on their savings. When you are allowed a little wandering, you must come: there is nothing to do except to look at the lake horizon, gentle and reposeful and such a rest from Emma; a little cure in the morning which must be good for *everyone*, and I hope is good for me; and then one can read. I have brought good solid books — Toynbee's Hellenistic civilisation, and an excellent little Penguin on Greek science, and Marchand's new Byron etc. It is a treat to read most of the day and all for pleasure. If you were here we would take easy drives along the beautiful shores, and you would not think of those beastly white corpuscles: forget them darling Dulcie, and think only of lovely things, as one did with friends on leave from the Somme battle who knew they might not return. Think of *new* things, darling Dulcie: new poets, new ideas, new horizons – like Socrates learning the flute. Think it all an adventure and forget those beetling crags: your good specialist will steer you round them and in any case you can *defeat* them, merely by disregard.

Love to Tommy and you – I think of you so much.

Your
FREYA

Montoria
18 September 1972

Dear Sir,

In the deep shock we have all felt over Munich,[144] we must not forget the initial injustice of half a century ago. It was unfortunately committed under our responsibility, although later carried on by the United States. A great number of people were deprived of their homeland, and left to fester for two generations in such misery and neglect that their lives have ceased to be of value to themselves. This catastrophe, and the threat of its probable end, were already visible when first I came upon Palestine and its problem in

---

[144] The murder of Israeli athletes by Arab terrorists.

1927: its final consequences were foreseen by most of the best and wisest of our officials out there during those following years.

A vision of the original wrong is essential to help us all even now. Reasonable and fair solutions have been offered (the Security Council of the U.N. for instance), but extraneous interests have always intervened. Britain and the U.S.A. were the two nations on whom the blame must rest, and by whom a disinterested, fair and decisive policy could avert, even now, more harm than has yet occurred.

Yours faithfully,

FREYA STARK

MRS. ALAN MOOREHEAD
Dallas,

Texas

16 November 1972

Dearest Lucy,

All went as well as can be and I feel much lighter without my unspoken speech inside me. It was accompanied by so much eating and drinking and two parties a day that I felt rather like a leaf in a wind; but everyone everywhere has been so kind, welcoming and hospitable and I am getting fonder of the Texans than ever. They were pleased with the speech and are printing it, and the adventure so far has had the unexpected result of making me an honorary citizen of Los Angeles! We went from there to San Francisco as soon as the ceremonies were over – the enchanting U.S.A. town still, as I thought it in 1944 – and this time got away to walk among the great redwood trees; then down to Houston over snowy ranges and the endless flat lands; such *pleasant* people and a dinner party of thirty in a house full of big dogs and French Impressionist pictures. From there I was able to speak to Dr. Ransom in Austin and am seeing him on Monday next about the letters. He told me he had been longing to meet for years, so I have hopes in spite of the bad moment. Anyway I will have done all I can.

Love to Alan, and to you and all of you,

FREYA

MRS. T. DEUCHAR
Dallas

16 November 1972

Darling Dulcie,

It is wonderfully like an oasis to get back here after such wandering – the last three days going to Houston (quite near the Moon station, but we left that alone). It was just like the stories of the American South read in my girlhood – the low rambling house full of fine furniture, dogs, photographs, an almost incomprehensible darkie maid, a party given for me with dancing after dinner – all so friendly and *warm* one can understand that South and North found each other very hard to understand.

Can you believe it? Two couples I know (and three others) are flying out from Italy for a charity ball here and a week on a ranch: of all waste of life and money! I however am very glad to have had an adequate objective and seen these new spaces.

Dear love to both,

FREYA

THE DUKE OF GRAFTON

Montoria
18 December 1972

Dearest Hugh,

It was a perfect weekend you gave me,[145] and wonderful of you to let me stand by in all my ignorance watching those birds. It came to me that they must feel rather like mountain climbers when a lot of stones come slinging down towards them – one flaps up just as blindly since there is nothing else to do.

We have the most lovely weather now, clear sun with a powdering of frost everywhere and every variety and thinness of mist curling in the valleys.

With love and thanks,

FREYA

MRS. T. DEUCHAR

Montoria
27 December 1972

Darling Dulcie,

This beloved house is sold.[146] A little family from Bassano, very simple people and nice, with a growing family, came yesterday morning and bought it. I hope the lira does not crash before they pay the last half at mid July – so that it gives you time to see the flowers.

I am exhausted, only just out of a new sinus and went to a Texan party as well as selling the house yesterday; and working hard at the letters.

All love: may all be better in 1973,

FREYA

145 At Euston Hall, Thetford.
146 For £80,000.

Montoria

13 January 1973

Darling Dulcie,

The climax of my house Odyssey seems approaching: Colin Bathers, for Bingo,[147] Mr. Punchard's colleague (Nixon of all names), for me, are converging towards Signor Imparato the notary and it is just possible that this sale may take a little less time and trouble than Vietnam. It seems almost incredible that a simple give-and-take can be made so complicated. There is a gloomy side: the new Swiss law now charges 8% on anything invested there, and the new Italian law together with Bingo's transfer are going to take at least 10 million lire off my little nest-egg. It makes me feel however that this is no world for living in big houses, and that for once I am being prudent. The work on Caroly's tower has started and I have seen, but not yet fixed, a flat of three good-sized rooms just above the Duse house.[148] It has a tiny terrace, a good view and easy stairs (it is second floor), and I would be able to fit in a bathroom inside my room. When you come you shall sleep in it, Dulcie dear, and I will move up to the tower which is in sight just above.

Dear love – I hope for that letter!

FREYA

Montoria

20 January 1973

Dearest Simon,

So glad to get your letter today (nine days on the way!) and I hope all may go smoothly to the Signature on February 1st. All seemed beautifully fixed until the explanation of the English way with documents frightened the poor little purchaser, and Colin had to struggle with him all over again and settled things perfectly for Bingo (leaving me rather to swim to shore as best I can loaded with Italian liras). If you hear of devaluing you will do me a kindness by telling me anything you can as early as possible. I had hoped to stay here till July, but it may be more prudent to move in April and the tower is full of workmen, and *very* nice. I hope also to have got a three-room flat just above Duse.

One problem is a garage, for both the little Stellina and the Dormo. I

147 Lady Gowrie had made a loan to F.S. towards the cost of Montoria, on the security of the property.
148 In Via Canova in Asolo.

would of course be most grateful to rent a home for them in either of Cipriani garages (and I shall be eating ever so many meals in the hotel as to be almost a semi-inhabitant).

I feel it an awful wrench to leave this lovely hill.

Love to all,

FREYA

HON. CLAUD PHILLIMORE   Montoria
                                                      25 January 1973

Dear Claud,

I feared there might be this news when I got no answers to my cards to Dorothea, and you are so good to write to me as you do.[149] How beautiful it has all been. Bertie, so easy in little things, and adamant in all his true convictions; and Dorothea beside him, trying to steer, but with her eye on the same stars always, and all the many years slipping by. Before the war, Bertie in his punt, picking one up off the dusty, solitary country roads; lunch under the great trees; siesta in the most beautiful *sala* in the world; music – eighteenth-century, and everything worn and loved that one touched or looked at. How many ages of the world's history go to make houses and *lives* like these? How happy we have been to know them. One cannot even feel sorrow when they go, so quiet and so dignified: just an immense gratitude for having known them.

Affectionately,

FREYA

LANNING ROPER   Montoria
                                                      4 February 1973

Dearest Lanning,

I have been waiting to write till Montoria was sold, and this happened two days ago and leaves me very sad. The garden most of all. But they seem to be a pleasant simple sort of family, with three young daughters going to school, and Papa has become a millionaire selling bicycle saddles to U.S.A. and now has got some kidney illness, and the being a millionaire doesn't help all that much. He liked the peace of these views and I hope won't spoil

[149] Dorothea Landsberg had died. Her husband, Bertie, had acquired and renovated the Foscari villa at Malcontenta, just outside Venice.

it and I shall try and instil rudiments of garden into Madame and have already explained that tulip bulbs are too late for planting now. I am writing to Hillier for one little bunch of five pink roses to plant as a parting gift — the very latest he has for autumn blossoming.

What a good ten years it has been, and what a dear friend you have been. *Things we do* go on although we don't, and all is well. I feel I am being prudent and that is an unfamiliar feeling, but perhaps suitable. Do come soon and look at all this. You will like the tower.

FREYA

P.S. U.S.A. was marvellous, such charming hospitable houses. I have been made an Hon. Citizen of Los Angeles — just as if I were a film star!

MRS. T. DEUCHAR   Montoria
                                                15 February 1973
Darling Dulcie,

Marina gave me a little eightieth-birthday lunch[150] and we were a funny old set, Mme Venini and I the only two over eighty, and rather more alive inside than most of the rest. I begged to have it small, and there were only ten of us. We sat in the sun under the beautiful portico and thought of old days.

Otherwise I am busy with the Letters and the house. The work on the new flat starts on Monday and should be ready in April: still rather chaotic but with Cipriani just at hand. I am sad of course, but hope it may be wise.

Dear love,

FREYA

JOHN GREY MURRAY   Montoria
                                                17 February 1973
Dearest Jock,

I have got back from my little jaunt for advice from Geneva, and come home a little more gloomy than I went. I am very tired with the house move and the finance and the Letters all together. How glad I shall be when this corner is turned.

The pleasant people are the old couple — so poor — who live at my corner

---

[150] At Maser.

and come in for odd jobs, and when I asked what they most wanted they said an inside W.C. to save them from cold in winter. So that is now being built and it makes me happy to see how much it means to them. I would like to offer a helping hand to the doctor with his house still to pay for, but he is too proud: such a mistake, when I haven't for years, if ever, been able to afford the luxury of giving presents and it is very enjoyable.

Dulcie's news is not good. What a year! One rather longs to be tucked up in Eternity – though not when the sun shines and this world looks so beautiful in spite of all. And I have had such enchanting birthday letters: about half a dozen from strangers who have read our books – ours before you abandoned me, dear Jock. But never mind. One can love each other in the 'choirs, where the sweet birds sang'.[151] It is the saddest of the Sonnets, but even for Shakespeare it was a passing sadness.

I had two lovely restful days with Anita of the Dormobile. She is getting to be a true friend.

Love, dear Jock,

FREYA

JOHN GREY MURRAY Montoria
18 May 1973

Dearest Jock,

A meagre little stream of letters begins to flow again and I am hoping for one of yours among all these stragglers. Meanwhile I am sitting in my empty room and my *eighty-seven yards of books* all packed about it; and Mama's beautiful painted wardrobe taken to pieces and pushed on. Even without its furniture, this room shows truly gentle and noble proportions; and now the curtains are down, all the views come crowding in – waves of soft greens and mists. I am dead tired and feel too old for these gymnastics, but a flicker of enjoyment over the new apartment is creeping in. Its walls are green and blue and the tiles of its tiny bathroom a beautiful warm yellow-gold. And we have reached the stage of driving the Dormo down to it with pictures.

So sleepy, dear Jock, but pleased to think of you and our many days as I sit by the fire.

Love,
FREYA

[151] From Shakespeare's Sonnet LXXIII: 'Bare ruin'd choirs, where late the sweet birds sang.'

MRS. ALAN MOOREHEAD   Srinagar,
                                                        Kashmir
                                                  20 July 1973

Dearest Lucy,

This is just Paradise: a perfect boat[152] anchored among the waterlilies –
and a tiny yellow buttercup lily in between them – and kingfishers of every
kind looking for their dinners on every pole that sticks into the lake. The
little boats with their awnings slip about on their own shadows making patterns that mesmerise one for hours – and today we have been up into an
opening in the valley to fish (first time in my life and with expert assistance
I took and landed nine trout!). There is a masseur who is gradually restoring
life to my legs, ruined by all those books and ladders in Asolo. I think you
and Alan might try Kashmir.

Love and soon I hope to see you,

                                                        FREYA

SYBIL, LADY CHOLMONDELEY   Asolo
                                                  23 August 1973

Dearest Sybil,

Days have gone by, nearly two weeks, and I am hedged away from my
desk every day by the most boring occupations, trying to make people do the
things that were all to be done before I got home. It is nearly finished now,
and only the most essential element – water – is still difficult in this new life
of mine. It should come in a week or two when an electrician can be got at.
Meanwhile in moments of frustration the picture of your staircase comes
before me and makes me happy as a proof that the best things do sometimes
get done. It is such an achievement, dear Sybil: it must give you happiness
whenever you think of it and it has *made* the west side, which always did
seem a little 'undressed' before. I like to think about it and it comforts me
when my Letters weigh me down; because both are like boats we are
pushing out into the unknown future, in thankfulness to the past which has
given us so much. How few people seem to care about doing that. Anyway,
in my new room, which looks like a very old woman's room with its rather
crowded mementoes, I sit at my desk for several hours a day and read those
old journeys and rather wonder at having got around so much. I wonder if
any of those pictures will come back as vividly to the people who read them
as they do to me?

152 Evelyn Lambert's houseboat.

I have been sent *Curzon in India* by a man called Dilks, and it interests me because it is all the background of what still seems to be 'The Great Game' in Afghanistan, etc. (though with America, not us). It shows Kitchener as one of the most objectionable of men. Did you ever know him?

Much much love, dear Sybil – and thank you for all you are. Such a refreshment.

FREYA

MRS. T. DEUCHAR   Asolo
4 September 1973

Darling Dulcie,

I have been thinking of you so much all day, because we started the life of the tower with lunch up there under the cypress, the guests eight charming young people you would have loved now staying in the Nevill house. Come soon, dear Dulcie, I have great hopes of this *healing* place; and I have thought of something you might really *like* to do – will you give a last look over Volume I of the Letters? I believe you would get absorbed in it and find that life and death and time fall into their places, and that in itself will give you so much better a chance. I know this as much as I know anything: not fighting, but accepting it and in the end of ends not minding – 'triumphing over Death, and Chance, and thee, O Time'. Oh, darling Dulcie, we are on a razor's edge always: it *can't* matter, and we will win through anyway.

Meanwhile I couldn't be more harassed as there is a block over the boiler and no hot water since I came to my flat; a complete want of response of all water in the tower; and dear Caroly just postponing all payments of workmen etc. till I could cry with fatigue.

The Sacheverell Sitwells are dining here this week; and one of the charming young men is Nutting's son.[153] A pleasant little stream of quiet people is discovering Asolo and the excellent hotel, and I find it splendid to mix when I feel strong and keep to my terrace (in lovely cool Pakistani trousers) when tired.

I am reading my own bookshelves: the Italian Renaissance just now and life must have been even more difficult then than now.

Dearest love,

FREYA

[153] John, elder son of Anthony Nutting.

Asolo
6 October 1973

Dearest John,

I am so glad I protested, because I do enjoy your poetry.[154] You are not what one might call a prolific writer, but the little things come out *quite perfect*, with no overstatement anywhere but the heart of the matter in them. *Please* let me have the next: or perhaps you might bring it? My tower is now furnished, and you look up over little hills and the mountain behind them, or south over old roofs to the plain; and I think the heating (with a *caminetto* and wonderfully energetic little electric things) is going to work. My lower apartment also has a very endearing view, embraced in a gentle valley.

I am reading old letters, which are to be published next year, and there is your first coming out to the old garden in Asolo, and lots of nice things said about you – ever so long ago.

Love,

FREYA

ALAIN NAUDÉ Asolo
11 October 1973

My dear Alain,

I have delayed in thanking you for your letter, in spite of your kind suggestion that I might write in English, but you asked me such a difficult question – to remember the books that most influenced my childhood and youth. This led me wandering down many forgotten paths to the time when (aged six) someone sent me the beautiful picture book with the story of Jeanne d'Arc. Then (aged seven or eight) were Kipling's *Jungle Books*, and a little series of penny booklets with the Seven Champions of Christendom, and King Arthur. All these romantic things are what I remember, together with Kings and Heroes, the Legends of Greece. A very little later was a book that I still possess – two stories called 'The Little Master' and 'Ondine', by La Motte Fouqué: the first was inspired by Dürer's etching of the Knight riding with Death and Satan defeated and this has remained with me, deeply graven, through the years. Malory and Froissart came next and the story of the *Iliad* and *Odyssey* for children: and then (aged fourteen or fifteen) more adult reading – a long history of Greece (G. Grote) and the great story

[154] F.S. had protested that John Sparrow had not sent her a poem he had written for Sir Maurice Bowra.

of Socrates which has been with me ever since. Romances were scattered – Walter Scott, the Brontës, Thackeray, Jane Austen, Dumas, all very classical; poetry – Walter Scott, the Border ballads, and an anthology are what I remember. And then (about seventeen to nineteen) I had a great time with Tolstoy, Shakespeare, and Carlyle (*The French Revolution, On Heroes* and *Oliver Cromwell's Letters and Speeches*). After that I went to the university and began to follow English history and literature in an orderly way. In looking back on this rather severe past I feel surprise as well as gratitude to my parents – for they were neither of them literary and their tastes went to painting and music: they allowed no magazines about the house, but a good library in which we browsed freely.

Have you passed your exams and are you free to live in U.S.A.? But will you *want* to?

Ever your affectionate

FREYA

MRS. DAVID PAWSON   Asolo
                                                          13 October 1973

Dearest Pam,

I had the inside of a week in England and, with my sick friend to see, had no other time; but hope for a good spell next year and *certainly* to reach and see your house. At the moment I am rather sorry for myself with sciatica and have been two weeks in a herbal nursing place where they keep one under poultices (doctors just having given all up: 'Nothing to be done after eighty'). But the herbalists do seem to be making it better.

It feels sadly familiar to be on the edge of war again[155] and I don't put it past Nixon to help destroy those so-called underdeveloped people for Oil – England will hold out against that surely, and it is worth while to show that one can die. In the last war I once heard General Jumbo Wilson explain (to someone who was scoffing) that it took us twenty-six men's work to produce one soldier at the front to fight, and these twenty-six were practically all 'Gyppies'. We owe them a debt.

Love to you both,

FREYA

155 The Arab-Israeli war.

Asolo

                                                          5 November 1973

Dearest Jock,

I have just finished the short preface to Volume II which that angel Lucy
is now tackling, and send it you, not for any reason except that it doesn't
seem right that my labours should go unnoticed even if you have abandoned
the poor exhausted laboratory. I am also sending you a copy of my invest-
ments (what a strange word, as if one were a cocoon inside one's finances) as
soon as I can write them out.

But meanwhile I must tell you of our expedition, with a very cold night
in Dormobile, up beyond that lake where you and I went years ago near
Cortina.

We woke with Pelmo and Sorapis and Antelao all powdered with snow
round us and the sun creeping down their precipices to our thin grasses *stiff*
with frost; and then went on to a lake off the Brunico road (Blaies), a cold
emerald under the huge cliffs, and hotel all shut. The others walked off
round the lake and I sat in the sun and looked across the ice-flecks of the
water at three great towers and dome of rock, their summits only alight and
their vertical waterfalls all solid ice. Only on tiny ledges here and there were
temporary things like pines or larches and bushes. All else was stone, and
nothing but Time could touch it: and I thought about Time till it only
seemed alive, progressing so majestic through the shapes of all things. And
I thought of the madness of those poor Letters of mine; yet here and there a
word or two has conquered and, whatever happens to them, they have made
their way in hearts of men. One fights on for that just as a regiment that is
being decimated. And as I thought this, a shaft of the downward-sloping
sun came across the mountain shoulder and hit the middle tower before it
went on its hidden way.

We have come back to mist and cold and I am glad to be in my cosy flat
with the hotel next door, and have bought a small electric stove in case of
petrol shortage.

Why should one envy the young? You say one should try not to – but I
can't imagine doing so. It would be so *awful* to go back when one is so much
nearer to the goal. I think you have got it wrong: one is old in this world,
but young oneself for the next step. I feel about it as about the first ball, or
the first meet of hounds, anxious as to whether one will get it right, and
timid and inexperienced – all the feelings of youth; and for that one needs
the comfort and companionship of one's own generation.

All love,

                                                          FREYA

Asolo

20 November 1973

Dearest Pam,

I wonder if this will follow you to Jerusalem? I do understand Derek longing to be back and it will be wonderful hearing all about it from you when you return. The whole of this set-up seems more like grand opera than real life: one can hear Verdi dealing with its choruses – the United Nations, or at any rate the Common Market, melting away in Oil.

I keep my fingers tightly crossed hoping that this time the Arabs just stick together till the deal is signed. After all it is not for nothing that they were the one great commercial empire between Rome and Britain: they do know all about bargaining. I wish Nuri[156] were alive, and Kinahan and Clayton[157] – so many who laid the foundations and saw no building. How I would love to make one little easy journey in a friendly Arab world again and see all the old friends that are left in Syria and Iraq. And we cannot help feeling that our 6,000 (was it?) little brothers have had some hand in this renaissance.[158]

You would be an angel to write and tell me what you find when you get out. A new Orient?

I am still handicapped but not so agonising as at first, and can manage an hour's walk, and of course the Dormobile on Sundays. I have had Colin Thubron in the tower and it seems beautifully warm with two electric stoves. I hope it may fill itself with godchildren to cheer these last years.

This may reach you after Xmas. It takes all love to both.

FREYA

Asolo

20 November 1973

Dearest Grey,

I hear you are launching an appeal for a poetry centre. I am so glad to hear of this, and I want to give you the present of an idea; it will probably not be of any use, but anyway ideas are fun.

The absence of patrons, and of the means of stimulating them into existence, seems to me to be one of our main deficiencies: it is just the good book

---

[156] Nuri as-Said Pasha, the 'Grand Old Man' of Iraq, murdered in 1958.

[157] Brigadier Sir Iltyd Clayton had worked with F.S. in wartime Cairo, where he was with Military Intelligence.

[158] The Arab Brotherhood of Freedom, organised against the fifth column.

that will not pay on publication that suffers from the want of them. Do you think it would be possible to elect a little band of patrons (discriminatingly chosen of course) whose privilege it would be to present and subsidise a poet? To make a sort of club, in fact, where good poetry could be found, and each patron would be able to select one member to come in under his patronage?

I wonder anyway what sort of circumstances do make good poetry? Do you need leisure? Or safety? Or danger? Is it a step-over, however disguised, into the time- and space-free world that is always parallel with ours?

Love and all good in 1974,

FREYA

ALAIN NAUDÉ Asolo
27 November 1973

Cher Alain,

I was happy to get your letter, and so deeply touched about what you wrote about the young people today. You found the words to say what I feel most constantly, watching them go so unhelped and unguided into so hard a world. Now, with the shadow of war again brushing like a vast black wing, it becomes almost unbearable. How nice you are to write to me. I feel we look out from the same little balcony over this vast and surely unnecessarily agitated scene: a world so beautiful, and made for happiness. Foolish men, looking always inside and not out where goodness and love are left to walk alone. One is divine, you say: I believe this, and we were made in the divine image – and how we spoil it!

I am not sorry to think of a world with fewer motor cars: there is already even in Asolo a certain silence in its streets and the sound of people's *footsteps* between the high old houses. I am afraid of America – afraid that she might try to grab (through Israel), and to trust to money to negotiate, not able to understand the Arab world. By the time this reaches you we shall know, and I hope you will write to say that soon you may come over.

You may feel, as I do, the old safety feeling that the medieval cities held within their walls, so different from my beautiful free Montoria: I think my Angel must have made me sell it this year, for it would have given me a very difficult winter.

Write again, and come back soon dear Alain to this battered old Europe.

With all affection,

FREYA

Asolo

4 December 1973

Darling Dulcie,

You seemed to be with me last night, I missed you so much, seeing the most impressive rendering of *Don Carlos* at the Fenice. It was magnificent scenery with the tremendous mortal atmosphere of the Spanish court about it, and all the voices were beautiful: the most touching to me was Philip the King in his long soliloquy – I found myself *weeping*!

Venice was sparkling beautiful, with a *bora* coming down on us from the snowless mountains: all the snow in *south* Italy. All here are rather cold except me in this beautifully warm flat where we have gasoline for a month. The absence of accidents on the roads is being noted for all it's worth and the first carless Sunday[159] went by quite well; but there is absence of sugar and macaroni – and the poor doctor could get only two gallons of petrol by running around everywhere. What a strange world!

I plan to do all by train and leave for Porto Ercole on 22nd – home on January 9th after my committee. Will miss you both so much down there.

Dearest love and for Xmas if it comes at the right time.

FREYA

Asolo

15 December 1973

Dearest Dulcie,

I am keeping my fingers crossed for what happens at Geneva – honestly not so much for all our prosperity and comfort with oil as for a decent Arab frontier and their own home in Palestine and – at last after fifty years – the hope that they may realise what they can do being united. Nuri gave his life for that idea (unity – not necessarily turning off the oil) during all the thirty years I knew him and so did many British advisers. Apart from everything else, it cheers me a lot to think that Faisal is turning on the whole strength of his modern world so as to pray once again in the Mosque of Omar. The Arab chiefs have bargained for centuries along the Silk Road of Asia and I hope will bring this off. And perhaps we may never again be quite so mechanical as we are at present or at least remember to be aware that there are other forces too? It does seem strangely irresponsible to build the whole modern apparatus on something that has only twenty years at best to run? The Tower of Babel seems the only comparable venture!

[159] The Italian Government, to conserve fuel, had imposed a ban on Sunday driving for private cars.

All the same I am regretting the Pullmino and my Sunday driving. I am leaving it uninsured for six months in its garage as I shall now be away till mid-January and later on in England I hope. It is ages since I have had my two months in England and there may not be so many more of these visits.

How lovely to think of my evening bag! One of the melancholy bits of Age is that one comes to have fewer wants and the art of spending gets reduced.

Darling Dulcie, all love: will write from Porto Ercole.

FREYA

MR. AND MRS. DEREK COOPER Asolo
10 January 1974

Dearest Derek and Pam,

I am longing for a good long gossipy letter about what is happening behind the very vague Italian newspaper façade – wondering how many of our little brothers were in the Egyptian army; and who will stand with whom. One is always terrified of a split and it will be a miracle if that Arab ship sails through with every oar in a different direction. The person I would like to meet is Yamani;[160] I read his interview in U.S.A. and thought it was the best of any statesman I had ever come across.

I was so worked up over the U.S. threat of force. I have had a hunch from the very beginning that America might try her big stick – too awful and strange if the shipwreck of our world were to be done by Nixon! Bad enough to have him as the only human signature on the moon.

I have been away with Mooreheads for Xmas, then Mortola, then Florence, then home to a much more austere state of things – thankful not to be in Montoria without oil, cook, or anyone near and no doubt lots of brigandage preparing.

Dearest love,

FREYA

THE EDITOR, 'NEW YORK TIMES' Asolo
10 January 1974

Dear Sir,

In 1943 during the war I was sent to the U.S.A. by our Ministry of Information on an unofficial mission to describe the Arab point of view on the Zionist-Israeli situation.

[160] Sheikh Yamani of Saudi Arabia.

I was very kindly received and found a great deal of sympathy and comprehension, but I still felt the deepest concern over an almost total ignorance among many people of influence and position. Their heavy responsibility in what even at that time was clearly a threat to world peace was a matter of anxiety even thirty years ago.

The threats published by Mr. Schlesinger and Vice-President Ford can only do harm. They have been answered by a threat to destroy the Saudi oil-wells altogether if a military action is started. It would be the most fatal error if such retaliation were not to be believed in. Months ago, during the air-lift to Israel, the possibility of such a development haunted me, and I mentioned it in a letter to a friend who scorned such an idea in a modern world; but it is almost impossible for a civilisation based on money to conceive of what is possible to people who are prepared to do without it, and everyone who has known the Arab intimately will agree on the madness of threatening what cannot but spell general disaster.

Yours faithfully,

FREYA STARK

MRS. T. DEUCHAR

Asolo

13 January 1974

Dearest Dulcie,

I came back from my tour two days ago, all very happy except for the sciatica which has made the doctor keep me more or less in bed and gives me so much pain that I can't sleep. You know how strong it must be to do that! The week at Orbetello was very pleasant and peaceful and the long journey to Mortola quite uncrowded so soon after Xmas: all the little Riviera towns dim round their darkened streets, but France blazing with lights. Cici very glad in a casual way to see me and I am glad I pulled up my old bones to go: I feel sure she does not realise that four years is a long time to leave one's only relative alone and the poor child has a lot of troubles – factory gone bust, and no share in what was left of it; Dronero house should be sold and isn't; peasants at L'Arma hopeless; and L'Arma itself, which should be wonderfully valuable now, is crippled by a neighbour who has the right of the only access and will not share it. The only bright spots are that these hardships are making her work at her painting and coming to say something with it, and the boy, Paolo, seems to be very nice and has got his degree and is now working in Turin. I sent £80 and I think he may come here to see me; and I shall then try to persuade him to take his mother's troubles on his young shoulders, poor lad (I had to do my parents' long before I was eighteen – and Paolo is now twenty-four). But I am so glad to have made this effort and seen Cici, who is a dear – with just the art of living left out; and who can wonder when one thinks of that childhood? The miracle was that my sister and I remained tolerably average!

The two writers near Lucca[161] were very agreeable and we made a charming expedition to Barga, a little town in a most beautiful valley where an unknown fan of mine lives among his Oriental books, with a fresh young wife I thought his daughter and three little girls. The whole place with the valley and its wintry brown trees was wonderfully remote in feeling, and we drove by stupendous views to the sudden appearance of a modern hotel with swimming pool and horses and skis and all the hills of the coast before it. I thought what a nice place it would be for you with the high air and superb view.

From there I went to my Florence committee and so home, and feel as if I would stay for good in this little refuge – and at any rate till the crisis is over that makes one sick with apprehension. I felt in November that U.S.A. would make a military grab at the oil wells, and everyone said 'Impossible', and now look at Schlesinger (surely a Jewish name?) and his threats. I also feel that this crisis will eventually make us choose between U.S.A. and Russia and that it will eventually be the latter: the American is a *rotten* civilisation, sentimental and bullying, with nice names given to nasty feelings. A wonderfully temperate good book on the Israel question has been sent to me – *The Broken Sword of Justice* by Margaret Arakia. I think Tommy might like it; do get it.

I am going to give myself a present I have been longing for for years – a good radio that will let me hear good music in my solitary evenings. I have wanted it so badly in Montoria, and now here it will make so great a difference – and after all I may easily be dead in three years' time. So I shall get that and my Paris dress and just economise on everything else (if I can!).

My letters are not 'corresponding' but more like tennis balls sent into an empty court, but perhaps this may conjure one up tomorrow.

All love darling Dulcie, as you know.

FREYA

SYBIL, LADY CHOLMONDELEY   Asolo
                                                  20 January 1974
Dearest Sybil,

Of course your letter came three days after mine had gone, but not yet the one before. Meanwhile I hate the thought of Houghton with no oil and hope

---

[161] sc. John Fleming and Hugh Honour.

this is not so in London? Montoria this winter would have been very difficult and couldn't have been left because of burglars; but this little nest is
wonderfully comfortable and a wood fire (I got wood at once and it is now
three times the price) would heat it all between its old thick walls.

My Arab jewels – I had no idea they were going to advertise them. They
are what I brought from South Arabia and not a girl among my young
friends would wear them at all easily, and I also have nowhere safe to keep
them; so I handed them to a Lebanese woman here who sells Oriental
jewellery. They are huge breastplates of silver beads, and bracelets like
handcuffs, and I have kept one or two of the more 'portable' ones; it is
rather a relief to whittle things down to what one really cares about isn't it?
Dear Sybil, I wish you hadn't had to whittle so much.

I think of you so often, with great love always.

FREYA

EDWIN KER[162]   Asolo
                                                          1 February 1974
Dear Edwin,

I am so pleased to get your letter, and here is the new address. I have an
old tower on the Wall with bedroom (and shower) and a lovely writing
room with view for guests, if you happen to come this way. So thankful I
sold Montoria, beloved but unmanageable, just in time, and now I am very
cosily settled at one minute from the hotel where I go or send for my food.

I discover that I am two years younger than you, and here we are hobbling
about and think of each other I hope as two sprightly young creatures leaping about Macugnaga glaciers.[163] I am trying to write about these things –
old age I mean – as it seems to me that too little has been thought about it
both good and bad: the old mountain habit I suppose of liking to know
where one's path is leading.

We are still mostly warm here but with all living prices very threatening.
As for our poor country, it is agony to see it rushing downhill. What is the
cause of it all, with both sides filled with good people? But am pleased of
course to hope the Arabs may get a fair deal at last, even if we suffer.

Thank you for writing, and all best wishes,

FREYA

162 A nephew of W. P. Ker.
163 Where they had both been in July 1929.

226

Asolo
1 February 1974

Dearest Dulcie,

Thank you for the dear telegram, punctual yesterday. You would have enjoyed my little party – Caroly and the whole Berardocco family, a huge cake with eight candles for tens, and one in middle for the first step on the slippery ninety slope; and a little present for everyone on his or her plate. Dear Caroly, thinking of my solitude, wanted to come with a television set but I have explained that, while still able to write, I must have time to think and television is an Enemy. As it is, I tried to circumvent the doctor by suggesting a stick, a useful present that wouldn't ruin him – and this he brought, but also a radio, and was so happy to have spent so much more than he should on his friend. I was so touched, because he has so many debts and four sisters as well as his own family to look after, and arthritis as bad as mine and forty years more of life than me to carry it along. I love, as you know, to have the things as presents that are always about me, so I cherish the radio and am enjoying two concerts a day – lovely classical music morning and evening. One has to tame these little mechanical monsters as if they were wild animals and learn their ways and hours.

You would laugh: I have just discovered that I can, more or less, read Lucretius and have this wonderful excitement in the watches of the night. He is a most thrilling person to meet and sees and makes one see the world's wonder. I have also done another short essay on death (part of Old Age) and will send it if you like: I don't think sadly of it and so it should not depress. Two more are in my mind – they come flitting around me like kind and healing sprites.

All love to you and Tommy. Is he well? I long to see you both.

FREYA

Asolo
6 February 1974

My darling Dulcie,

I have taken two little walks these two days, one to the tower, full of peace and restfulness, and the other down the road to lunch with four elderly ladies and two husbands, not very exciting. I am so happy sitting here by myself while the essays are slowly taking shape: one now on 'The Written Word' which lets me say a lot of things I have long been thinking. So much pleasure this little wireless is giving me too: they give lovely Bach to go to sleep on. It is curious how, in my ignorance, I feel I know what a very

227

few musicians – only Beethoven, Bach, Mozart and sometimes Schubert I think – are *saying*: a feeling of straight meaning clearly spoken as in good literature. Most music leaves me dissatisfied (not opera, which is people).

All love,

FREYA

MRS. DEREK COOPER   Asolo

9 February 1974

Darling Pam,

I am typing because of the sciatica which prefers this to writing. So glad of your letter – that little procession through the streets of Jerusalem made me weep. And now it is heartbreak over England. I can't help thinking that the miners insisting on a strike just for the hell of it is going to do them harm. I was rather on their side to tell the truth (because no one can come out of a coal mine and not have at least an hour to get *clean*). But this last produces a very British reaction, and I imagine will do so with a lot of people.

What has happened I suppose is that we had a fairly large educated class educated and geared to run our empire (one fifth of the world) and that may now be redundant, anyway till it finds something else to do. A quiet revolution in an English way may not be the worst that could happen; if I had a vote I am not sure that I would not vote Labour as the best for the Conservatives in the end. But I don't believe the country will be bludgeoned into a revolution, and anyway another three weeks will show.

I am writing an *old* version of *Perseus*,[164] all on age and death but not I think depressing. Anyway sciatica is one of those things one *knows* one won't take with one, and that is something.

Love to you both,

FREYA

EDWIN KER   The Old Parsonage,[165]

Ashmore,
Dorset
28 May 1974

My dear Edwin,

I have been so harassed by changing plans that I can't remember if I thanked you for your letter of 1 May, which I enjoyed for all its opening

164 *A Peak in Darien.*
165 F.S. was staying with David and Pamela Pawson.

avenues. Now as to my plans – I have an excellent surgeon, have decided on the operation,[166] and got a bed fixed at Sister Agnes Hospital (not *quite* as expensive as the others) for July 29th: nothing earlier to be found, and the National Health *minimum* wait is two years! But the doctor gives me some remarkable pills for the pain, and I hope to spend these months seeing my friends, though not any moorlands till I can walk again – perhaps next year, who knows.

The Letters are coming out (Vol. I) end of September and perhaps the essays can be done in hospital. My two assumptions lead me down a high-road full of surprises (to me anyway). I can't *see* people there, but can *meet* them free of all barriers and Socrates should be accessible as any next-door neighbour. What continues to live in us is turning out to be some element indivisible from divinity itself, i.e. a part of the divine (as indeed the Greek fathers taught long ago): and even the date of this accession of consciousness in this world can be guessed at, sometime between the physically mortal world of rocks and trees with anyway the early animals – and the first pre-Greek philosophers: some time in this period a question was asked and an answer given. In this timeless peace to which we acquired access my two assumptions eliminate, as far as I can see, *all* our mortal virtues except love and delight which keep their timeless divinity across the border. And all this has led me to the most difficult question of all: as to how/if this timeless immersion can be harmonised with the retention of some sort of personality? This major question will I hope keep me happy and anyway occupied through the rather drastic time that awaits me?

But how astonishing it is how many people step over their border without taking any real interest in what they are stepping into?

I must end this, with all best wishes,

FREYA

EDWIN KER   King Edward VII Hospital,
London W.1
19 August 1974

My dear Edwin,

I must give you my news, which is good so far: I walk up and down the long corridor on two sticks only, now, and can bath myself and feel very much happier than I did before. Tumblerfuls of my good red blood seem to have lost themselves in pockets and have to be thrown away, so that I think

---

[166] For a new hip.

vitality is 'low'; but life comes oozing back and even at eighty that is a pleasant sensation. I had Wellington's Life to read and that was a good choice and very healthy to have the Peninsular War as a standard by which to measure one's trials. What a story! And what makes one man able to play to such a tune that the roughest, 'the scum of the earth', can listen? I am not yet fit to do anything but just exist: shall go for a week's convalescence at Osborne and then (about September 7th) to Jock Murray and on to Italy a week later.

Let me hear news in Asolo,

FREYA

MRS. T. DEUCHAR   Osborne House,
                                                          Isle of Wight
                                                      6 September 1974

Dearest Dulcie,

I found myself very tired when I got here in spite of the kind motor drive (quite beautiful country). So they kept me in bed for a day and today I have been beginning treatment, learning to step over things and walk, and all seems hopeful. I took a slow half hour walking on the lovely turf, looking down glades of *mown* grass to the sea between trees. Inside it is quite unique, a bit of the Victorian Age and not selected for its special beauty but for what its two inhabitants really loved – their children, dogs, animals, classic figures, huge pictures or statuettes in bronze, so that with its curtains and cornices it is a whole history that appears. And the feeling of a past age is naturally alive too – all of us old crocks who have done something or other in our day and look back to some far corner of the past world with nostalgia.

All love,

FREYA

MRS. T. DEUCHAR   Paris
                                                        1 October 1974

Dearest Dulcie,

I think this will get to you as soon as if my young escort had posted it, but the truth is that in all the bustle it was forgotten. It was a charming, animated journey: in perfect comfort reclining in armchair and on footstool, with the gentle Kentish hills rolling away to Dover and then the Hovercraft, more like a whale than anything since Jonah, waddling up its beach towards us on its fat rubber flappers. The sun shone, we waddled out and crossed, splashing and spouting foam, till we landed in a delightful quiet way on a sandy beach by Calais, and motored off with thoughts of a little country inn for lunch. We passed along the coast I remember from nine years old, and stopped at Montreuil-sur-Mer where Harry van der Weyden, a very good artist, used to live and my father brought us a toboggan suitable for racing down sand-dunes. All this simplicity sems to have gone and the charming little town has got a very chi-chi castle hotel, but excellent food — and my dear young couple got me safe to the Monnets, and settled to sleep in the middle of Boulevard St. Germain with perfect privacy and success, and a morning wash in the pub of Les Deux Magots. I gave them lunch at the Brasserie Lipp and got a whiff of the Left Bank, half genuine gaiety and half tourist, and then went for the fitting. M. Jean has to take in all the seams and implores me not to get fat again, and the suit looks *beautiful*, a ravishing simplicity with a little beading on its jacket so aristocratic that it simply can't be seen! With any luck, and the efforts of all the Grès who love me much more than their millionaires, I should take it with me by air on Saturday, and am so glad in spite of the extravagance which includes this Paris pause (though keeping rigorously away from shops).

I do so long to be at home now and among all my own things, although it doesn't look like a very easy winter in Italy. I will write and let you know all the news, darling Dulcie, and am so happy to think of the last weekend and that my little essays may help in the way they are being written to do — my whole heart is in them.

All love to you both, bless you.

FREYA

MRS. T. DEUCHAR   Asolo
                                                          25 October 1974
Dearest Dulcie,

I am feeling better, in danger of getting fat again, and very glad to be at home. I have another essay done, on 'Tradition', and hope now to get on though it takes me almost a month to deal with each essay, thinking it over and over. How strange it is that people (publishers included) never seem to realise that a certain time has to go to the *thinking*. I don't believe I shall write any more when this little book is done, but sit on my terrace and *draw* if any time is left.

We are lunching today with a man who is rightful King of Hanover –
didn't know this existed!

Dearest love,

FREYA

MRS. ALAN MOOREHEAD   Asolo

22 November 1974

Dearest Lucy,

I do rejoice when I see your familiar envelope: one feels rather like a
desert island just now, with little news and surrounded by daily kidnaps and
murders. Lots of them seem centred on our quiet little Veneto towns – and
I must say if I were Agnelli or Montesi I would *give away* my money so as
to enjoy my family in peace. Evelyn Lambert took me to Venice yesterday
in her expensive Mercedes and a protest of *agricoltori* was moving about
Piazzale Roma. We were dressed for *città* (going to Victor Stanley's
memorial service) and for the first time ever in Italy I saw looks of real
sullen hatred.

Asolo keeps its friendly atmosphere but Cipriani does look a bit less prosperous, though Kamener goes about with his Napoleonic smile. I gave a tea
party for all my Asolani friends (and yours: lots asked after you all). There
were over fifty and it was touching, all pleased to see each other and welcome
me back as if I belonged to the little town – we have a very gregarious feeling and will no doubt help each other through whatever is coming. Meanwhile I have got the Dormo with a fine Swiss number plate and feel happier
knowing I could get across a border if necessary (a feeling left over from
the German 'pincer movement').

My leg still hurts but quite bearably – and I can take an hour's slow walk
up and down hill. I keep a good heart – the doctor says he has never seen a
better, of a purely mechanical sort.

Love to you all,

FREYA

MRS. T. DEUCHAR   Asolo

23 November 1974

Dearest Dulcie,

We are back in this isolation of war, which is so poignant to me as it
brings back those days when my mother was in prison and nothing could be

done. There is some child or young thing kidnapped for ransom *every day*, and apparently no end to people who can pay several milliards of lire to get them back. And the centres of all the fascist plots (which seem to me by far the most dangerous) are all in our quiet little towns – Verona, Padova, and now Treviso. We are all economising of course, but one can only do so on what one eats oneself. I couldn't bear to stop my masseur as he tells me that all his clients are doing this and it is his livelihood: just saving up to marry too! Caroly carries on but looks very tired and her girl has tonsilitis; and so it is – every problem made difficult by what is really a state of war.

The bank manager helps with taxes: the Swiss have just put 12% on foreigners' deposits (it is amusing for *me* to have to pay more than the wealth tax!). The faithful doctor comes every few days; one couldn't have more friendship around one and there is a feeling of all standing together in this little town. Its darkened streets (saving oil) have gone back to what they were built for and cars are getting fewer. Most people I know here are having a struggle and I felt so anxious to do something to cheer them up. They take any little gleam that comes along to let them be civilised and happy.

Dear love,

FREYA

JOHN GREY MURRAY   Asolo
25 November 1974

Dearest Jock,

A new essay is started – on 'Landscape', the difference as seen in age or youth. It is one of the few things that improve with the passing years and I try to find out why. When I sit on my little terrace and look over the beautiful valley and try to manage the labyrinths of words, I am very happy – even if there is little at the moment to make one cheerful. Some things however, even more now in the general strain: the gay little people so much enjoying their new prosperity are pulling in all their smart new belts and rearranging their lives with the hard experiences of all their centuries behind them. I cover my pearl necklace when I go out as one might have it torn off! Carmelo the driver and his wife took me out to lunch in a little pub yesterday, full of young students – I drove the Dormobile, not too bad after all this interval. I told Carmelo that, if I still have it, I am leaving him half a million lire to get an Italian number plate for the Dormo which he is to have: he had no idea of anything of the sort. How much their *gentilezza* helps through the hard lives. My doctor was so upset because I sold my picture for the operation: why not go to him, he said – and he has a huge debt to pay for his

233

house. This decency has helped Italy through all their black markets etc., and something will help us through too. I am more hopeful too for the Middle East – the Arabs will win through; no one can now think of depriving that tough young generation of a country. It is pretty grim to think how their murders have helped. The oil too, but not that only.

I love you very truly,

FREYA

LORD GOWRIE   Asolo
25 November 1974

Dearest Grey,

I hear you are married[167] – I am so glad and send every good wish I can think of, and wish you had brought her to see me before I left. You must come here as soon as you get a chance, and meanwhile find time for a letter to tell me how life is treating you – or is it how you treat life? It will be interesting I know, and I hope you have a companion to walk along together. I like to think of the lovely house *alive*!

I am writing a tiny book: not religious but trying to see how far the reasonable and non-revelation evidence carries, for prosaic people. It goes quite far.

Do come and see me, dear Grey, and bring your wife and stay a little, and I will find a wedding present when I see you.

Love,
FREYA

JOHN GREY MURRAY   Asolo
30 November 1974

Dearest Jock,

The first volume of Letters is here on my desk and it doesn't yet seem true: such *years* (I can't remember now if three or four have gone since the typing began) – and all those sums to incapable American typists (my poor little French gowns very inconspicuous in comparison!). And now it is done, and if we get the second safely off next summer I shall feel that the other volumes will follow even if I die – there will be people to see them

167 To Adelheid Gräfin von der Schulenburg.

through I rather hope and I am leaving all as settled as I can. I think of all this, and how it has really come through with Lucy's labours – I could never have done it alone. And then dear Jock I think of you and feel sad that it is not one of our green books that is lying on my table – and am writing so that you should not feel forgotten or not cared for, on this occasion which means so very much to me. You had to decide, and you kept off St. Crispin's Day, and neither you nor I will live long enough to know whether you were right – but I want to write just now to thank you, dear dear Jock, for all the other books you and I have written. I do this with a very full heart, and am glad you are taking on the last one (essay 14 I enclose).

Dear love,

FREYA

MRS. T. DEUCHAR

Asolo
Christmas night 1974

Dearest Dulcie,

It is late on Xmas night and I am here alone in my little flat and think of you and Tommy – your lovely red roses on the table beside me – and I wonder whether we might not be here together next Xmas and what will have happened to the world. I read my Plotinus (so grateful always to you for that book) and think so often how like our world is to the one he knew when Rome was falling down. How firmly he fixed his gaze on what was beyond that sadness. How wonderful that that faith, so firm and reasonable, could come through to reach us, to inspire Christianity itself. So great is the *idea*, beyond any other strength in this world.

In the meantime I have been having my Asolo Xmas, rather pensively gay under the shadows – the young nearly all away skiing and the little town taking round flowers, or wine, to their friends. Lunch today with some Yugoslav exiles, nice people who have seen everyone killed and themselves in prison; and last night was driven to an old villa in the plain, a young Islamic Art expert there with wife and daughter and a fire in huge fireplace, and lots of books and easy talk.

My leg gives a bit of trouble but the young masseur is quite happy about it. He still comes because it seemed too unkind to deprive him, but when I paid him before Xmas I told him he mustn't spend it all over the holiday (very long this year because of unemployment). 'I have spent it all already,' said he: 'I have bought a little gold watch for my *ragazza*.' I can't help liking this sense of relative values so like my own, and he was so happy at having managed his Xmas present, but I wonder if these values are going to carry Italy through? They keep her cheerful in great poverty meanwhile.

Must stop and go to bed, and send my loving thoughts to both.

FREYA

Asolo

MRS. DAVID PAWSON

3 January 1975

Dearest Pam,

So glad to get your letter, just come (other one never materialised). Oh Pam, how could you ever believe you could bear anything wet and damp after Greece? I am glad to think of you back in Athens even for a month.

I on the other hand am thankful to have slipped out of almost every responsibility and feel again like a Pilgrim, however stationary. The hip will carry me for an hour slowly, and grateful if the landscape provides a stone to sit on now and then. I go about looking for little forgotten paths that have no asphalt. I begin to like just to sit and do nothing, but am as a matter of fact slowly getting on with my little book of essays – dividing into two parts, Timeless, and Temporal.

I hope to get to Turkey in the summer, so glad to have that vision of England in May to remember – Francesca in Hell (Dante) remembers the little brooks that tumble down the Tuscan hills, and I shall never I hope forget the May hedges in Dorset.

All love to you both. Do come to the tower as soon as it gets warm.

FREYA

Asolo

JOHN GREY MURRAY

14 January 1975

Dearest Jock,

There is chaos on my desk and I am trying to get Letters off to Lucy, delayed more than they should have been by the essay on the Negative Virtues – obedience, chastity, permissiveness, and the sense of duty. Such a fascinating tangle and I think may come well. I agree with you about the poverty of the titles: 'Last Horizon' must go (though not egocentric; it is *everybody's* last horizon, though not so visible till after eighty). I thought of calling Part I 'Timeless' and Part II 'Temporal'? And one might imitate those chocolates and call the whole thing 'After Eighty'? Anyway the title will come. You will now get the typescript complete as far as it has got. The only people I would like to show it to are Dulcie (also to fortify her) and Colin[168] who has a very delicate ear for prose. I hope I may see him here and go through it with him, poor man; but I would do the same for him!

I have no news whether Letters are selling, but *very* nice letters from friends full of warmth and I do believe sincerity; and this of course is the most difficult volume. No time for more except love always.

FREYA

LORD KINROSS Asolo
15 January 1975

Dear Patrick,

How nice to be the least Wykehamical Wykehamist! Thank you for the poem and the wishes. I felt that Italian posts were best left alone at Xmas so did nothing except sending of thoughts. It is very pleasant just to receive and say thank you, thinking of you sitting in your book-room on top of your seventy years. The decade after was one of the happiest in my life; I hope it may be the same for you. One could be happy now if it were not for war just round the corner – luckily the Italian papers are nearly always on strike so one can't read them.

Asolo is a kind little Cranford place in winter. There is no snow; primrose and hepaticas and Christmas roses are out; I will soon be able to make my tower warm enough for visitors – when you can think of a little pause in the Ottomans. All wishes for the next ten years and after.

FREYA

THE DUKE OF GRAFTON Asolo
24 January 1975

Dearest Hugh,

I have been thinking so much and so badly of all the beautiful houses – Houghton with Sybil watching its last years, and so many others – and your struggle to save them. And now an idea has come to me and I would love to talk to you about it – but will do my best writing it meanwhile. It came to me while reading an old (1893) good book by Seeley – *The Expansion of England* (if you would like to read it I will send it you). It makes a great

[168] sc. Thubron.

point that our colonies, i.e. the Dominions, are radically different from the Spanish, Portuguese, etc.; they are nothing like colonies at all and they have no mixture of population but are really a *part of England* merely separated by distances which today need scarcely count: it has been a long mistake to look upon them as something so separate. (This made me think of Canada where I lay in hospital by the sea and used to hear the young men marching to the harbour and our war – in my father's little town everyone of possible age had volunteered.) Now don't you think that if you could find a suitable person to put it to them, they would provide us with buyers for the beautiful houses which have otherwise to be doomed? It would be good both ways: helping us out but also giving them a new and vital tie with England. Do think it over, dear Hugh. It would be like the eighteenth-century nabob who came back and settled and became an M.P. and J.P. and all, among the traditions to which he belonged.

Now this very instant a telegram from Patrick Plunket[169] asks if I have got an invitation for Buckingham Palace on February 11th (letter not arrived of course), so I am taking an aeroplane from 5th to 15th February for a very hasty look at you all: perhaps a meeting in London? I don't yet know where I shall be but Jock will know as soon as anyone.

All love,

FREYA

NED O'GORMAN Asolo
2 March 1975

My dear Ned,

It is so hard that we have to grow with pain: no other way. But I hope you are coming through – one does, you know, and so do I – and the world is still beautiful and only less so than the greatness that made it. And I am now eighty-two and getting very near (though fine, with this new hip beginning to get normal). I sleep like a navvy, but now and then at long intervals get a dream, nearly always in landscape unknown and among unknown strangers; and one came the other night – a vision rather than dream and strange because I am not worthy of visions. I had been thinking of my first love and thinking kindly though he had not deserved it; but all the sorrow had faded and only gentleness remained and from that the memory of the true deep love came (also divided, it was, by Time). I fell happily asleep, and the vision came – *nothing*, but only an overwhelming

[169] Lord Plunket was Equerry to the Queen and Deputy Master of HM Household.

presence, which enveloped; it was not inside me but I in it, and I felt an incredible joy that I was it and not a self any longer. From nowhere (because I was not aware of myself any longer) I asked 'But where am *I*?' and my attention was directed (again by this awareness and not communication) to a little bit of black gristle charred and deformed on the ground. I was filled with a joy greater than I can tell you, knowing freedom, and that I was a part of *love*, not possessed or possessing, but intrinsically one – I can't describe it all and the only human description I can think of that comes near it are the frescoes in the Pompeian villa. They give the irresistible which is so because it comes as already a part of oneself. It is the *whole*, of which we know so many partial varieties as we travel along. I thought you might like to hear about this event, because you are able to understand it even through the insufficiency of words; but I don't think one can describe it, at least I can't.

I am here till July and would love you in my tower. Am still feeling my hip but not in a *menacing* way.

Love,

FREYA

SYBIL, LADY CHOLMONDELEY   Asolo

1 April 1975

Dearest Sybil,

So glad to get your letter and to hear that we have only our familiar pains to worry over. I tried your gymnastics and certainly felt the stretch. I do a rather similar exercise, holding a chair-back and making a semicircle as high as I can with the poor leg, and I am also trying now to do little *jumps* from one carpet to the next (alas, I was once described as a beautiful *leaping* creature!). But never mind; we can manage for everyday life and what a blessing that is!

I am just back from the Engadin, having stopped to deal with finance (I hope successfully) on the way. The Dormobile took me up and then left over Easter with guide and wife and was held from fetching me yesterday as the roads were blocked with snow. A little local train still went down the Bernina and we sat blocked for two hours but got down in a lovely landscape – I never remember such whiteness and softness of snow. Down below a mile or more of cars were going home to Milan etc., crisis or no crisis, and we got home after midnight and I got no driving at all – the road much too bad.

I have the little Stewart goddaughter coming out for a fortnight: but she is bringing a friend so must take on the tower – which is still pretty cold. However, their hardships are nothing to what we took gaily in our youth.

All love, darling Sybil,

FREYA

COLIN THUBRON   Asolo
                                                11 April 1975
Dearest Colin,

I have taken your excellent advice and cut out most of the double quotes, and have also and with true delight finished the Cyprus tour.[170] You have a marvellous range of observation – I was wondering if you are conscious of it at the time or if the pictures come back so vividly that your *memory* can observe? It is a splendid gift and has grown so much since the earlier books; one really travels with you. I would love to talk it over and ask some more. There is a little sadness I would like to see more victoriously submerged in the triumph of history and time – but optimism is hard put to it just now. And now Burma! I think you may do wonderfully well: having so short a limit, you will be led to a less detailed but perhaps more sweeping landscape. I believe it will suit you. I had a week only, and it is still a whole gallery of fresh and lovely colours. Do go to Pagan which Marco Polo saw being destroyed. And all the old capitals round Mandalay. I wonder if you would like to use any photographs of mine? It takes an awful lot of one's precious time to take all one's own and I have some lovely ones of Burma and very glad if you liked to use them.

Your book is really fine – I am so pleased and longing to see the novel.

Love,
FREYA

JAC CHAMBLISS   Asolo
                                                20 April 1975
Dear Jac,

I am so glad to get your two letters with news better and better – that wonderful feeling of settling back in the saddle again. I have so many ill-nesses to look back on and now always see them as the time of good thoughts that come and go in a relaxed sort of way unattainable in perfect health. Next year I hope will see you in Europe if there is a Europe fit for travel; at the moment Italy seems ready to explode no one quite sure whether right or

170 Colin Thubron's *Journey into Cyprus* (1975).

240

left, but certain that all is near idiocy in the middle. U.S.A. too must be a sad quagmire just now and England just negative and poor. But in spite of all I can't help feeling that good may come and the world barriers be less high than they are now when this huge revolution is over. The murder of Faisal was a sorrow — he had wished to pray once in the Mosque of Omar in Jerusalem, but he certainly must have gone straight to his paradise. I once met him as a young prince dining at the Savoy — I was dining with Jack Philby, who was a friend of his, and we went to the table where he was sitting extremely bored with an equally bored little blonde. I heard about the murder from a friend just come from Saudia and it was a purely family affair — a young man's revenge for his grandfather, who was one of the Shammar rulers defeated by Faisal's father in the north. The young widow was taken, Beduin fashion, into the conqueror's harem and this boy was born to avenge the family feud. So it goes on. One does sometimes wonder how the human race survives. But as for Israel, for their own sake they should accept the Security Council's plan: it was moderate and good — the Palestinians along Jordan, the Golan Heights *neutral*, and Jerusalem international. (What city has more reason to be so? And yet this is the stickiest problem of all.) But only America can obtain this by cutting off armaments and Israel has the big vote in New York!

I am reading early English history — 1,100 years of it *before* the Normans came in 1066, and we had already seen the 600 years of Roman civilisation, the Celtic, German and Danish fall to ruin. I believe that even our feelings of every day go back for thousands of years.

All love and wishes,

FREYA

MRS. T. DEUCHAR   Asolo
                                                          26 April 1975
Dearest Dulcie,

Do you like this photograph? I think it expresses the right relationship of age and youth, and also makes me look intelligent, which hardly any photos do. I thought it might do for the Essays but Jock likes it only *single* and that makes me look intelligent in a vacuum. Intelligence is a correspondence (like letters, oh Dulcie!) and when alone it should be just meditation and give a reposeful look. You will see that I have definitely crossed the barrier of old age; and have been strangely saddened by the decision to sell my little car — Caroly and the doctor imploring me to do so almost on their knees and there is not a hope of getting my licence renewed next year. That happy little companion, always responsive though sometimes capricious, must go – with Lesbia's sparrow and all that. How strange that one should mind about a piece of machinery.

There is a threatening atmosphere here only too well remembered – Asolo itself quiet and lovely, but every big town filling with chaos. It is just sheer violence that is getting us down.

All love,

FREYA

MRS. T. DEUCHAR   Asolo
                                                          18 May 1975

Dearest Dulcie,

I am just back from two days in Venice, beautiful but tiring with so many steps to go up and down. Evelyn has got a lovely little flat in the Polignac palace (where I used to go when the Chavchavadzes were alive). She has done it up and made it entirely her own with the modern of the modern, and because it is all what she really likes it makes its way even to my ignorant mind. She asks after you and is a very true friend. While I slept through the afternoon she and a fellow Texan worked away and by the evening had all the furniture placed and a table laid with Peter cooking a marvellous dinner and an Arabian Nights atmosphere all about it. We went to the Fenice for a Ravel and Schumann evening, came back for our dinner party and got to bed at one, and came home a bit jaded yesterday morning in the right atmosphere in which a holiday should leave one – pleased after all to be at home again.

Lucy and John are coming up this week, and Michael Stewart on Wednesday. I still have one essay I feel is needed for the book. Darling Dulcie, I think of you all the time – keep a good heart for anything: it is truly *all one*.

Your
FREYA

SYBIL, LADY CHOLMONDELEY   Asolo
                                                          25 May 1975

Dearest Sybil,

It doesn't seem possible but it is nearly a month since we made that stormy little crossing in Venice. I wrote once but thought of you more often, sad at

242

the thought of change in Houghton which must be painful to you. The last two days I thought of you in Mantua – Michael Stewart, who is spending a week in my tower, drove me there. It still has a feeling of being unchanged with its great castle holding the side of the *piazza*, and the Mantegna – I think my favourite of all the Italian pictures – with the great staircase leading to it, up which you could ride a horse. The damage left by the war has been wonderfully obliterated and the whole town has recovered since I went there with everything half-wrecked; and I had not seen the Pisanellos lately discovered: fascinating to see a great picture as the painter *sketches* it, with a freedom which of course it loses later. I wish you could have been there; I would love to look at little Italian towns with you, dear Sybil.

All love, and thanks again for the little holiday – only wish it had been weather like today.

FREYA

LORD DAVID CECIL

c/o Lady Crawford,
Balcarres,
Fife
17 August 1975

Dearest David,

I was so glad to hear from you and deeply pleased as ever by your approval of the letters. I had hesitated so much before deciding to publish them, and it reassures me very much indeed that you should think them worth while. It is anyway a present to the Future from the Past from which we take so much while giving so little.

I am delighted at the thought of your anthology.[171] Both my little bits come from *Beyond Euphrates* but I haven't got the pages as I found them in *The Journey's Echo*.

As you see, I am in this most beautiful home enjoying lovely conversation and looking out to Scotland with its sea and that sort of a radiance that makes me, so strangely, think of Greece. I am going north to see the tip of our island before I die: it has been a fancy and wish for years, and this summer has been as it were a leave-taking from various tucked-away corners. The zigzags could not be made to fit Dorset or I would have reached Cranborne – but I hope for another chance there.

All affection to you both,

FREYA

[171] *Library Looking-Glass.*

243

Achentoul,[172]
Kinbrace,
Sutherland
23 August 1975

Dearest Jock,

This holiday is so beautiful and so nostalgic, melting away into a peaceful and happy goodbye to so many faraway Scotch days and people and seeing the landscapes they loved. Such beauty too – a great and very simple dignity in the hills, a sort of heart of immobility in great flowing lines – and the heather out, and the deer easy and friendly till October. They know the hunting season. The party is all ages and its middle ages fish while the two extremes (I am the only old one) look on and have the pleasure of walking on turf by a stream that seems to curve for fun in this open naked valley. In Glasgow I saw Edwin Ker, not in bed as I expected but up and coming to dinner and very alive though one side still paralysed.

After Glasgow I stayed with Mary Smith (not seen since Lionel's death)[173] and then was taken to Balcarres, where the Earl is one of the most charming people I have ever met and Mary has all the abrupt charm of the Cavendishes.[174] The castle looks out over the Firth of Forth and is full of the treasures – mostly Italian Renaissance – collected by three generations, a sort of oasis of civilisation from which one comes away renewed, hoping in spite of all that what was possible once may be so again.

Must stop dear Jock. I return to Euston on the 27th.

Love,

FREYA

SYBIL, LADY CHOLMONDELEY Achentoul,
Kinbrace
26 August 1975

Dearest Sybil,

The days have rushed by and I meant to write before, but then waited to be able to tell you about our visit to the Queen Mother. It was in her castle

[172] F.S. was staying with the Nuttings.

[173] Lionel Smith, sometime Rector of Edinburgh Academy, had first become a friend of F.S. when she went to Baghdad in 1929. He was Adviser to the Ministry of Education there.

[174] She was a daughter of Lord Richard Cavendish, brother of the 9th Duke of Devonshire.

by the sea[175] and more like a fairy tale than real life – the castle so right, with its pinnacles and towers and flag with many quarterings, and the gates open and none but one old retainer at the door. And herself so simple and royal in her welcome, so that one felt the genuineness of everything about her; it was a wonderful atmosphere of true and basic things. There were only two other charming people – Lady Mulholland and Sir Martin Gilliat – and they made us (Nuttings and young Nicholas stepson,[176] and Henrietta FitzRoy[177] feel happy at once, and took the young up to the highest tower while the Queen showed me her garden and then took me down to the beach where she has a little seat that looks over the sea. The tide was out and the long ribs of shore lay below in slices of stone as if they were the good beef we had at luncheon on the way. The Orkneys were far away, but just visible in a silvery mist, and this delicate northern light lay on everything – the long low green headlands of our island, and the far outlines, and the changing iridescence of the sea. I forgot it was the Queen as we sat there, two old women with most of our world behind us but happy in what we remember and what remains. She told me how she found this castle, falling into ruin, and on a sudden impulse decided to save it, and made it the quiet remote treasure it now is. How much you must have understood this, dear Sybil, and how I understand your love and regard for someone so true and so *human*. We all came away with this *human* feeling about us, after tea at a long white table out of our childhood. It was a great day anyway, and that sight of our northern frontier, the long green headlands with their small groups of houses and cattle browsing, and the feeling of remoteness and the long hard winters all about them, and our history so wrapped between south and north and so visible here – it left me very happy to have seen it all.

Dear love,

FREYA

JOHN GREY MURRAY

c/o Nuri Birgi,
Istanbul
8 September 1975

Dearest Jock,

I am so far on my way and yesterday left the house on the Bosphorus after five happy days. Sevim and Memduh no longer there, but the feeling

---

[175] The Castle of Mey in Caithness.
[176] sc. Beatty. Diane Nutting had been previously married to 2nd Earl Beatty.
[177] The Duke and Duchess of Grafton's daughter.

of them all about, the little garden at the water's edge still full of children coming over the grown-ups in occasional waves, and people landing or leaving by the lapping water. Ayesha and Ahmet have taken over and there is a younger face wherever an older one has gone and the same tradition and friendship. The little boys are now out or just getting out into their jobs and coming to the tower as they go by; and the oil-ships of every nation go by rather grim as there is never a human being in sight on them. The feeling of history going by makes it impossible to do anything but look out over the great shining waterway – the new bridge straight as a pencil across its horizon.

Life here just as uncertain as everywhere else but it is extraordinary how natural this atmosphere is as soon as one reaches the Mediterranean and especially the eastern end. My Turkish practically gone but coming back – more easily if my friends wouldn't all talk French. I do no sightseeing but let the East soak in. Send news to Bodrum – poste restante – to say all is well.

Love,
FREYA

NURI BIRGI

Hotel Sami,
Gümbet,
Bodrum
13 September 1975

Dear Nuri,

I have happy days to thank you for. It was like a dream to look at Istanbul again and from the frame of your windows, and the Spirit of Turkey *speaking* in your house. It is so rare that anything happens just to coincide with what you wish and need, and this was one of those times: I do thank you so much – and hope you will not remember too acutely that I was the guest who made you get up at five o'clock.

The journey landed me here about 5 p.m., very jolted because the road is being remade now and far too much built over as you come to the lovely Menderes valley, but it was a great joy to come here and see the castle and bay and the exquisite far mountains just as I remembered them. The view is one of the best and I hope you will come down with Rhoda and let me give you dinner either here or at the Halikarnas.

I was distressed, dear Nuri, to think what you have suffered in America; I know it, because I have felt it myself. It is hard for our generation who have known very heroic and splendid times – hard for you as a Turk but even more so for us English who have watched one fifth of the world melt away from us as if it were snow. I don't think you need fear for the Turkish future: it is geography that counts and you are the bulwark of the Mediterranean and I feel sure that with modern changes that centre of the world will come back into its own. But we are out on an Atlantic solitude with no one but America to be in close communication and the next generation will have to choose whether to convert her or be converted. I am very much afraid and most who worked for my generation, if they are still alive, carry a deep sorrow in their hearts – such as your ancestors must have felt when the Turkish tide receded and the hard days came. You can look back with such pride on how those days were met.

I leave this sad topic to thank you again for your friendship and kindness, with affection dear Nuri.

FREYA

SYBIL, LADY CHOLMONDELEY   Gümbet,
                                                                                            Bodrum
                                                                        13 September 1975

Dearest Sybil,

I hope to find letters when I get home on October 10th, but at present am cut off from all except the sea. It has renovated me already after one bathe this morning, the air like a living warmth all round one. A little hotel very clean and new has sprung up in this which was the solitary bay I used to swim in. It will be spoilt in a year or two as there are camping places, rather gay and still innocuous, but soon obviously to be too big for their beaches; but now it is just what I need and I wish all the time that you were here also, and shall live in the water all day long till I leave and get my tame jeep to take me into Bodrum to see its lovely view – the castle very black and the sunset cutting like a sword across the bay, and the far mountain outline with the impossible quality of being wild and horizontal at the same time. The little town is beautifully tumbled all round the water and looks no different from three years ago – and I am so happy to be here. I had ten days in Istanbul on the way, first on the Bosphorus, delightful for all except its bathing, and then with Nuri who has been really shocked and loses all diplomatic reticence when he talks about America. He has made himself a dream of a house and garden, and looks across the water at the whole great curve of the city with its six mosques and minarets on the skyline, like a bow so

247

gently and evenly curved; and the ships of all nations still wait in the sea outside to steam in – for petrol from Russia.

Love,

FREYA

MRS. T. DEUCHAR

Gümbet,
Bodrum
30 September 1975

Dearest Dulcie,

I leave tomorrow morning and hope to get into Venice on Saturday. I am a week earlier than I meant (money ran out completely: it makes me feel young again!). Anyway swimming has justified itself as a cure, and I am back at the stage where I can do up my dress at the back. I have also got back quite a lot of Turkish, with my nice schoolmistress every two days; but to learn a language with age and deafness against one is very hard and the really quite good Turk I had in 1963 has gone for ever. But I can get about again and be treated like a *nice* foreigner, which means quite a lot in Turkey just now.

I don't wish for you here, Dulcie dear, because you would collapse under the cooking. Even I notice that it is bad and in a few years there will be a *plage* and houses everywhere. As it is, the bay that was so completely solitary now has three groggy little wooden piers, and the hotel (very clean) has rows of rooms on two floors with much higher numbers than themselves – all a family affair and a good pretty woman with three charming children making up for continual subservience to a husband she has evidently long ago ceased to believe in. But the women are taught to be amiable whatever happens, and perhaps this is a good arrangement so long as there is divorce?

Nothing has yet taken away the *speaking* beauty of these coasts – no mountains ever seen more lovely than the range, delicate as a miniature, that runs to Mysidus into the Carian Sea. I look at it and wonder how the ecstasy I first felt twenty-three years ago can come again as deep as ever. Looking at them one can understand that Civilisation was possible. The hills are brown now, the olives also – a brown that one does not see but *feels* through the dim green; and tamaris fills this bay with its tufts of pale blossom, always tossing in a soft wind, so pale it is scarce visible – as if patches of sky came through. I have followed the west wall from Alexander's gate to where it once commanded the harbour – and yesterday was driven by

248

jeep to where the huge bend in the north let in the Greeks. They have half dug up the theatre – seats like new, but a motor road in front.

Looking for news and all love meanwhile,

FREYA

JOHN GREY MURRAY Asolo
28 October 1975

Dearest Jock,

So very glad to get your note from Cumbria – what a very cumbrous name! I can't tell you how relieved I am to think of you taking a proper spell of quiet; W. P. once said to me, 'I haven't wasted my life: I took a holiday whenever I could.' And now I have a wonderful feeling – another two and a half years to go (*inshallah*) and letters and books will be there not to be worked at but only to be enjoyed; and if Providence is kind I may be given still a year or two just to sip at the loveliness of life. When one loses this feeling one is most truly mixed up with Death. And I believe darling Jock that you were wandering off the road – trying to make yourself believe what you don't really believe, that business is business. It isn't – and I think this mistake may be what is wrecking our poor world. I don't believe that, among many mistakes, I have ever made *that* one.

Something went wrong: I think it was those Twenties whose pinchbeck a whole generation took for gold. The good old Victorians were not just 'business'; it was something else – a use of material means for a beyond-material purpose – and it is this *direction* I do believe that has gone wrong. One mustn't make money for money, but to do something with it (like Pericles building the Acropolis with the allied funds). The object must remain not the prosperity of the firm but – as a *main* guide – the production of the superlative. And it is so in everything – and how one can believe in the Gospels and not believe this passes my understanding. It is not our war, dear Jock, dear Diana – I am too old and you came into a bewildered age. But there is a longing in many hearts and surely a speaker will come.

Meanwhile poor Anita can't come down because people are looting along the motor-way! I drove the Dormo up (with Carmelo beside me) – a 200-kilometre day to beechwood under pinnacles and snow. Such beauty: lovely to do nothing but look. When will you come and try?

Love,
FREYA

249

6 November 1975

Dear Paul,

How glad I am that you like getting letters. I have been so much alone that it has gradually become my easiest way of conversation – one has intervals to think over whatever the subject may have been and presently the pleasantest of patterns shapes itself, a little hit from each side and gradually the shape of its own emerging. I am now writing to you well ahead of the arrival here of *Country Life* so that you may realise the impartial quality of friendship apart from any of the kind things you may have been saying, and I am so glad you approve the idea of the Old Brewery[179] – Chesterton would surely have approved of this sort of commercial venture?

But as for Christmases, my memories about them seem very vague and the one in Afghanistan far the worst I should think to live through. Mrs. Butler, a gay and sprightly old lady, once came to dine in the house I stayed in as a girl and told us how the Government of that day allowed her to *pose* the army in the middle of a charge so as to have it accurate. The disgrace of the Afghanistan retreat was redeemed by a later expedition who were instructed to hand out a punishment which would make the Afghans feel how wicked they had been, and (as feelings by that time had become quite friendly) the C.O. commanded the destruction of the fine old bazaar – so that no human life and only Art need be destroyed. Now isn't this one of those rather difficult points you come upon so often with morality in action?

I was asked to write a Christmas speech for Lady Lampson[180] in Cairo in 1940. I thought it would be a good idea to tell these poor men in their desert camps how like their Christmas was to the original setting (apart from Peace on Earth of course) – and I let myself go over the desert scene. It was rejected with scorn – quite rightly I think. Snow and candles and plum pudding were put back in their place – and this is the only Xmas abroad I can visualise. I only *feel* Easter in the Mediterranean.

Affectionately,

FREYA

---

178 The novelist, author of the *Raj Quartet*. He had enthusiastically reviewed Volume One of the Letters in *Country Life* and was due to review Volume Two.

179 The Old Brewery, Tisbury was at that time the address of the publishers of the Letters.

180 Wife of the Ambassador, Sir Miles Lampson – later Lord Killearn.

Asolo

12 November 1975

Dearest Sybil,

I have been meaning to write for so long. Your lovely letter about the Queen followed and caught me just as I was catching my boat at Smyrna. The sea, and Cape Matapan, and the grassy, empty western coast of Zante were too riveting for the next two days; then I reached my desk here and have been trying to clear the accumulation ever since.

Do you agree with the attempt to interfere with the Italians having a Communist sprinkling in their government (than which nothing could be more inefficient at the moment)? It seems to me that the velvet glove is missing on the hand that thinks it runs the world. I don't believe living was any less harassed in the Renaissance than now – only better art!

Sybil dear, do you sometimes think of going to look at something, like Palmyra for instance; and on to Risafe with its Byzantine gateway so lonely in the desert? Sudden longings for these places come to me and they would not be difficult and we could leave poor distracted Beirut and go in from Turkey by Aleppo – and back by Damascus according to the outlook of the day. Dreams – but not impossible. Meanwhile I too am having to find a maid as Emma has been found out and goes around looking like Catherine de Medici contemplating St. Bartholomew.

Dear dear love,

FREYA

Asolo

16 November 1975

My dear Paul,

Am I really like that?[181] The review has come and leaves me very deeply moved and happy – happy mostly in the knowledge of a true friendship which has sparkled so kind and spontaneous out of those old days. Thank you – very very much; I had forgotten that I discovered the discomfort of notoriety so soon, but that has not left me at any rate; and the virtues you list, it is a *wonderful* list so sensitively chosen. Oh my dear Paul, I hope you will not find them all rubbed off by life in its later years! Anyway I must tell you that four young people, calling in on their way, asked to see the review and instantly bought a volume each. Apart from the personal happiness this

---

[181] In his *Country Life* review of Volume Two of the Letters, Paul Scott had referred to F.S.'s 'rare and precious gifts'.

writing of yours has given me, I must tell you what a great delight your accurate use of words constantly gives me; it gives that precise outline which is so rare and makes one feel so safe in a shifting world. I am glad to be your little water-carrier in the desert![182]

FREYA

PAUL SCOTT   Asolo
30 November 1975

Dear Paul,

I ought to be writing duty letters, but this habit of written conversation is too beguiling, as you will see in the coming volumes – when great friends were there to be talked with; and I have been missing them so much and am so happy to find a person ready as I am to use a little leisure in written conversation. It seems to me that the difference made by actual presence is smaller than people imagine. Anyway I was delighted to get your letter yesterday, and to hear that it was the Afghan Christmas you chose. I have a little Staffordshire model of Lady Sale on horseback: I will leave it to you in memory! She managed the Afghans very well and they were of course perfect gentlemen, and still are.

Meanwhile here in this civilised country I am packing away all my silver etc. as two bands of young *malviventi* are wandering about with sten guns looting houses and shops. It is fascinating to see how shocked the Italians are by visible violence and how little by corruption.

I have been vaguely thinking of an essay on horizons: it would suit the Mediterranean of course. The fascinating thing is, don't you think, that we share this exciting thing, this rim of the unknown, with every living creature: an ant must have his horizon just as we have, smaller but yet dividing all immensity as far as he is concerned? But I am not yet writing: a new, nice maid, the people with sten guns and a quite futile new lock being put to the door – too many distractions.

Affectionately,

FREYA

[182] The review of the Letters had concluded: 'For me they have the blessed smell of water in dry country.'

Asolo

20 December 1975

Dearest Dulcie,

I wonder what sort of news you like to get and if there is anything in this one-way traffic of my letters that you like? I find I can't read for long now and it is such a deprivation; but I discover that in a strong light I can still embroider (rather badly), and my little effort went to you I hope for Christmas. There is no Christmas feeling here, and four cars were stolen from the Asolo square last week. All the outlying houses are 'visited' and someone rang my bell at 2 a.m. two days ago. Of course I didn't open, but sat inside the door with my pistol for quarter of an hour. I do read before getting up, and have just finished the 'Paradiso' of Dante, deeply moved. One has to have lived a lot to see its vision. (I have found an excellent edition with notes to explain it and with the illustrations of Doré, which I am giving to the doctor's son, Livio, who is now doing Dante at school; the beautiful drawings may help.) Oh Dulcie, what a hard world these young creatures are going into! But the 'Paradiso' has been making me happy – there is a radiance, loveliness of joy which no other poet has that I know. Milton is the loveliness of earth, but with Dante one is truly away in a bliss that transcends this earth; and I don't believe that any other poet has ennobled love as he has: the laughter of Beatrice, the 'sun of my eyes' – it spills radiance over the wonderful economy of words.

Love, dearest love,

FREYA

Asolo

1 January 1976

Dearest Tommy,

It is New Year's Day and I am longing for a letter from you – not to tell me that Dulcie is better but that she keeps along her level and gets no worse. When I hear nothing it gives me a feeling of desolation as if the world were sinking; and perhaps it is. And I would like to hear how you are – so strong, darling Tommy, but terribly hard to go on so long. I feel too old to do anything useful, but I think of you and wish I could do something too – and by hook or crook I will get over just to see you both in spring. I hope things here may get a little better with the longer days; there is nothing very hopeful in the air just now though the hotels are all full and people spending all they have as fast as they can.

253

I am joining a Committee for Human Rights, not very hopefully, and will try to go East to Yemen and Arabia in spring, and later in the early summer to Turkey to try and get rid of the arthritis which is slowly creeping up me; and between these two journeys I will make a little air-loop to see you both. I make these plans long ahead as travel has become difficult even for the simplest journeys.

Much love dear Tommy to you both. Does Dulcie like to get my letters or do they tire her?

FREYA

EDWIN KER

Asolo

2 January 1976

Dear Edwin,

Christmas is over and the New Year is in, and I hope it may be better than last one for all of us and especially for you.

I feel very old this year, much more than one year more than last, and one of the saddest things is that I can't go on reading for hours at a time: the brain just goes on strike and refuses to take in any more. I have just read Dante again and found that I must have changed: 'Purgatorio', my favourite, is now not nearly so beautiful as 'Paradiso'. It may be because I have found a fully annotated edition. W.P. first led me through it and explained the geography and would quote it among the mountains whose steep grey rocks and pinnacles seemed to be like those living words. What will we find more beautiful than words when we go on?

If I am strong enough, I hope to travel in February or March – Egypt and perhaps farther, but in an easy way; but I will be here long enough to have, I hope, good news from you – and send you best wishes meanwhile.

FREYA

MME ANITA FORRER

Asolo

21 January 1976

My dear Anita,

I must tell you that the four-volume novel by P. Scott arrived just as I was being packed off to hospital. I had suddenly become unable to walk and thought the other hip might have gone, and have been four days in a ward (with two such nice old peasant women, a strange and touching experience);

254

and luckily it is only arthritis, but very painful. I am back now and in bed and hope to be active again in a week or so. The novel was just what I wanted and saw me through wonderfully. It is very interesting, though I think there is a little unfairness over the army in India: we are in an anti-army age, and although I saw all the bad manners which the author describes (I was in India for five months in 1945), there were always a great many among the young men who loved the country and its people. There is an affinity between England and Arab which seemed to me not to exist with the Indian — but affinities are beyond human control.

Dear love,

FREYA

MRS. T. DEUCHAR   Asolo
                                                 30 January 1976
Dearest Dulcie,

I have got disorganised in my letters, making my way through a little chaos left by these four weeks of illness. I can now walk again, very gently and not much farther than the Cipriani, who are giving me a far too lavish lunch tomorrow all for nothing. In the morning I got Sandro to drive me in to Treviso for passport photographs and the landscape of the plain had suddenly plunged into depth of winter, and the seagulls had evidently left bad weather beyond the coast and were flying over a pit of refuse: it was all covered with the grey shimmer of their wings. It made me think of all the good familiar moments that come to comfort one in life — hot tea for instance when you come back tired, and the warmth of the bath in the morning, and shafts of sunlight and plots of shadow, and a spring of water if you have a piece of bread to eat beside it. All this small furniture of the vast room: how poor we would be without it!

All love to Tommy too: I hope to have a letter.

FREYA

JOHN GREY MURRAY   Asolo
                                                 30 January 1976
Dearest Jock,

Thanks for the kind winged words: how many birthdays you have sent to! On the eve of this one the essay proofs have gone to you, my last book I truly think.

Your rigidity over punctuation reminded me of a dinner where you put Max Beerbohm and me together and we had such a happy time over punctuation lasting to the dessert. We agreed in being unorthodox. I keep semi-colons and colons like a jerk of a stop to ask for attention, and he graded , ; : according to the length of pause he required, and we came to the conclusion that our use of these signals was really the same. It is one of my regrets that I never got to know him better with Rapallo so near – he did of course have a very tiresome wife to begin with.

I hear you are back at work and in great form, but I am anxious, dear Jock: please don't forget my letter – one is given such short little runs as time goes by; and John must be thirty-three – the climax of Alexander. The time-tables do keep us very humble. What I find rather sad is the forgetting of every language I have ever learnt.

When does the *Peak* come? And please tell me you are keeping Evelyn her fifty volumes.[183]

Love,
FREYA

PAUL SCOTT   Asolo
                                                                1 February 1976
Dear Paul,

Since writing to you there has been an event in my life and that is the reading of your four volumes. I would not say this if it were not so, but I very rarely read novels now and only enjoy them if they are like stepping stones – as good novels surely should be? Anyway, these came just before I went into hospital for a week, and I read through all four books and spent the time in India to all intents. I am longing to hear more about your Indian life – how early did it begin and what made this noble great expanse of writing come into your mind? It is all that the reviews said, a really great monument, and I am longing to know the India that stands behind in your life? When you come upon Volume V of my letters you will find me in India for five months, trying to make a plan for Lady Wavell to enlarge the W.V.S. This was of course quite hopeless, but I did make a plan to work in with the Indian women's own efforts and I wrote to Lady Wavell from a number of places, finding on the whole great help and sympathy. The Wavells became close friends; the army people who were about him were

[183] Evelyn Lambert was arranging to sell copies of *A Peak in Darien* in Texas.

256

perhaps exceptions, but one couldn't help feeling that they made a good empire structure and I wondered whether the clue to our failure could not be found in the different systems on which civil and military seemed to work. I thought the army was still wanted but practically everyone wished the civilians to go (1945), and was it because the army was *paternal*? I wondered whether a *deification* of the Viceroy and his wife could not have saved the British rule? I would so like to hear what you think: it is out of my parish and so different from anything in the Middle East.

Volume III is being printed and I am, I hope, putting in the interval with a visit to Cairo – just to let the lumbago sniff the desert air.

Affectionately,

FREYA

MRS. T. DEUCHAR

Asolo

9 February 1976

Dearest Dulcie,

I am hoping for your news from Tommy, and to hear of the last blood test, a week or so ago? He must write or I shall be gone: I am fixing up a month's tour – Cairo, Yemen, and if all goes well a glimpse of the pilgrim route at Medain Salih, where Doughty stayed. It may not come off, anyway not beyond Cairo, but it is, after all, only a year or two that can now be taken from me and the desert air may make it a pleasant year or two. At present the arthritis is behaving in the most sadistic way, although we have perfect days, mountain ranges' snow, and the first snowdrops in the valley just along the edges of the mist, which twists like a Chinese dragon in the plain.

In Cairo, Francis Witt has asked me to a house 'full of servants' where he directs his bank, and in San'a I am asked by Hugh Leach, at the Embassy. One goes there twice a week by air, over the pass where I camped with a broken-down lorry in 1940, and everything has become accessible and probably not improved by that. Meanwhile our crisis here is, at last, producing a certain glumness. A woman just out from England was asked how the English are taking it: 'With their usual rigidity,' she said.

Dear love to both,

FREYA

Asolo
24 February 1976

Dear Paul,

I was delighted with your letter and have been thinking over it and India and how it must have struck you as your first Eastern impact and what the difference would be from your and my Arab-Mediterranean approach. This fascinates me so much that I must write about it, though I ought to be packing for Cairo-Yemen.

The point I would like to tell you about is a meeting with Nehru at the Simla Conference (1945), when I had two long and very friendly talks with him at the hotel one morning. I was doing my job for Lady Wavell and in the evening our whole party came down from the Viceregal Lodge and there was Nehru talking to some Congress man and looking at us all *to see if we would bow* – which I did of course but everyone else was very busy talking and no one else even saw him in the shadow. But as I noticed this sad little nuance, I remember thinking how if that had been an Arab he would never have bothered to notice whether we were saluting or not. I still think that is the centre of the knot. We like the people who stand on their own feet: Turks, Greeks, Spaniards, Arabs, Afghans, Pathans, Muslims in general...the French as enemies, the Italians for fun; not good with the sensitive *receptive* – Indian, Persian, Egyptian etc...I sometimes wonder whether this does not go back to some largely forgotten Celtic world which ruled before the Christian – Mediterranean – Greek went north? However this lack of sympathy came, it seems to me the blame is not all on one side or the other but fairly equal? That quietness in taking sorrow touched me – so patient and unobtrusive. And then I remembered how I reached the U.S.A. in 1943 and heard how the Halifaxes had gone out to the Embassy there and were invited to a State banquet; and the news of the death of Peter, their youngest, had just reached them: but they went. But what belongs to all the East, I believe, is that evening light, that *yesterday*, as you say, so visible today. It draws one for ever – I sometimes rest myself with the thought of it.

I am very insecure – not really ready for long journeys, but everything had been so beautifully arranged; so, optimism as usual. I hope I may come back and then encourage a visit to Asolo. I have a volume of Wavell's letters. He became a great friend, and I had them bound as an heirloom, and I think that true greatness of his comes through.

Love,
FREYA

San'a,
Yemen
8 March 1976

My dear Anne and Frank,

Our letters are divided by such continents: I picked yours up as I came away from Asolo and flew by Rome to Cairo. Rome was having an out of work young men's demonstration and I found myself walking nervously through it, as one hears of people thrown down and their coats taken – and I am now a timid old lady about falling down. Then Cairo, terribly down-at-heel (two wars of course), and the graceful *galabias* I remember now rare in her streets. Francis Witt is there, very happy running a bank just opposite the Embassy which keeps the graceful shape of its imperial splendour and reserve and still had the old *cawass* in service (fifty years) and most hospitable friendly Ambassador[184] who gave me a ten-day home. Francis sent many messages and we talked of the good memories and I had a good day at Sakkara with sand blowing about, gold in the sun. But the near pyramids look as if a disease of jerry-built concrete had crawled about around them. I left by air at 1.30 a.m., the aeroplane hired out by Britain to the Yemen, and got here in four hours on to a fine aerodrome and asphalt roads – it took six days from Aden in 1940! So glad to see it all again and, apart from too many cars, not really different. The tall stone houses and their white-painted windows are clustered just the same, and the crowd more friendly than 1940. I am so happy to see it all again and had forgotten the incredible beauty. My host is Hugh Leach, a new young friend who has made himself a garden with lawn and flowers in the old walls, and loves and knows the people. All my old friends dead or gone. But the country is open and I have been driven north through a wonderful mixture of volcanic peaks and sandstone, flat-topped cliffs, and villages on rocky ledges.

Dear Anne, I think of you and how brave you are, and realise what you feel with the landscape in sight and that growing inability to go and look at it, and know the feeling – not cruelly imposed but still perceptible at eighty-three. Sometimes I wish it all over, for I feel so deeply that what we go to is a happy sharing in all that makes the beauty we enjoy. But it is the little casual things that perhaps we shall miss?

Love to you and perhaps a sight of you in autumn. I am a bit vague but think it must be Asolo in October.

Love,
FREYA

---

[184] Sir Willie Morris.

23 March 1976

Dear Edwin,

I am sure that a letter from you must be waiting for me in Asolo, but I am still far away; in another world, and on my way to London this evening. Dulcie Deuchar, a friend of many years now, died just as I was leaving for the Yemen, and I hope that I may persuade her husband to let me take him to Asolo for a short spell away from all his sadness. So I did not rush back from here to the funeral (which I feel like walking behind a used-up dress however loved) but shortened my Yemen visit to a week and switched this flight from Venice to London – and when I get there will find out what I can do. Even so, in those short days, the magic returned: thirty-six years since I was there, and about three wars and several assassinations, and now there are moderate 'progressives' in power and tribes still fond of explosions in the north, and ever so many motor cars; but the new concrete hasn't drowned the tall stone houses with their whitewashed decorated windows – houses that give one the feeling of mountains (just as Manhattan does to me) and which I knew so well in 1940, going up and down their steep stairs to the harems at the top.

I stayed with a friend at the Embassy there, in one of these old houses, and was taken over as much of the country as my week could manage – a fairy-tale country of mountains, and plains held bright in their arms, like jewels; and villages clinging and cut out of the mountain stone. They are slim, quick people, with faces that go to rather pointed chins unlike the other Arabs, and very friendly now. I no longer saw the striped black and yellow gowns with great sleeves that I remember in the streets but most of the women still wear their ponderous veils, though the eyes are not often left out between nose and forehead to smile at one.

I loved it all and felt at home, and Arabic words came back one by one, and I think if I am spared I might go back for a month or two once a year to read through the Koran with a teacher. The Arabic is still there, but Turkish words keep on interfering.

I hope for good news of you when I get home, early in April.

Love,

FREYA

Cairo
23 March 1976

Dear Mary,

I have such a nice letter of yours written long ago, and have been meaning to write and want to do so now that I am on the way home from the East, where it is such a joy to feel happy as ever. I had to cut it down to a week in Yemen, but a friend now posted there took me over mountains from north to south – the six days from Aden to San'a (the capital) now shortened to hours, and an asphalt road. I think there are three now – from Ta'iz to San'a over the mountains. There is a pass near 10,000 feet, and you look down from it into round valleys lying about like cups filled to the brim with terraces of a drug called *kat*, which is the most precious plant they have. It is such a troublesome thing, and more so now than ever, to see so much labour given to tiny plots of earth. The drug apparently does no harm though not much is known about it, and our driver, when tired, runs into a wayside shanty to buy a little bunch and bite its green leaves. The mountains that toss about above these valleys are so jagged they are more like spears in motion, coloured by the sun, but hardly any green till the monsoon. I am happy to have seen it all again and like to write to you thinking of your lovely view with the Firth and the grazing cows all in the same world!

I hope to be in Asolo early in April.

Love to you both, and to the beautiful home,

FREYA

Asolo
5 April 1976

Dearest Juliette,

There is a bit of May clear and very welcoming before I leave for Turkey on the 22nd – but I must tell you my rather inadequate hospitality: it is just the old tower on the city wall, with a magic view and a shower (one of those you have to be very brisk with) and an old woman who brings you breakfast and sweeps and dusts, but that is all that happens unless you like to share my picnic of ham, tea, and a little bread and butter in my flat in the evening. I find this régime satisfactory and little trouble, and have one good meal in the day at the hotel next door, where of course it is lovely if my friends will come on their own and join me. (They are usually out exploring in the day.) But I can't do anything for them there as it is too expensive, and it rather naturally refuses to charge less for visitors, though it takes a little off for a permanent inhabitant like myself (who also consumes less than half their *porzioni*). This explanation reminds me of the Scottish landlady who told my godfather that she liked him and his party because 'sandwiches and the beauties of nature were enough for them' – and I wish I were a Lucullus to do more. If this tempts you, dearest Juliette, in this little blossoming town, you know how happy it will make me.

Love,

FREYA

SYBIL, LADY CHOLMONDELEY Asolo
11 April 1976

Dearest Sybil,

I have been busy and only just finished clearing my desk of a month's letters, as there was no forwarding in reasonable time to Yemen. I can see that it is almost impossible just now, but if a chance does come and you feel like it, do send a telegram and fly out and you shall have my room and I go up to the tower and it would make me so happy. Any time till May 29th when I hope to fly to Turkey and spend a month bathing somewhere along the beloved coast. I am making a collection in my mind of places *unprogressive* and *quiet* where I can sit for a few months a year in these last years and practise their languages quietly. Am rather planning to go back to Yemen for November, which they say is the best month (and they talk good Arabic). Saudi Arabia, which I wanted to visit, they say is quite objectionable now, talking only of money.

As for this country, it is gusty with those winds that mean a revolution. The Demo-Christians are really despicable and their great men, I am told by my Swiss friends, have bought up pretty well all the villas of Ticino. To hold up a revolution by a tussle over abortion seems more like a Mozart opera than real politics. Anyway the divergences (which could have been tided over peacefully) are now blatant and ending in an election which no one can pay for and which will only help on the Communists – whom very few really want in power (including perhaps themselves). Anyway, for the *third* time in my life I have been packing away the silver, etc.

Let me have news of you, dearest Sybil. I think of Houghton with such a mixture of love and sadness.

Your

FREYA

Asolo

                                                          13 April 1976

Dear Paul,

I am going to choose one or two of my most treasured and small objects
to give to Jock to take to England in a fortnight when he comes. The chief
will be the two volumes of my godfather's and Wavell's letters, and I will ask
him to let you see them before he puts them into the archive. I shall be so
curious to hear what you think. W.P.'s I think comes straight through in its
conciseness from his great store of wisdom and knowledge; and Wavell's –
like most soldiers' – one has to guess through the rigidity of training. If I
had been a man, I think I would have been a soldier and am often touched
by the humility of their conscious solitude. 'You must not think we do not
love the beautiful things though we know so little of them,' was once said
to me by a young guardsman long ago dead. I suppose that not many realise
how they live in a dedicated solitude and have to rely on its corporate atmosphere – but the Wavells did realise it and Archie once explained to me how
it was only the actual majesty and compulsion of the art of war that made it
a possible profession: he was lamenting that Archie John his son lacked this
dedication. He too was a very dear friend and would tell me how much he
longed to devote the rest of his life to the educating of the army and did not
really enjoy being inside it. But you will find all these things in the letters
better than I can tell them. I think often of the last pages of your fourth
novel; I know of no finer climax so nobly carried up from the everyday
triviality into their splendour. Very great skill dear Paul; how happy it
makes one to meet it.

Let me hear what you feel about the letters. Meanwhile I am very enthusiastic at the thought of a *Times* article written by you. Lucky I am.

                                                          Love,

                                                          FREYA

Asolo

                                                          5 May 1976

Dear Edwin,

I am so glad to have good news of you from your hut and to think of you
back there looking at the year and its changes among the things you love. I
too am having a very great delight in the past, re-reading Doughty after
fifty years exactly. I was learning Arabic and he was sent me, two huge
volumes I thought would last the summer, and I read him all in a fortnight,

unable to put him down. No other traveller I think makes one share his adventures so vividly, so that the reading has the same quality as if one were journeying oneself. When his second edition came out he read it over, after twenty years, and found not a word to alter! He never uses an adjective that does not mean something. Looking back now, I believe he was responsible for the travelling part of my Arabian days, and it is great joy to recognise the everyday life of the Beduin so that the little touches are of things that I have come to know for myself.

What an adventure life has been and I feel sure it goes on. On May 20th you should get the little book of essays, I think the last.

Love,
FREYA

SYBIL, LADY CHOLMONDELEY   Asolo
14 May 1976

Dearest Sybil,

Your telegram was so welcome. This was the sixth earthquake in my life so I took it calmly when the lamps began to swing about – and there was no noise here which makes it so *humanly* frightening. I was most worried, you will sympathise, about my china and put my beautiful glass lamp from its column on to the floor to be safe; then remembered my bedroom wall – an old one nearly a yard wide, and got into its doorway; then remembered rather belatedly the old lady of ninety-two upstairs and went up to find her just coming down all neat and ready for the road – so we came down hand in hand with that splendid British 'rigidity' we keep for occasions; and then we went to bed and slept all through the second and quite a lot of succeeding shocks, gradually lessening. But they go on in Friuli and the weather has been quite uncertain and there it is, one more detail to this unenviable year.

I leave for Turkey on 29th and hope to come back by way of the Leigh Fermors in Greece.

I long for your news, dear Sybil – wish you would come to me in autumn?

FREYA

PAUL SCOTT   Asolo
20 May 1976

Dear Paul,

So *interested* in your letter, but sorry that my beloved godfather didn't come through. Is it perhaps the Scotch that leave so much unsaid? He never did what someone said a gathering of bishops should have done: 'Ils ont perdu l'occasion de se taire.' I am sure you would have come through into the unseen country if you had known him; and he would have liked and talked to you, because you are interested in humanity as well as literature, and the inarticulate must after all have someone articulate for any conversation at all. W.P. knew fifteen languages and their literatures and an Italian friend once asked 'Does he speak in monosyllables in all of them?' But he talked to me, and many of his sayings I still remember, and so do many of his friends – did, I should say, for this was all long ago! Wavell too was no talker, and once told me that he would give almost anything for the capacity of a little 'drawing-room chitchat'.

The earthquake began here quite quietly, only the lamps and little tables moving horizontally, and then – even last night – we go on with tiny quivers. The Friuli people have asked to be allowed to rebuild their own houses – full of strength and courage and wading through government help as if it were froth. I hope it isn't.

All luck, Paul, in Oklahoma.[185] Do write and tell me about it. You will have all the emotions of the Election year?

FREYA

JOHN GREY MURRAY   Alanya
                                                2 June 1976

Dearest Jock,

I got here safely yesterday – so nostalgic a drive, seven hours from Smyrna, now hugely overgrown. But we came out among the soft Ionian hills, saw the small remembered airfield a baby now in the landscape, saw the Seljuk citadel, Byzantine walls and Ephesus below, and then up the Maeander valley first travelled when there was no road but only the railway twenty-four years ago. Now it is asphalt and the villages have been turning into towns and the edges of the valley, the strange decayed ridges eaten by the ages of sandstone gritting on sandstone, are almost hidden by the luxuriance of this most fertile of valleys, like a Titian woman in its full maturity: crowded plantation, fig trees and peaches and maize and poplars and willows and houses with roofs only showing besides their running streams. And the ways I had travelled were as I once saw them but richer now with all those acquired years – Nysa and Aphrodisias left and right, till we came out into ampler lines and wider pastures and Maeander a flowing river

[185] Where he was going as Writer-in-Residence at the University.

265

already winding in serpent curves. We came over the highlands, by Burdur where I once found a train at four in the morning, across the stone hills to where the plain opens and the Antalya mountains rise in their incredible majestic tumult from the sea. But Antalya itself is a large ugly seven-storeyed city I have no wish left to stay in, and Alanya too (I now am looking down on it from a climbing garden of the old Greek citadel) has now grown away from beauty though the Taurus surrounds it with its great bay. The McGhees were so kind and sent a car all those seven hours to meet me, and have this house that climbs uphill filled with bits of furniture and sculpture and ceilings from Phoenician, Greek or Roman, anyhow.

No more now, but a bathe.

Love,
FREYA

JOHN GREY MURRAY   Bodrum
                                               10 June 1976
Dearest Jock,

I am writing by moonlight: a little sunset comes into it, but it really is the moon, almost round, filling the bay. The place has become a little more elegant – blue cotton for the waiters – and naturally more expensive, but a warm welcome: kisses from the hostess and the washerwoman, the children two years taller and that climate of civilisation which goes down to the poorest and one seems to lose between the Mediterranean and the Celtic fringe of Dartmoor and Scotland. It was a marvellous drive up from Alanya: the mountains with clouds like fighting dragons, snow on the tallest; the Maeander showing its perfect valley-shape, gathered in a basin so wide you might call it a plateau, except for the high prison lines of the barriers that hem it; then gradually the valley forms (below the lake where the flute was invented), still very wide and lush, and every plant seeming to grow into a tree, and the river rolling down smooth and mostly invisible, carrying its history and with it the memories I took there twenty-four years ago. It all looks more prosperous now in spite of crisis, the industrial age coming with a natural Turkish untidiness that makes a ruin of a building just begun!

Your letter with the review reached me before I left; thank you for sending. I feel it was meant most kindly, but to put two long paragraphs of one's own notions on death as an introduction is enough to put off any reader. I tried it on my hosts and saw the sad result. Surely the reviewer ought to have learnt by now that the photographer's light should be on the object and not on himself? Do you remember Harold Nicolson's gay and charming

266

reviews? Oh goodness how long ago. Meanwhile I must go swimming while I can.

Love,

FREYA

SYBIL, LADY CHOLMONDELEY   Bodrum
11 June 1976

Dearest Sybil,

I have been seeing such lovely 'old, remembered things' – some not seen since 1952 – and I thought of you as I went along, wishing you were here and not walking about those loved rooms of Houghton with trouble and fatigue not really due to our years.

When I got to Alanya my hostess was ill and being taken off to Istanbul and I had a week with two charming girls full of ardour and quite unaware that life is difficult, and no Turkish except mine (very poor now) to rely on. But the maids were of the old sort, in tears when their mistress departed, and she recovered so that I met her by staying an extra day. They have arranged an old Greek house on the castle slope, with the headlands of Taurus as a view, and all sorts of pots etc. from Minoan and earlier which Mr. McGhee is allowed to collect by promising not to export. The staircase is old wood and old ceilings above it, and it all feels as if washed up from time and sunning itself on its old slope. There must have been a Roman ribbon development along this coast.

I have been bathing – to everyone's surprise; it seems not to be done after eighty. This bay is held with a narrow opening in easy slopes, and the wall attacked by Alexander climbing just out of sight behind windmills, and three camping grounds that are as quiet as can be, being Turkish (as are all the people in this only hotel). I am here till early July and then by Istanbul to Greece, ending with Leigh Fermors I hope, and Asolo before the end of July.

Love, dear Sybil,

FREYA

COLIN THUBRON   Bodrum
18 June 1976

Dear Colin,

How pleasant to be reading your letter here in a quiet bay where people come to enjoy themselves and to think that our friendship is maturing like

267

wine. I am losing a lot of old friends – not so much age, as most were younger than I am (Patrick Kinross for instance), but just vicissitude, a word that seems to me to give just the feeling it expresses – a jumble of the unmanageable consonants of life.

The main point of my plans is that I hope to be in Asolo before the end of July, and long for friends in the tower; and meanwhile I go here and there. The Alanya coast with its skeleton of mountains is overwhelming as ever; forms so tightly packed, as if the *feeling* of the Himalayas had to be got into a small suitcase for travel. Nothing wilder than the mountains west of Antalya – and a city of jerry-built skyscrapers to face them. Here my little solitary bay, so gently embraced in its brown hills, is turning into a resort, but with a few years still to go if you avoid July–August. In fact I like this atmosphere of quiet bourgeois who have worked hard for their fortnight's holiday; and what one notices coming from Italy is a complete exclusion of *violence* – none of that Renaissance feeling so interesting to read about and so hopeless to live in. I am wondering by the way what is happening at this moment in that poor country. What is so strange here, as in Greece, is how the vividness of life comes through these hills that are as brown as the coats of lions and with the same sort of power that strangely expresses itself.

Do write Asolo and tell me news.

Love,
FREYA

EDWIN KER
Bodrum
1 July 1976

Dear Edwin,

Your letter finds me here (just), as I leave tomorrow to go slowly home – Izmir, Istanbul, Greece – by end of July. I am sorry about the hip; mine too hurts a little after exercise, not enough to matter but I will ask about it when I get back. To my great joy the swimming doesn't trouble it and I can now do 1,200 (gentle) strokes a day. Have you thought of this exercise, if you can find it anywhere nearby? (Must not be very cold however.)

I am here trying to make up my mind between three languages. I feel that one of them could still be my companion if a few more years are left – but they all need to be recovered with some months' study and a visit now and then; and it is a difficult choice. Turkey has this lovely sea but no great literature I long to read; Arabic I think would be easiest and I would read the Koran all over again with deep delight; and Persian offers Saadi and Hafiz

268

which I have never read. Almost as difficult as the choice of Paris: I love all three countries and peoples. Life is just rather short!

Love, dear Edwin.

FREYA

EDWIN KER
Kardamyli
24 July 1976

Dear Edwin,

I get home in three days' time (unless there are strikes or a Turko-Greek war in the way), and hope to find better news of you. It is very like travelling in and out of crises in 1939 – only that one is older.

Paddy Leigh Fermor is giving last touches to his book[186] – a journey at eighteen from England on foot to Istanbul. We talk of titles and I am saying that 'journey' is not a good word now for a *walk*; and that 'winter journey' suggests age: it is the heart inside and not the time of year that counts.

I have had such a happy nine days here above their rocky little creek opening to the Peloponnesian Sea. The third prong shows when the light becomes manageable at sunset – a high rounded hill hiding Pylos and the bay of Navarino somewhere near. Their house is loved and lovely, full of cats and books and stone benches under olive trees, each with a separate view. When the sea is calm, the cook and gardener husband fish for little fish. Even the shadows, the olives more particularly, are full of light.

I hope you are better, dear Edwin. Not at all sure you ought to do housework.

Love,
FREYA

JOHN GREY MURRAY
Castle of Mey,
Caithness
14 August 1976

Dearest Jock,

This is a sort of fairy-tale expedition and I am in the enchanted castle looking out to the Orkneys — a perfectly fine still day yesterday and the whole of the Royal Family to lunch and tea. They left the *Britannia* and came driving over this quiet countryside that slopes with a wonderfully gentle peacefulness into the sea, with sheep of an almost incredible fatness

---

[186] *A Time of Gifts.*

(to anyone used to the Italian kind) browsing almost to the water's edge. One has the feeling of a landscape almost basic coming down from the days of that old captain who described the North to King Alfred. The Royal Family, wonderfully polite and easy, with the youngest members handing cups and glasses, and even Hanover represented by a charming German-speaking pair. They had left the *Britannia* to turn the northern corner while they came to visit the Queen Mother. Our houseparty is all young except me, and I was put between Prince Philip and Prince Charles, both easy and pleasant to talk to and the latter launching out so readily into the Abstract that I offered him a volume of *The Peak* straightaway. It is most fascinating to be given as it were a foresight of the future in the hands of these young people who will be busy with this island's future when we have gone.

They left after tea and came sailing by as near shore as is possible, and we greeted their passage with rockets while they replied. The *Britannia* a lovely yacht and its sailors aligned on deck as they passed along in front of the Queen Mother.

I was writing in my room and must go down now, but thought you would like to hear about this memorable day.

All love,

FREYA

PAUL SCOTT   Asolo
                                                    1 September 1976
Dear Paul,

I came away from London as usual with half my good and pleasant intentions unfulfilled, and people I had hoped to see unseen, and you among them – and I had not heard and am sorry to hear of your divorce. One can't go through that without a tearing of the heart past or present; I hope it is the former, because then you will have the reward of the wonderful feeling of liberty: it is like the sight of your climb below, when you have reached your mountain top. I hope it will come to you. It is like a key that opens all doors; I am still happy with it after twenty-five years. I have now and then a Puritan scruple that one ought not to be made happy by mere elimination, but this is not a real feeling: the reality is the good and varied world, the delight of the unexpected. How ungrateful we are for the *unknown*; how sad a world it would be if we could see round every corner. There are many good contrary arguments, I know; but you must let me break a lance in favour of the unexpected.

Meanwhile you are no doubt surrounded by it in Oklahoma and this is really to wish you a good stay there. I hope it will not be too far for Volume III to reach you and am sad if it takes away my best reviewer.

All luck,

FREYA

JOHN GREY MURRAY   Asolo

20 September 1976

Dearest Jock,

I have just had a week's visit from the charming Morrises who were so kind to me when dumped on them by Francis in Cairo. I took them up to the tower and they promptly left Kamener and the hotel and picnicked there and left early this morning, just missing a Sheikh Abdulla who says he was a friend in Wadi Du'an just forty-one years ago. He and his wife are driving over tomorrow to lunch and I am going to the Cipriani to see that we get them a suitable menu; I am so pleased to be able to give Kamener and all the waiters such a new guest. But I am reaching the age when it is either work or conversation but not both.

Love,
FREYA

JOHN GREY MURRAY   Asolo

5 October 1976

Dearest Jock,

Sue Pugh, whom I insist on calling Susie, spent a very cheerful weekend to discuss our possible programme for the B.B.C.'s 'The World About Us' – with Venice and the opening of its new (regional) university, Evelyn and her Futurist Villa and a Sunday here with the really so charming talk of Anthony Hobson, wife, and daughter. He told us the *dreadful* story of Evelyn Waugh's review copy (I think) of Cyril Connolly's book – *The Unquiet Grave* was it? – and Connolly finding the most hideous things referring to himself inside it – thinking too that it came from a friend. I wonder if Evelyn W. ever thought he had a friend?

I gave Susie six countries to choose from and our common choice is the raft down the Euphrates (easiest too for me) and possibly with Mark and

271

wife to join. It is up to her to solidify this vision, and I will be seeing how I get on along the edge of things in Yemen in November. The young are always ready and their risk is a lifetime; after eighty it isn't much more than a year or two anyway. Why should *anyone* hesitate? I am thinking of it with pleasure and hope it comes off.

Awful weather here and a little tremor they call mere 'assessment' now and then.

Love, dear Jock,

FREYA

MICHAEL RUSSELL Asolo
6 October 1976

Dear Michael,

It is a fine Volume III. Caroly's copy has come and I hope Dr. Hofmeyr[187] will be bringing some for me. Meanwhile I have been looking at Caroly's: how skilful Lucy has been with Miss Caton Thompson;[188] one is just getting a bit tired of her when the good open world restores sanity. It seems to me that the end bit comes to a fine climax of opening war?

The *Peak* has had two perfect reviews and others medium. We however have a four-page letter from the Queen Mother written in her own neat charming hand with ER top and bottom. She says she is reading only one or two letters a day to make them last longer.

May all go well, dear Michael, as we go on with all these storm clouds round us. I hope to start early November for a month in Yemen.

FREYA

MRS. ALAN MOOREHEAD London
17 October 1976

Dearest Lucy,

My flight to Damascus is fixed for 7th November. It seems rather touch and go with Syria, and a sadly familiar state of disorder to travel through,

---

[187] Dr. John Hofmeyr had kindly offered to take out copies to F.S. when he went to Italy on holiday.

[188] The archaeologist whom F.S. had accompanied on a contentious expedition in the winter of 1937–8 in Southern Arabia. The letters for that period were somewhat acerbic on the subject of Miss Caton Thompson, and F.S.'s views seemed not to have mellowed over the years. Lucy Moorehead, making her plea for editorial restraint, added that Miss Caton Thompson was after all still alive. 'Typical,' F.S. replied.

but *Allah Kerim*! there is nearly always one country out in the Middle East, and this is a trial run for me to see how I travel, as the B.B.C. are doing a television. A nice girl came out to organise it and we decided on a trip by raft down Euphrates as a background, I take it in March or April whenever the river-current is suitable.

> Death closes all; but something ere the end,
> It may be we shall touch the Happy Isles,
> And see the great Achilles, whom we knew.

I remember coming upon this poem and being enchanted when I was about ten years old and quite unable to understand it – but I do now, after seventy-three years!

Hugh Honour and John Fleming were here from Lucca. Tell me, how is Tommy?

Love,

FREYA

EDWIN KER

San'a

13 November 1976

Dear Edwin,

I left Asolo on the 7th and had no news of you for quite a time and do hope all is well. I flew to Damascus in the present squalid manner, but there suddenly revived: those bleached, sun-drenched hills lifting the bright new houses on their shallow slopes; the new buses, bright blue, taking pilgrims day and night to the pilgrimage and Mecca; the poverty and riches and the feel of a world in which there is room for all – it came back as if there were no forty-eight years in between.

How hard it was to get to the East in those days. And now, as I stayed two days at the Embassy, a bevy of young men and maids came to dinner all lodged for the winter in various Arab houses to learn the language and the ways. One thing can make us happy about this world in which we grow old: there is far more mixing, a feeling forgetful of barriers, than there was in our youth (not that I ever felt any particular barrier, but lots of people did).

In Yemen too the changes are coming and the incredible landscape remains – but this is merely to send my love and wishes for Xmas and ever, and to tell you I should be back in Asolo by December 8th for news.

Love,

FREYA

San'a
16 November 1976

My dear Anita,

It is strangely happy to be here, living my old days (thirty-six years ago) in an unreal way as if in a landscape seen through water. I can no longer *do* much, but am taken by car sometimes on sometimes off the new roads (Chinese) to look at the hills beyond hills, the blue ridges behind their long sandstone cliffs that look as if Titans had laid them in long terraces of stone. In the arms of this fierce landscape are the terraces of millet and maize and the little square one-room houses crowded round their towers and fine palaces, all cut from the mountain side and ready for defence; the tall houses beautiful with decorated windows, the little ones with their (often) only door as an opening, painted; and the whole looking like a bit of the armoured earth to which it belongs.

The people too belong to the fierce land, breaking into friendliness but with an expression not naturally smiling. They are small, with faces coming rather triangular to a pointed chin, very different from the Arabs I know more. The country women are still veiled: even the littlest girls come from school in the villages with a black band from chin to eyes – but free enough otherwise. I have only been out twice for any distance, and sit in the lovely garden with its old earth walls and two or three of the beautiful old houses in sight around it, and try to read my Koran. A blind lad comes to teach me – no good as teacher, but I get back into the spoken language: it is thirty-three years since I have used it and very rusty. But all the few English here talk it, mostly very well, and it is nice to be back in the gossip of the East. The economics of this land are very strange. A large part of the people go to work among the rich Saudi Arabians where a labourer makes over £15 a day. *Après nous le déluge.*

Dearest love,

FREYA

Nr. Zabid,
Yemen
29 November 1976

Dearest Sybil,

I must write you a little note, just to tell you that you are the only one of my contemporaries who would, I believe, enjoy this journey. What fun it would be to have you here! As it is I am being most kindly looked after by two young diplomats, Hugh Leach and John Shipman, and am now sitting quietly on a house-roof in a village. A wide land, mostly sand desert dotted with little flat-topped trees that I remember, stretches to the sea, and the inland mountains through which we came down are hidden in the warm damp cloud that floats up from the water. I came up here in 1940 in a lorry, six days from Aden to San'a before the Chinese and Russians had built their roads. But there are not many and we have been bounced about in and out of coastal villages built of reeds and bushes round, and their roofs all pointed, so that they look like a sort of embroidery against the sky; and when one drives through them, each in its little brushwood enclosure, with dogs, cats, camels, goats, sheep all about, one suddenly realises that our lives are made rather barren by the lack of *animals* about us. We camped in places as far from villages as we could, but even so there were strips of plough, maize or millet here and there. A kid was bought and cooked for supper, but the second night a little white one with odalisque eyes, dreadfully appealing, was brought and began to make friends and it was really impossible to eat it. I don't think one can make such a huge gap between us and other creatures, do you? Only by not seeing or anyway talking to an animal can one think of it as food. So we had a meal of eggs, much better for us, and the little white kid is here in the compound with other animals, though I doubt if its life will be long. I have done my best with the driver and pointed out to him that it is a 'guest'.

My Arabic is imperfect but coming back and good enough to make me wish to have it better; the women of the house come up to have a chat. The roof has a thick whitewashed wall all round it: one can stand tiptoe and just look out, but there is a pattern of little square holes worked in the mud of which it is built, so that one can look out and not be seen. It has shade, and a lovely soft air, and the sea-clouds travelling up towards the hills; and falcons floating about on their big wings and dipping down to see if I am alive. I am so happy to be here and grateful to the two young men who put up with me and introduce me as grandmother.

All love, and please write to Asolo after Xmas.

FREYA

MRS. ALAN MOOREHEAD   Damascus
                                                        6 December 1976

Dearest Lucy,

Am waiting here for Susie who is due tomorrow. The television plan is going ahead — it sounds as if the Syrians want to be in on it, and last night at the Italian Embassy I met the engineers of a paper mill on the Euphrates of all things, with an Italian from Vicenza. They are ready to produce charts of all the ups and downs of the river, and to welcome us with an apéritif as we pass. I have also heard of an archaeologist in Aleppo who might keep an eye on the raft builder – the most tricky bit of the plan *I* think. Anyway, there it is: I am in the hands of the young and am glad to have a little swan-song in that chorus – a new, ominous, but interesting world opening and it is lovely still to be wanted by this tough and yet untried generation. I can't imagine anything better than this fancy journey to end up with – I really think I will have to rest when it is all over.

We ended in Yemen with a glorious week, camping out in the north, where the flocks came out from their little pointed rush villages to graze round us in the dawn – and then south to stay with Hugh's driver in the country which I crossed in 1940, sticking at intervals in the sand. We saw Mocha and the Governor's tower where I had a strange adventure so long ago. How one ever got over that country before Land Rovers were invented I can't think: we used then to roll wire netting to pull out of the sand. The last three days were given to the Feast of Sacrifice and the wedding of the driver's daughter combined. Both Hugh's friend and I collapsed under the strain of so many little immolated kids and lambs and goats and I think seriously of becoming vegetarian: all those patient little creatures taught to expect nothing but kindness from human beings and led off like the September Massacres with the mild eyes of their little groups following them into darkness. The little bride too, just fourteen, was led in with her face covered and a brocade cover over head and shoulders, the black veil all wet with tears and her fevered little hands limp when I pressed them. And yet the old women who survive it all have a wonderful serenity.

We slept on the roof in this hospitable home with a little wall *just* sufficient for modesty between us, and the wonderful procession of the stars, immense and so grandly moving, above. I saw for the first time how Orion had to be called the Hunter: he was trying to get at the Great Bear across us all the night till he sank into his horizon and the dawn came with its swift southern speed.

I don't think I shall do much of this again, dearest Lucy: it is a strain (eighty-four next January) – but it was very good. I think with joy of your coming and send this to Porto Ercole with Xmas love to you all.

FREYA

Asolo
                                                            13 December 1976

Dear Hugh,

It all seems like a beautiful dream, those weeks in Arabia: they grow
as I think about them and have a strange living quality as if I could go back
again and again and find them living as ever. My little goat, the beauty of
the stars (*hours* of night spent looking up into them), the nice kind women
and the little bride, and you and John and Mubarak all so thoughtful for
this aged traveller. I came away very much touched and happy, and prepared to go on as long as Time allows to see and be a burden to my friends.
The journey back was an anticlimax – Italy wrapped in a sort of funeral
garment of fog, but not so my own view which shines in sun and is as good
as when I left it. I hope you will see it in 1977 and I send you all best wishes.

I had a great emotion flying back just south of the shoal of the small
Greek 'rocky' islands that, by some trick of light, were shining white as
foam in the sun. The mainland cliffs too were white and the sea smooth
blue, and it all looked alive as if playing a game in a private sea. We will
have to carry this Greek civilisation through somehow: one can't do without
it.

                                                            Love,
                                                            FREYA

Asolo
                                                            11 January 1977

My dear Susie,

How splendid, your letter just come. You can't think how delighted I
am with it all and give you full marks for everything, and especially for
getting £15,000 out of the Syrian Government. You are quite right: they are
old experienced bargainers and can see that this may be the first link in a
happy series of 'tourism', an opening of peaceful intercourse with decent
people. Golden Age on the Euphrates!

I next want to congratulate you on the raft. How splendid to find a model
– I agree, better to have it made in Syria if you can find the expert for the
model. Is it a *kilik* or a *shahtur*? (I will recognise the shape if you give its
name.) It sounds as if you think of those poor horses *swimming* all the way,
but I rely on your kind heart. Do you think we could have a plan drawn
beforehand, chiefly because of the distribution for living on it? i.e. they like
to tuck one into an almost air-proof shelter to sleep and it may well be hot: a

little canopy of dry *leaves* which lets the air through and gives shade by day (as well as view) is essential, with just a more private corner for dressing (they don't undress so it is only us). Give me the dimensions too; and tell me how much luggage I can take – with a suitcase at base perhaps.

I loved to read what you felt in the first impact of that magic world; it made me feel young again and I recognised it all – that first view of camels at large, and the tawny hills. You are enslaved for life, my dear Susie. And I am so happy to see it all over again through your eyes and to find them in their views the same.

I am working to get my poor forgotten Arabic into shape and might go out to Damascus a fortnight earlier to practise it. And am also looking for quotations. If you can get my *Rome on the Euphrates* I have marked pages with quotations here and there. The two great Roman journeys were Trajan and Julian and I will collect what may be relevant.

Let me hear more, dear Susie, and go ahead; you are well on the road. I like the idea of concentrating on 'transit' as a subject: it opens every door. There must be a caravan and caravanserai and a desert night with Beduin; and shops and towns, and no European groups; their tourism can come later! But I am not concentrating on the speaking till I have prepared more reading. Poor old brain!

Love, dear Susie,

FREYA

MME ANITA FORRER   Asolo
                                                  11 January 1977
My dear Anita,

Such a strange and happy thing has happened to me and I am going to try and tell you, for you are the only one of my friends left who would understand what I try to say. It happened as I lay in bed between waking and sleep a few mornings ago, and I was suddenly *freed from myself.* I can't describe it, because I think we have no words for it. I was afloat in a pleasant vague atmosphere of light and gossamery clouds and I was without a self. I was a part of everything: indeed not a *part* for that too would have a contour. I *was* everything and nothing. It was freedom and unity and a ravishment so indescribable that even now it lies upon my world like infinity, a garment which for some moments I wore. It faded imperceptibly away as I lay there, and left me filled with an inexpressible gratitude, and is for me a complete answer to that question of personality which teases us with doubt: there was no personality, but a ravishment beyond it.

You must not think, dear Anita, that I am given to such things. Many years ago when I was fifteen or so, one such came over me: I had gone out in the summer moonlight on the moors, and the same sort of rapture enveloped me so that I thought 'I need never worry about anything again'; but then, to my sorrow, the memory of what happened vanished and I can remember only the effect but not the cause. This is why I write it now because it too may fade, but the certitude of that rapture will remain and take away from me all fear of solitude or death. So I would like you to know, dear Anita.

Love,

FREYA

MME ANITA FORRER   Asolo
24 January 1977

My dear Anita,

Both your letters are here together and what you say about my vision is such a comfort. I feel all the time what a great gift that was – to have an answer one can believe in, to the question of questions. I shall go dancing to my death and, dearest Anita, I hope this happy certitude will help you too, for we now share it. I have just come upon a quotation which says that the human race makes the main mistake of building on *past* and not on *future*. This goes very deep I believe, and is true of our religions: the Muslim goes a little way by omitting the personal effigy of God, but even there, and much more so in Christianity, and even in the Indies, there is always a *separateness* which builds a universe which is human but not divine. A revelation is always given by us as if it were *final*, as if it could be final when we human beings know how young we are in our world, with the pattern only just started and (unless we destroy it all) with the future stretching immeasurably before us. How *could* we have a final view any more than dog or horse who are only a few steps behind? Only, or almost only, the late Greek Christians held that we ourselves are part of the moving Divinity; at least, many must have felt but not expressed it. That indescribable happiness is like a talisman to hold against all troubles.

Do come in March!

Love,

FREYA

279

My dear Susie,

I am really very troubled about your programme, because it is something quite different from what I had understood and something I am not able to do except with many weeks' preparation (and wouldn't do anyway). What I had understood was: the raft expedition with *conversation* as the landscape went by, pointing out this or that as it caught our eye – but not a sort of Baedeker which requires condensed and accurate information in a rather boring form. I take it the film is for an hour; and with fourteen places to film it is roughly four minutes for each place – some more, some less.

What I had thought is that we would start from Birecik and go along talking of the *theory* of the Romans' wars of Mesopotamia. Have you got my *Rome on the Euphrates*? It contains all I know about this country, and I could read bits or mug them up – to accentuate the main events (the Battle of Carrhae and desert war; the descent of Trajan to his crossing from Euphrates to Tigris, and description of his boats, etc., and the main theme – the Emperor Julian, slipping down to defeat and death). Small details, like Zenobia founding Halebiya, or Risafe in the desert (I see you have not included), or the Greek civilisation in Doura, could all be slipped in casually as the landscape went by; but the main line would be a half-hour talk on what Rome felt she was doing there, while the visual details of the landscape would go by unexplained.

What I had been thinking of as a plan was to open on Asolo and its landscape and close that preface with me walking down our old street and opening my front door ('Nothing like home,' I could say to the audience); and then have either my terrace or sitting room and us over our drinks discussing the place. You would give the programme, and I would say that what I had thought and prepared was slightly different and more of a conversation, with the landscape slipping by but not (except once or twice) specifically referred to. I would say that the spectator must be trusted to enjoy the landscape, and the producer must enhance it with a living interest, and I had thought of five human beings (if we go to Carrhae) to make this river and Palmyra *live*: 1) the first, Alexander, whose ghost hangs there like a shadow, crossing at Zeugma; 2) Carrhae and the story of the battle (my book, p. 114); I have been told it is the best description of the tragedy and I might read it out? – it has I think the feeling of that desert edge; 3) Trajan taking his fleet down the stream to the crossing for Ctesiphon and the breaking up of his dream – dreamed no doubt when he stood in the room where Alexander died (we could discuss why one succeeded and the other failed?); and 4) our last of Euphrates – the Emperor Julian, his strange sad character and defeated death; and 5) when we come to Palmyra, the portrait, fascinating, of Zenobia.

Love,

FREYA

SUSAN PUGH
British Embassy,
Damascus
5 April 1977

Dear Susie,

All well so far and the most beautiful sunset ever seen over the hills of Crete; they were holding in their arms stretches of sea – the purest gold. After that we plunged into an unnatural darkness and found Damascus being pelted with rain. A man from the Embassy and a very nice television man – Costandi Hamati – were there to meet me; James Craig[189] was off to a Bulgarian dinner party and left me with a charming woman journalist; and this morning I am taking it easy in the garden enjoying the desert air. The Arabic gets along, incorrect but just enough for conversation.

The news of the raft is fine and all are full of admiration for your organising. Costandi tells me that it will be 'quite easy' to lift the Ark over the dam! (They will have to do this of course if they want to make it a tourist proposition.) He also said happily that the man who takes us has never steered a raft before and this is to be the first that ever was on Euphrates; and it is wonderful to find again this happy Arab attitude to the unknown which on the whole succeeds. Must send this – so looking forward to all your arrivals and grateful for so much care.

FREYA

JOHN GREY MURRAY
Hotel Baron,
Aleppo
9 April 1977

Dearest Jock,

All seems well so far and I am here till the 22nd when all the company arrive, and giving all time and energy to the Arabic while I have the chance. Its old charm comes back without a wrinkle: it is made out of the charm

189 The British Ambassador.

of the people themselves, their politeness, their easy way with life, taking all its trials with a patience hardly recognised as patience, it so pervades the thousands of years behind them. Two most efficient lady-journalists have interviewed me (and the second one was in Arabic for better or worse) and a charming young man, enthusiast for his language, gives me two hours a day which stretch to four and leave me *finished*. He says the shapes of the letters have been made to follow the mouth's shape as it speaks them: it is only the Arabs that I have known to play with their language in this way.

When Easter is over I shall begin to revisit the bazaar, and a few old people whom I remember. It is thirty-eight years since I came down here from the mountains, to hear of Donald's[190] death before our own war started, and it is all still vivid though the pain has gone. The city has grown, but still lies on its green slope in a curve of the white stone that makes it beautiful. I brought a little present of Asolo weaving to Koko,[191] the Armenian and his English wife who keep this hotel which the Government has taken from him and he now keeps for them! It had a splendour in its day and still has fine proportions and things that were beautiful and old servants go tottering about it and quiet travellers come through it, and it feels as if straight out of a Balzac novel. Koko's house is close by and had an Armenian circle celebrating Easter, and it was the same old East of knots of people gathered into their own groups amid the general welter. I feel very old, coming back into it all after fifty years!

Love,

FREYA

MRS. ALAN MOOREHEAD   Aleppo
25 April 1977

Dearest Lucy,

That raft has slowly materialised out of all those years when Hubert Young[192] first talked to me about it. Years passed and then I was travelling between Tigris and Euphrates, and a raft-builder and I agreed on the raft and I came back to Birecik on the appointed day and the river had sunk so low as to be dangerous with its pointed rocks to the goatskins on which the raft was floating; and so it had to be given up. More years passed and I told

[190] sc. Lennox-Boyd.
[191] Koko Mazloumian.
[192] Sir Hubert Young, the distinguished Arabist, and his wife Rose had been friends of F.S. from the early '30s.

this story to Susie when she wanted the list of countries to travel in, and we both chose a second try with the raft. And now it is *built* and ready to start day after tomorrow from a little cove below Birecik where Leonard Woolley dug at Karchemish and the Taurus Express crosses the river just below the ancient mound. I have not yet seen the production as they want my ecstatic expression to be roused for the camera when all is ready, and we still walk about bargaining in Aleppo in crowds which show that TV is still new. We have a pleasant friendly team, three for the camera, Colin[193] and Susie chiefs, Mark and Arabella,[194] three Arab drivers to run along the shore road (out of sight), a charming Palestine Christian, and a finance man from Syrian TV — all full of friendliness and optimism, and my Arabic has now returned, not to perfection but good enough for ordinary talk. While the rest went yesterday to see the boat in its cove, Arabella and I drove to St. Simeon and had a lovely morning looking out over the country I had ridden over in a long-ago spring. I think it was 1939, and my heart so sad for Donald, but the beauty of it all came back to me, the strange landscape of hills all turned to rock by the wasting of the good earth away from them to the fertile plain below and only their mass of flowers left there in the rocky cracks where the horse stepped carefully from hole to hole. All this land south of Antioch is starred with flowers and the clouds roll down from the north and are rebuffed by the desert air.

I must go down and send this. I feel I shall need a rest when the film is finished and will go to Asolo and on to London later, I think about last week of June.

Hurried letter, forgive: and all love dear Lucy. How is the new Caroline baby?

FREYA

Jerablus on the Euphrates
30 April 1977

JOHN GREY MURRAY

Dearest Jock,

Such a sad story. The raft too beautiful and a wonderful welcome when we drove up by the little sandy hills which surround it, and found a huge crowd massed on all their summits, clapping their hands as they saw us. The raft looked very cosy and just like its picture, opening over rush matting and a layer of dry hay, with my little raised apartment (one room with a loo) at the back and three armchairs in front. We decided to sleep there, and the

---

[193] sc. Luke.
[194] sc. Lennox-Boyd.

sun went and the crowd dispersed and we were really rather happy and slept wrapped in sleeping bags and warm, while the great river tossed its waves past us at great speed, pushing us more and more into our little inlet and rising round us as the clouds massed up in the direction of Iraq. At about 5 a.m. I woke up and thought the pleasant clucking notes of the waves much louder, and looking out, saw the hay and matting on our north-west corner submerged and a lisping of water all over it. I waited to finish doing my hair and then thought better to call to Arabella and Mark and we watched the little corner getting slowly more submerged. The details of this squalid story are too long to tell you, but anyway by that evening we decided to sleep here in the hotel (very clean and amiable and kept by a Circassian). The raft was stripped and we went down next morning across a subsidiary stream where a small crowd and three cars were gathered. The stream covered an asphalt road which had come to grief and split the rubber wheel of the last car across it (with a bit of iron girder) and the governor's order had come to suspend all traffic. The governor himself arrived, a plain but kindly elderly man, and listened unconvinced while one very nice A.D.C. explained the necessity for reaching the raft; and we were rather despondent when he seized my arm and said, 'Come, let *us* cross' – and so we did, shoes, stockings and all, the water not more than knee-deep and not too cold. Just over the hillock, with its crowd gathering, the poor raft lay with all the baggage on the bank beside it, a rather soppy wetness over everything and the rest of the morning spent stacking our woeful household into a police hut nearby. An old Russian launch and a little one beside it were there ready for anything, but the fact is that the river is more or less at its height and this is the third morning that begins bright and drifts into an evening storm. We spent the afternoon visiting a village on the bank of another subsidiary stream to look at the *shahtur*, the ferry-boats used to cross the river, and think of taking two of these and forgetting the raft which is obviously very shaky. (How often did I beg them to have some Western overseer at its construction?) It floats but tilts one end up if the current catches it.

Dear love,

FREYA

JOHN GREY MURRAY   Euphrates
                                                   4 May 1977
Dearest Jock,

My letter didn't get posted and now days have passed and the raft is sitting on the shores of the lake (dug out of this landscape about ten years ago). It is still giving us shade though all our luggage is sitting forlorn in the sun while motor transport seems to be lost along the one and only road and a lovely basket of fish bought this morning will soon be feeling the heat. The raft has been a great success in spite of being stranded five times (always in the middle of the river). If it had really floated on goatskins they would have been shredded to bits by now, but the oil-drums seem to have held and the only thing wrong was the timing, which of course the difficulty of coinciding with film production made inevitable. A fortnight or so ago the river would have been deeper and the raft would have floated without these hesitations; but in spite of all this the venture has been very successful and Mark and Arabella toy with the thought of it another year. The film people are pleased and feel they have got all they want and therefore it looks as if the dam just down the lake (if only these cars would come and take us to it) will be the end of this venture. We have got very fond of the raft; all Mark and Arabella's loving little bits and pieces have been stripped and the lake has been swishing over its edges with little biting noises as the Syrian launch (looking like a veteran gunboat) towed us across. The lake is fifty miles with low white gentle outlines round us. The raft really looks better without its ornaments and practically unsinkable, ready for any flood to overlap. It has given us three lovely evenings – Jerablus to Serai.

The moon has come to the full, silvery over these white hills. We had a camp on a field by the steep little stony path and all the village to see us: the women stand by themselves and make a lovely field of colour in the bareness and are most friendly, especially as I go up to the oldest, most wizened and tattooed and say 'We are the same age you and I.' This seems to be most popular with old and young!

The second night we spent under a great Arab castle which I had ridden to in 1939: no time this trip to go up, especially as one of our worst strandings was just below it in the twilight, and we slept very easily in the raft, and last night came down the valley that looks more like a plain to the northern shore of the lake.

7 May 1977

Another hold up, dear Jock, and in this interval we have been from the great dam to Aleppo, just time to see the friends there and on to Palmyra. After thirty-eight years I had the joy of seeing it more beautiful than ever – much of the old town dug over and what is left of its carved capitals and arches replaced and glowing, the white stone turned rosy like some of those yellow roses as if light were inside them.

The end of our journey was really the new dam, a look as it were into the future from all these landscapes of the past. It seemed in its own way to fit in with them, just a turn in the dreams of men. The Russian engineers who have built it would have been understood by the builders of Palmyra and it was beautiful too, lying in a great curve with the Euphrates spreading again among smooth sand banks. It comes down to these in nine smooth snakes of water that look like pure strength embodied, a sort of muscle of earth. The lake that makes it is nearly fifty miles long, still naked in its hills, which will no doubt have trees in twenty years or so.

We are now back in Damascus.

Love,

FREYA

MME ANITA FORRER Asolo

21 May 1977

My dear Anita,

I am just back and must tell you that all went well. I was spoilt by my own troop and petted by the Arabs, and handed up and down the steep places and on and off the raft as if I were very fragile porcelain, but I wasn't fragile at all and all the better for sleeping out (glad of warm sack and padded trousers), and quite ready for the extraordinary variety of the incidents that happened every day.

We got back with friendly feelings unspoilt by the small ups and downs of our days, and in fact we were all a very pleasant friendly company. I enjoyed the glimpse into an unknown art and its construction, very exciting there where the acts of man have left their most ancient traces. It is wonderful to look at panoramas in old age – I mean a view of things wide enough to combine their consequences with their causes. This procession so old and still continuing is like an easy chair where age gives us leisure to sit and watch the curtain, which will rise at any moment now and show us the reality of the play behind it. I thought of this as I sat on our raft stuck in the river with a wide expanse of racing water on every side of it: the young lads were saying they could swim in it, and so were the girls – but I knew I could not, and contemplated this with the absolute peacefulness produced by my dream; only I was glad that we had not after all taken the three horses on board! The little launch appeared beyond the shallow zone and threw a rope, and dragged us off with the grinding noise below which I will now always associate with gravel. The petrol tanks resisted – the ancient goatskins would have been torn to shreds and the ancients used to take huge supplies of them in reserve.

From the dam we returned overland to Palmyra, where I would like to linger for a fortnight just to draw. Then Aleppo, Damascus, a night with the Beduin in Jordan and home. On June 16 I fly to London for a fortnight, and then again in September to see the film; but otherwise quietly here I hope. Is there a chance of your coming? Or I might stop in September on the way or October on way back if you have an airfield near?

Dear love. Do send news.

FREYA

Asolo

24 May 1977

My dear Elizabeth,

I have just been shown a copy of your talk on Gertrude Bell and am writing, much moved, to thank you for the kind words with which you end. I am indeed happy in my women friends as well as men, and you are among them. I thought you did *brilliantly* and got all the essentials in their right proportion, so difficult in so short a space. She will always be fascinating to read about and I am sorry to have been just two years too late to see her in Baghdad. I used to hear a lot about her from the men there who had known her well – Ken Cornwallis, and Lionel Smith and Vyvyan Holt:[196] they all gave a picture of sadness in the last years when the war and her time of great usefulness was over and there were plenty of young Arabists about, eager to make their own way. The Foreign Office letters would be sent round so that she did not see them and V.H. told me that Faisal, in those last years, never once mentioned her name (no doubt she was too evidently on the stage for an Arab king). He also told me that the 'Office' often paid her dress bills without telling her (surely a charming trait in a Government office?). I used to feel that she could have been happy if she could have brought herself to retire from active politics and run her museum and all the building up of that ancient world which was then so exciting, and she would have been the person one visited for advice which needed never to be published or even admitted. But that is the feminine way of running the world and I think it is pleasant only to people who look on this life rather as a passage than a goal.

Dear Elizabeth, I hear tiresome news about your throat? And long to

195 Elizabeth Monroe, an old friend who had been with the Middle East Department of the Ministry of Information.

196 Captain (later Sir) Vyvyan Holt had been Oriental Counsellor at the British Embassy in Baghdad.

hear if you are on the Incense Road? I had one night in the great tent of Mut'ib ash-Sh'lan where four frontiers cluster round it and the camels were just moving from Jordan to Saudia. The desert air as good as ever and I found I still felt happy in the saddle and would like more of it.

Next year Volume V should come out with the letters from America. I showed them to my Texan friend and she says they are 'very tough' but should be published.

Love and all good wishes,

FREYA

EDWIN KER   Asolo
                                                                5 July 1977
Dear Edwin,

I am so glad of your two letters, one found on arrival two days ago and one this morning, and it is good of you to write and reassure me, for I was very sad thinking you more disabled than you are. I don't think we are very different in being *receivers*, only I have gone far afield to get a horizon clear of interceptions and this is perhaps more necessary to women whose lives are usually so tied and enclosed in other people's lives. If ever I write anything again it will be an essay on what is given to every living creature great or small: the midge and the elephant share it – and it is the *horizon*. Its width does not really depend on space, and it is lucky when one gets old to look at the infinite from one's own door; but the fascinating thing (to me anyway) is that the meaning of a horizon is that there is something beyond what he sees for *every living creature*. 'Et homo factus est' – but not surely the end; and that I think is why I could never *specialise* in any religion and think it more than steps on the way. It seems to me unreasonable to believe that the final explanation has been given when this world itself is so young with all its development before it?

I hope you will see the film of our raft at end of October. I will try and reach you then – but will you be in your cottage?

Love,
FREYA

GERALD DE GAURY   Asolo
                                                                9 July 1977
Dear Gerald,

That dinner in which I look forward to hearing the gossip of well over a generation should be in October: I hope to have a month in London from anyway the middle, as the film is promised for the last Sunday. I hope you will not be put off from inviting me by the fact that I look about 120 in the TV: every wrinkle part of the documentary, for which, they say, no beauty treatment is allowed. Truth is what the documentary goes in for. It does promise however to be a very amusing film as every mishap seemed *made* for photography.

I had no time for anything else in London. Sheikh Mut'ib Sh'lan turned up and had to be entertained; he brought along a pretty and quite inoffensive tart – modern progress.

I do look forward to a good gossip dear Gerald – and love meanwhile.

FREYA

MRS. ALAN MOOREHEAD   Asolo

14 July 1977

Dearest Lucy,

The R.G.S.[197] made me miserable as always beforehand but was charming when it came off. I left geography to the *four* experts who were lecturing on their explorings, and just gathered the thanks of my lifetime to that beloved Society which has always been a little Paradise for me – and thanked everyone from the early Presidents, Admiral Goodenough, Percy Cox (even Alan can't go back so far!), to the Secretary and Mr. Allen in the map-room, and ended by thanking those whom no one ever thanks – all the *animals* that have carried our desert burdens through our lives: long files of camels, mules, donkeys and horses. (English audience applauded and perhaps an Arab one would see the point, but wasted in Italy.) Anyway this was, I think, my last speech and it was lovely being in that atmosphere again. With Lord Hunt our new President (a most gaudy medal round his neck) and the young lecturers all out on their discoveries, I thought it would have been indelicate to lecture on the B.B.C. jaunt which can't be packed in with 'exploring'. So it goes dearest Lucy, and what a lot we have seen, good and bad.

Dear love to you all,

FREYA

[197] The Royal Geographical Society had invited F.S. to speak on 29 June. She had had a long and happy association with the Society during her travelling life, and had been awarded their highly prized Founder's Medal.

JOHN GREY MURRAY   Asolo
                                                      21 July 1977

Dearest Jock,

It seems impossible that three weeks have gone since I came back, and my desk not yet clear, and a sort of languor over us all with weather more like a damp summer in the West of Ireland than anything else I can think of.

All here, except expenses, seems static. Violence and speeches fill the gaps. We went up a mountain valley last Sunday amid a host of cars. Cipriani very expensive and very full. My teacher in Aleppo writes as one used to write to me fifty years ago: 'I do not know how this relationship of learning came between us, over so great a distance, but I discover that I lose my happiness when you are far away.' What a language, warming to the heart at eighty-four as ever! The feeling is there and why should one not know how to express it? W.P., in my youth, once signed himself 'Yours affectionately', and then added 'but affection is a *weak* word and love is strong.'

A little book has just been sent me by Ian Greenlees[198] from Florence with the speeches of our Anglo-Italian celebration at Lucca last year. I am writing for copies to distribute here among the Italians who seem to have forgotten that this was ever a united country.

Love always, dear Jock.

                                                          FREYA

T. DEUCHAR   Asolo
                                                      22 July 1977

Dearest Tommy,

It is nearly a month since I came back and I would like to have news of you. Lucy adds a little word to all her letters as to how you are, but she is I rather think on her way back and anyhow very crowded out with that growing family.

I flew back in great comfort as I had the happy thought to ask for a chair at Heathrow (that long walk nearly does me down). They asked me to give a reason for asking and I just said 'Eighty-four', which they understood at once and out of pure kindness put me in first class to a splendid lunch. So it must be BEA if you ever thought of coming, dearest Tommy, and all you need say is 'Ninety' and they might include champagne.

[198] Head of the British Institute of Florence.

All is well here, except that I have too much work: a few years ago it would not have felt like work at all! If all goes well I hope to be seeing you again by end of September, so keep well and bless you dear Tommy.

Your loving

FREYA

JOHN GREY MURRAY
Asolo

26 November 1977

Dearest Jock,

Safely back in my little refuge, though with a really alarmingly piled-up desk to greet me, and a feeling of remorse for that huge bag of this and that left for the poor La Valles[199] to bring. Rumour has it here that they may come in their *small* car, for which my belongings would be the last straw (if straw is a word for anything like my bag). I have asked them to call in at No. 50 and look at it, and, if they quail, do you think it could be sent by air as freight inside a large cellophane bag to discourage theft? How awful if La Valles did what everyone else is doing and went on strike? I have a beautiful Arab dress for her at Xmas, but if I told her now it would be a bribe. Do you know that with all my years in the East I don't think I have ever bribed anyone? It has always been some voluntary kindness and a present afterwards – the only civilised way!

England was a joy, and the sight of so many friends, but I do feel tired and probably unequal to travel on anything but a raft or possibly a little pony with a faithful retainer to organise every night's stop. Meanwhile the new maid has made my flat as clean as a new pin, and Caroly has a cold but is otherwise cheerful, and the world's disorder seems better in small places. It will be so wonderful if the Middle East peace is brought by Sadat – a brave man!

Love to you all.

FREYA

P.S. Mrs. Beach[200] has left me 500 dollars – so touching coming out of such a distance of past.

---

[199] The La Valles (she came from Asolo) periodically drove to Italy from London, and always kindly offered to bring packages to and fro for F.S.

[200] F.S.'s mother had spent the last year of her life staying with John and Lucy Beach in California.

Asolo
                                              26 December 1977
Dearest Jock,

Your little notes have been flittering in like butterflies and very welcome.
Nigel and Marie[201] turned up for a Cipriani Christmas and it has been very
pleasant in spite of my choosing the *festa* to be almost immobilised by
lumbago as well as everything else. I remember Vyvyan's advice so many
years ago which said that 'trotting is good for lumbago' and went up with
the Clives (but in a car) to see the Dolomites shining in a north wind, brilliant over snow. It is a lifting of the heart to me even to *look* at a mountain,
and there they stood row behind row, breathing in their sunshine.

It is tantalising: I keep on getting lovely ideas for new essays but the
effort of writing is at the moment beyond me – and in my next venture into
mortality I would like to be a painter!

Love, dear Jock, to you all,

                                                        FREYA

Asolo
                                              11 February 1978
Dearest Jock,

There are signs of the end because it now tires me to write even letters –
not a bit of hope for your little odds and ends of prose! But I am getting such
endearing words from friends – all stirred by television to reminiscence on
good days gone, so many of them, and all gone so quickly. Looking back on
it all I have no complaints, though eight very narrow escapes from death
by either accidents or illnesses. I am now just a bit tired and the dear conscientious doctor who does love me wants me to tell him exactly how long
it takes for irresistible sleepiness to come over me when writing letters: no
sign of it yet dear Jock but this letter may stop abruptly and you will know
what has happened.

Michael Russell is due to come out in ten days, so you may get rid of that
bundle of mine which disfigures your waiting room. It also has every bit of
clothing I really need, so do be firm with possibly Michael and otherwise
La Valles, who are due for Easter.

In spite of this calcification and what I believe to be an unavoidable war in
the Middle East, the plans for Aleppo in March still hold. Only true firmness

---

[201] Nigel Clive, 'my young p.g.' in Baghdad in the war, had had a special place in
F.S.'s affections.

could get conditions out of Israel which a people asked to give up their 1,300-year-old homeland (I am thinking of the Palestinian Arabs) could possibly accept. The question is fundamentally simple: one is morally uplifted by giving presents, but surely only if the present is one's own property and not someone else's? It is a constant surprise what ethical blindness seems to inspire reasoning as soon as it steps beyond the *defensive* in war.

Love, dear Jock,

FREYA

SIR MICHAEL STEWART   Asolo

12 February 1977

Dearest Michael,

I was just thinking of you when your letter came, and thinking what a long time it was since I had seen any of the family. I meant to reach Ditchley or rather Combe[202] and also see Oxford friends – Shuckburghs and Cecils and John Sparrow – but time just ran away and brought me here rather exhausted. Evelyn Lambert wanted me in Teheran for a regal party, but I was much too tired to move and you are quite right – it is a risk to look again at places loved long ago. Before this 'long ago' happens, do come over again with my goddaughter. I would like to give her a little treasure – an ivory-handled tiny parasol my great-grandmother must have used in an open carriage – and I *might* part to you with one of my two treasured Sung vases: it is so much a nicer feeling to give presents than to *leave* them (a poor word anyway).

I plan a quiet summer here but hope to be able to go for a month to Aleppo a month from now, if there is no war. I suppose the real tug is between Carter and the money-threat in U.S.A.? I can't see anything but war ahead and am glad to be old – though when you have children you must want to keep alive just to see them turn the corner.

Here the Italians are busy showing how Guelphs and Ghibellines managed each other in the Renaissance: amount of talk unbelievable and someone dead at every street corner. Dear love, dear Michael – do come, and we will go and look at a mountain from below.

FREYA

---

202 The Stewarts' address was now Lower Farm, Combe, near Newbury.

293

Asolo
                                          21 February 1978

Dear John,

   I am delighted to get your letter and I am wonderfully tempted by your suggestion of a week in Jedda. If my poor old physique – which is rather like your description of the Embassy car – stands up to it I hope to reach Aleppo about 20th March. Very soon after two Italian friends (one is Professor Pesce who has written the Jedda history you must have) are to visit Medain Salih which I have longed to do ever since my long romance with the Arab world began with reading of Doughty fifty-two years ago; and they suggest taking me by helicopter, an unworthy but I hope feasible affair. Would you have me on the way from Aleppo, somewhere about end of March? And could you use the remains of our Imperial power to get me a Saudi visa? If all this goes smoothly, I will hope to turn up in Damascus for a day or two and on to Hotel Baron in Aleppo and a little much-needed practice in Arabic until the Medain Salih trip takes shape and lets me stop in Jedda on the way. It makes me feel much stronger just to write down these names, and I hope all may be well in the good desert air, far better than any doctor's tonics.

   Hugh[204] seems to have managed to get into the thick of Middle Eastern complications. It all makes one feel when reading the early travellers as if they had been enjoying a rest cure.

   I hope to see you dear John and all luck to you meanwhile.

                                                    FREYA

Asolo
                                          26 February 1978

Dear Edwin,

   Your letter took just three weeks coming and that is about the normal time now – back I suppose to when the 'penny post' started? I was so glad of news and like to think of you in Bon Secours while your cottage must be buried in snow. Here it is mostly rain, with a few flakes half drowned here and there – a poor sort of winter, and I am now getting giddy (from those calcifying bones in neck) so that walks along the little hidden paths are more difficult: they say no one would know where to look for my body! Anyway, even a bad weather is better than none in a world slowly becoming all mechanic.

   [203] The Foreign Office friend who had been one of the party in F.S.'s Yemen journey in November 1976.
   [204] sc. Leach.

I enclose a little scrap. It is by way of putting my religion into as few words as possible for a Miss Spain who has been making an anthology of the religious ideas of her schoolgirls: most interesting, she says, and is now adding a collection of the old as well. I include my contribution; I think I should have added what I do believe, that we would have done better to make our Messiah a Messenger rather than a God (as the Muslims *did*). The Greek Fathers were on this road, and why I wonder did their great theologians come to an end so soon?

I like climbing books if they give what the author was made to feel apart from the technique – just as travel books must not *concentrate* on one's dinners and bodily distresses. But I have A. E. Housman's essay: I rather think W.P. sent it years ago, and it is splendid, I thought – then and now.

You will be getting back soon to your cottage I hope, and finding spring flowers. I enclose a little bunch from Monte Grappa, with love.

FREYA

SYBIL, LADY CHOLMONDELEY   Asolo
                                                        6 May 1978
Dearest Sybil,

I got back from Damascus late last night (airfield strike in Venice) and find your note and am very distressed about the wrist and what a month left-handed means to you at Houghton. But Sybil, one does get very *brittle*, you mustn't twinkle along so fast!

I have been practising semi-prudence and found a lovely little Arab mare in Aleppo. I made three days' little trial rounds and felt quite happy in the saddle and got two small proper rides on the hills that lie like the rise of a saucer round the bustling little chaos of the town and its citadel. So beautiful it all is, and the skyline goes gently rather like my Dartmoor, with hills in misty distances uncultivated and gentle. I trotted happily but felt prudent about a canter as the earth is all hard flattened stones.

I had two days in Damascus on the way home and went to see my friends of 1928 – no longer the gay young man of picnics among the gardens, but father of six *lovely* young women all at work in the American Secretariat, and one son, the youngest, just going in to be a lawyer. My friend, who was then a beautiful girl in her twenties, was there, and a charming beautiful wife at least twenty years younger than her husband. My Arabic has recovered just enough for a fairly easy conversation, so that I enjoyed this return to the past, with the whole impetus of Civilisation, not just money, behind it. The family used to live in their own Azm palace which is now a museum. I thought of you and Houghton as I wandered there, and how the spirit of man is the same and blossoms in such differences of loveliness.

My plans are quietly Asolo till mid-July and then I hope Turkey, but only its little coast-village and some bathing. Dear, dearest love and do please send news of your wrist.

FREYA

JOHN GREY MURRAY   Asolo

8 May 1978

Dearest Jock,

Life is like a Beauty, fascinating but exacting. I am back, happy to be in Asolo and even more so with my month in Syria, but rather overcome by the fact that there seem to be *two* films in the offing. You seem to know all about C.B.S. and Susan Stratton says she is telephoning on 15th; but I have no idea of what they think of doing. I have a really good subject in hand, the old Byzantine summer ruins spread along the beautiful Antioch hills: stone churches, and villas with their square windows of stone still looking out, their carved gateways open, their olive-presses empty, only the wooden roofs missing, the olive trees cut away and the earth itself melted down by a thousand years of rain. The ruin came with the Arab-Byzantine border wars, when Antioch was so burnt down that householders could not recognise even the *streets* where their homes had stood! But no doubt they could still find their great summer villas. I spent a week there riding over that country, still roadless now, and have been thinking what a super film it would make, camping and riding from church to church or villa to villa and sitting over a tent-fire talking about life and Time and all. But it should be in spring, April, when the burnt hillsides are just carpeted with flowers.

Dear Jock I can't begin to tell you how nice everyone was to me, Arab, American, and English – but must get on with the clearing of this desk.

All love,

FREYA

JOHN GREY MURRAY   Asolo

23 May 1978

Dearest Jock,

So exciting – a p.c. from Crete turns out to be you and Diana. What a good thing to do and please let me hear more about it. I am just sitting at my desk trying to get to Greece or Turkey, dodging in and out of summer guests at the tower. I think I can get away for September and trot around from Athens by Kardamyli (if they are there) to Istanbul – Bodrum (if no war over Cyprus). But Crete always eludes me and I am getting rather inefficient at finding lodgings and all the unexpected that entails. (Going to Florence for my only committee next week and find the railways are to be on strike.)

What a nice letter from the lady in Kenya. What a pleasure it is to find people who *coincide* with one. I am sending you one of such, a young man (forty) called James Coyne who wants to write and I have an idea might do so, about Arabs. I have told him you are sometimes to be found after hours at your desk ready for a talk?

Love,
FREYA

SYBIL, LADY CHOLMONDELEY   Asolo
9 June 1978

Dearest Sybil,

I think of you so sadly, your letter has just come. I know from nursing days that one's hands are the most painful bits to recover because all the nerves run down them, and age too comes along and makes us slow to recover. But you must also think that pain is *forgotten* as soon as it passes and that day must now come soon. I am sad for you meanwhile, and knowing how little help you have.

I have just come from my Florence committee and enjoyed it all, and Lucy coming up to talk about Volume V (due in September). I distinguished myself on one of those dark, stone, *Palazzo* stairs by missing a step and catapulting to hit the stone wall below: it is extraordinary what time one has to think while hurtling through the air, but my skull must be very hard, and though it went on slightly bleeding for several days it seems all right now and the femur (also bruised) quite unprotesting. I am encouraged by all this to go for a fortnight's riding on Dartmoor (a gentle pony is offered): but it will be the shortest of visits, though I will dash up to Norfolk if it is only *hours*.

Every loving wish, dearest Sybil,

FREYA

Asolo
13 August 1978

Dear James,

Here is a fine big sheet for answering questions, and can begin with thanks for the snapshot: it is a nice cheerful face and has a holiday feeling about it altogether and I am so glad you sent it. One of these days I will send you one of mine, even perhaps on a horse. Since riding about Dartmoor in ease and comfort I have broken a rib in my bath; if it had, just as easily, happened off my pony everyone would have called me foolish. It just shows how accidental life is.

I have, and read, Soane's *Kurdistan* and made a little pilgrimage to the beautiful plain where the Lady of Kurdistan used to live, and he was still remembered, and the Kurds sat round of an evening with their great turbans telling me stories about them. He had died by that time and I had met his widow who was quite uninteresting but I shall never forget the plains of Kurdistan with their garlands of mountain and sheets of flowers.

The rafts were and probably are quite common on Tigris but unknown on Euphrates – and of course we discovered why. I think it is not only the caprices of the seasons that holds them off, but also the fact that this great lonely river (unlike the Tigris) had no large towns to buy their timber; but now that it is being gifted with a town at the barrage the rafts may appear.

I have met Wilfred Thesiger once or twice and do love his *Arabian Sands*, but agree about this sadness of what we call civilisation. I have taken all the care I could in simple places and don't think I ever made Turk or Persian or Afghan or Arab feel ashamed or apologetic about his simple things: and it is, it seems to me, *more* civilised to be able to live well with little than with much. But what will happen now? The fundamental Arab feeling, which makes us love them, is that the true values are independent: perhaps they will stand the strain?

Some friends are leaving for England and I have given them Alan Moorehead's *White Nile*, of which I have two copies, to post to you: it may be a new stretch to explore? There may be some more books, and someday, when my rib improves, I will make a list of what I would like to find a home for. I have three that are very good and rare but more history than travel, but they deal with North Persia and have quite a lot of Arabic inserted here and there. They belong to the E.J.W. Gibb Memorial Trust, and are lent to suitable people who are asked to hand them on when they read them no longer. But do you think of North Persia as a country for your dreams? I will gladly send them, for I shall go no longer into those jungles.

All luck to you both,   FREYA S.

RICHARD WALLER[205]   Asolo

                                                          24 August 1978

Dear Richard,

I have been meaning to write ever so long just to thank you again for that perfect holiday. It makes me so happy to think of it and to think of the moor still just as it was, and the ponies and sheep and cows grazing about so that it makes all one in my mind with the years that have gone by. Now I had just planned to be off again – to Turkey – but I slipped in my bath of all silly things and have a broken rib which takes ages to cure itself.

I have an American (Texan) female friend about twenty-five years younger than me, and talking of this and that I said I would still like to see Nanga Parbat before I died. 'I will go too,' said she, and we fixed on November 1979 as a good date (mountains visible etc.) and wondered if you would think of taking such an aged couple to ride up on these tiny ponies and just look at it. The whole object would be just to spend a few days looking at it in all its beauty and come away perhaps by some of the Indian cities of the north – all dreams still unrealised. This is a business proposition I am asking you and you must let me know and give me a sketch of its feasibility.

I think of you and Yvonne with you with love and the feelings that have ever been clustered round that dear corner of your world. Bless you dear Dick.

                                                          Love,
                                                          FREYA

JAMES COYNE   Asolo

                                                          22 September 1978

Dear James,

One of my eyes started to need attention and I have been away and only found your letter on my return two days ago – and now your letter of 14 September has just come. Gertrude Bell and her biography: it was not want of admiration that made me refuse (I think *Amurath to Amurath* one of the best travel books I know) – but merely that I can write my own feelings direct but have no experience of describing those of other people. I would have perhaps liked her and certainly would have liked to meet her, but she would probably not have been kind to me as she had no use for other women learning Arabic. I heard a lot about her when first I went to Baghdad, and there was no sort of feeling of 'sisterhood' with women about

205 Lady Waller, his mother, had been a Varwell. The Varwells had lived at Thornworthy, the neighbouring estate on Dartmoor to the Starks' Ford Park (sold in 1912).

her (rather a nice feeling I think.) One bride told me how she had been taken to be introduced and Gertrude turned from her to the man she was talking to, saying 'I can't think why they bring out all these uneducated young wives!' But she was a fine traveller all the same.

This brings me to your plans and the fact that I do think the language is essential. You might learn it out there but it would be far better to have enough to get about with when you go. I have a Linguaphone course of Persian which I go through for two months or so before going there and I have long been thinking of getting an Arabic one if I can find something better than the Egyptian dialect one. (I rather think that a more classical one is now to be found.) I would only want it for two months – say February–March if I were going in April – and I would gladly buy it and let you have it for the rest of the year (and permanently when my little candle goes out). It is quite a manageable little parcel to travel to and fro. I have heard of the Koran arranged for gramophone but this is not what we need: the records must begin very slow and simple and reach ordinary conversation when they end. If you can discover this I will gladly buy and lend it to you for ten months or so of the year. But when you do go, I should not advise Medain Salih as a *first* trip: I have looked down on it from the air and it is very fierce. But there are lovely countries with a little more cultivation.

The sad part is the political: Sadat's new move and the U.S.A. between them are making war almost inevitable and throwing the Arabs inevitably into Russia's arms. I still hope to go out there, but very sadly.

All good wishes,

FREYA STARK

SIR GEORGE TREVELYAN, BT. Asolo
25 September 1978

My dear George,

I was so pleased to get your letter. I had to go to Switzerland and came back through the Mont Blanc tunnel and the vision was out of this world both sides, though nothing I think is more dreary than the *inside* of a tunnel. It was lovely to get a glimpse and drive down the Val d'Aosta thinking of old and good days, up to Cogne one side and Monte Rosa on the other – a happy week spent ever so many years ago looking at Rosa from the ends of all her passes. How lucky was W.P. to step from this world into the next from a mountain side.[206]

[206] Professor W. P. Ker had died suddenly during a climbing holiday in July 1923.

Do come out whenever you can, and look at Venetia from the guest-tower on Asolo city wall. It sees the Venice lagoons and the Euganean hills where Shelley wrote 'Many a green isle'. But not more beautiful than Ross-on-Wye. I used to go there to stay with the Balfours – nephew of the old philosopher who seems now to have been busy preparing a Third World War.[207]

Dear George, I will be so happy to see you again, and so glad that all is well with you.

FREYA

COLIN LUKE

Asolo
12 October 1978

My dear Colin,

I am delighted to have news of you – was wondering what part of the world you were in and how your China film turned up. I would like to see it for another view of the Great Wall. Am glad too for the date of our film's repetition to tell friends. I have been reading old Eastern histories and find the raft referred to in pre-Christian times, and *lions* walking up and down along the river.

Lord Pembroke – if you remember – suggested a film, and I told him that I had fixed myself to you and B.B.C. if you wished for it; and you told me that you and he could probably fix it up together. This would suit me, as I would feel very safe in your good capable hands, and you already have made friends in that bit of Syria where the old Byzantine ruins are ready for a background. A week's riding about could do it with the *flowers* out and Mark should be available at Easter. But I am very old, dear Colin, and would not like to venture unless you are managing it all!

Am now going to Turkey for three weeks and then I hope a quiet winter at home.

FREYA

JOHN GREY MURRAY

Bodrum
30 October 1978

Dearest Jock,

I have a letter of yours to answer but it is packed somewhere and I will get at it in two days' time when I unpack again in Istanbul. My time here has

[207] A reference to the Balfour Declaration.

gone very quickly, but I caught a bronchitis on the way and it got worse instead of better, so that a kind American woman took me to a doctor, and I am taking antibiotics with good effect. It is anyway much too cold for any bathing and great clouds with lovely sunsets bring rain at intervals. Otherwise this little place is still unspoilt in spite of ominous building on its hills. The nice family feed us on everything around us, vegetables, olives, grapes, fish and pomegranates. Between holidays I am the only guest and the little bay is empty, its four little piers going out like Japanese drawings into the sunset that is flame-coloured now above two mountain ranges – not high and threatening but spread, beautifully Greek, along the west horizon. The Greeks left after 1920, but one is constantly coming across some likeness in the faces here.

I am so glad to have come – my Turkish is slowly coming back though it would need another two months at least to be good. But it is enough now to get about with. I go to Nuri Birgi for three days tomorrow and Asolo on 7th.

Love,

FREYA

JOHN GREY MURRAY Asolo

6 November 1978

Dearest Jock,

I got back three days ago after a very long journey. The afternoon aeroplane for Venice was overcrowded and I believe I got the last seat in the evening one and spent five hours mostly sleeping (my most useful capacity). It is so good to be back, and we are having a belated summer and cherry-trees all over the hills like bunches of fire. And I am enjoying life with no book to write and the *Iliad* to read. There are things one must try to do before going on, and this is one of them.

What I am feeling during my research into the early civilisations (7000 to 500 B.C.) is the incredible length of time that must have gone to make them as complete as they were: if you take away the top layer of sophistication, the remainder was very like ourselves today. 'Had I but world enough and time' I would write another book about it.

Love, dear Jock,

FREYA

Asolo
                                                           20 November 1978

Dearest Sybil,

I came back four days ago and was happy to find your letter, but not so over the news of your wrist. We are all getting on, darling Sybil; but what good lives we have had — something Homeric about them. I am reading the *Iliad* (for the fourth time) and carried away as ever by that continuous excitement, that greatness of the stage which is ever there, dominating and inspiring the greatness of its people and power of its incorrigible gods. I weep over Andromache and Hector as I did when I was fourteen, galloping about in those chariots quite independent of roads, with eternity round every corner and here and there friendly voices of the gods who happened to like you. With fifty years of writing behind me, I can be fascinated by looking into the *structure*, which draws itself up out of life's very depth — and does it so unerringly out of its crude materials, not trying to disguise them. What a poor world it becomes when people only try to be clever.

I had rather bad luck this time and got bronchitis, though was tucked in on all sides by old friends and lovely places — driving up from the south by lakes and hills into Caria. Too cold for bathing at Bodrum but from there along the coast — promontories and islands — to Izmir (quite spoilt) and Istanbul.

It would make me wonderfully happy to hear that you have a proper staff at Houghton: so please tell me. Love always,

                                                                FREYA

Asolo
                                                            9 January 1979

Dearest Mark and Arabella,

Xmas is over, and we are being snowed in with a steady little persistent snow, and the news of the world is as unpleasant as it could possibly be. I am wondering what you are busy with — an election I rather suppose?[208] I am anxious to hear whether you are settled in Lancashire already or whether I could still find you in my home from home at No. 11[209] in the spring? as I am planning a very short visit to England, with a week or ten days in London in March or April. (I feel I am getting too old to take more than

[208] Mark Lennox-Boyd was elected Conservative Member of Parliament for Morecambe.
[209] sc. Cavendish Avenue, London N.W.8.

that of the hurly-burly, but so longing to see you all.) Film project is dormant and I very much doubt its being alive at all: a thing with a long name has been getting into my neck and is liable to make me drop down off anything I might be riding; how wonderful to have been able to snatch that last little spree out of the grip of Time.

Italy is more Renaissance than ever though not as artistic as the Cinquecento. I am leading a quiet life, in my warm flat with a perfect maid for six hours a day, and reading as many as I can of my history books in sequence: they have brought me from 8000 B.C. in Anatolia to Greece, and it is a fascinating way to get at the *development* of history, moving with all its curves down the valley of Time.

I would love to talk with you about it all, and this goes to you with all dear thoughts.

FREYA

RICHARD WALLER   Asolo

RICHARD WALLER

Asolo
29 January 1979

Dear Dick,

Your letter was waiting for me here when I got back from Turkey and was more or less swallowed in that unmanageable mass that collects on one's desk in absence; and then of course Xmas; and also the absence of my American friend who was to share the expedition. She is here now and we are both sad about it but see your point: I imagine that everything even remotely spaced between Russia and China is going to be precarious for a long time now. I am enjoying myself with my own books: they are all sorted now in order of time and I am reading from date to date, lingering in Greece at the moment. I don't think I shall live through more than the Dark Ages, but it is a very fascinating thing to do, to watch the gradual stream of civilisation winding slowly down, bulding its temporary pictures, and with its geography settled by the unexpected discoveries of man – the discovery of the horse for instance, on which the Hittites built their empire, standing in their chariots and carts, until the stirrup was discovered and made possible the cavalry that took Alexander to India. The great revolutions always made by some new means of communication: the British Empire built on train and steamship and the vaster spaces coming in with the control of the air. Where will it end?

Love,
FREYA

Asolo
                                                              5 May 1979
Dearest Jock,

I am getting to feel so old and incapable that it has an effect I remember
about sixty years ago, a feeling of longing to *find* oneself again and climbing
a mountain to do so. This was Monte Rosa in 1923 – but now it is a less
reasonable urge with the remembered outline of the Himalayas, and you are
partly responsible by publishing those splendid books by John Keay. I have
been tracing a glorious route and all depends whether one can ride or must
walk over the passes. I rather think this daydream will not come off – but
anyway I will buy Dervla Murphy's Himalayan book[210] if you will send it to
me, and will then write to her if it inspires anything feasible to me; and I
would also like to buy what seemed your excellent handbook for India. (All
this comes of waiting in the Murray waiting room!)

All this written in a state of great feebleness surely due to the awful wet
weather as well as age. The plain lies below like a great sponge.

There is bad news about Costanza in Lausanne:[211] a possibility of partial
recovery one can't wish her. I would go to her, and will do so if and when
Paolo[212] thinks it advisable; but I have no good effect on her alas! Paolo
himself is most anxious to do all he can and has written me most kind and
good letters; and this sorrow has anyway made a bond between us.

Bless you, dear Jock, and all the family.

                                                              Love,
                                                              FREYA

Asolo
                                                              15 May 1979
Dear Anne and Frank,

How good to get your letter, and just as my mind too was beginning to
wander off on journeys so that it seemed to meet you on the way! I was in
fact wandering with you in spirit led by the magic word Afghanistan. Do
you think one could ever get a visa for it now? Together with one for Russia
next door and already unpopular? (I am so glad!) I have been reading *The
Gilgit Game* by John Keay and a great longing comes over me for another
glimpse of that roof of the world (but to me more like an *altar*). I would

---

[210] *Where the Indus Is Young: A Winter in Baltistan.*
[211] F.S.'s niece had suffered a stroke.
[212] F.S.'s great-nephew.

like to meet the Indus where I once crossed it below Peshawar, and go up to where (I take it) no road goes on beyond Hunza, but I like to imagine that those little ponies get across from where one leaves the Indus, and reaches Oxus by passes (Baroghil) to what look villages (Sarhad-i-Wakhan and Bouzai Gumbad), and goes down into Badakhshan. If I could do it I don't believe I should at all mind dying on the way because after all one can't complain of departing from this world at eighty-six. Can one deal with height by taking oxygen? I am going to enquire into these things but not really with any solid hope, chiefly because of those two little bits of frontier paper. I have done no proper travelling now for years and can't tell you with what admiration and vicarious pleasure I read your itinerary. If there were to be a road for Bistritza over the Pamirs would you not come? I wish there were, just for such a chance!

But as it is you must come through Asolo one day *soon* and we could find a sunny day or so across Dolomite passes before petrol disappears.

I was so glad to get your letter and send love as always.

FREYA

MRS. ALAN MOOREHEAD Asolo
10 July 1979

Dearest Lucy,

I have just finished re-reading the letters and can't possibly tell you how much I admire your tact with them. It has really been a great and devoted work and I am writing, dear Lucy, with a heart full of gratitude. How wonderfully, wonderfully lucky my life has been in its friends.

The doctor would not like me to be writing. The trouble was a *sciopero* of the heart but seems much better. It does look as if riding may be over.

So many thanks for all dear Lucy, and love to the house on the hill.

FREYA

SIR MICHAEL STEWART Asolo
11 July 1979

Dearest Michael,

The whole of October as well as say a week of September are free as air and I hope for a sight of the high mountains before I die. Would you like to risk it? Nothing very adventurous is possible because I have just found that riding is over (most depressing little story of the heart giving trouble after twenty-five minutes' trotting: not the sort of thing that happened in my young days!).

One would gladly travel all that way to see a beloved face and that is what a mountain is to us eccentrics. The *beautiful* plan I had made is useless (no visas from Russia or Afghanistan) apart from the altitude; but there are jeep roads and indeed asphalt and we could go out and browse from Peshawar along the Gilgit road and into Swat: and dear Michael I am just on the crest of a little financial wave so we could spend £2,000 or more if needed. Now do send a telegram in response as there is an awful lot to do.

Love to you both and the children.

FREYA

SIR MICHAEL STEWART   Asolo
12 July 1979

Dearest Michael,

Carrying on the story from yesterday I must tell you that the gods seem propitious. I took up a pamphlet of Serenissima Tours of this year and there was the country in question, the North-West Frontier all branching out from Peshawar and Pakistan. I have written to ask if this year holds for the tour and would join it (if it does) from 29th September to 14th October: splendid if you came on it (£995); and otherwise, and if I emerge undamaged, if you would like a further little wander from 1st October onward (an excellent month for that country)? My good old heart has been X-rayed this morning and turns out undamaged, so the ponies might be possible after all.

Love to you all,

FREYA

MRS. JEREMY SWIFT[213]   Asolo
18 July 1979

My darling Caroline,

I have been sitting with all the crowding pictures of the happy years, so many, so unbroken, such dear days ever since the first day of meeting in Cairo, with Lucy and me on the edge and Alan in the middle of the desert war. Never a wrinkle on our love after those days – and a feeling ever

[213] Her mother, Lucy Moorehead, had died in a car crash in Italy on 16 July.

growing for Lucy's dear depth and sweetness and courage. Dear Caroline I am so deeply your friend and deeper than ever thinking of you all, John and Richard too and Jeremy and children, as all part of one deep friendship. May it go on till I too get called. I won't write now, but want to know where you will be and if you come north if you would stop here for a night on the way: all can be settled between tower, flat and hotel.

I have had times very near death and my dearest ones have all been there suddenly very near: you will never feel Lucy far. Bless you all and love, to Alan too.

Dear love,

FREYA

Kardamyli
6 September 1979

MR. AND MRS. SHAN SEDGWICK[214]

Dear Roxane and Shan,

All went well and here I am after the morning bathe, finding house and sea and friends as good as ever. It seems impossible to think of having been so many years away, and I think of you in Athens too in the same way, so lovely to find the milestones of our way still in their places and to treasure the good talks we had.

Joanie and Paddy are flourishing and just the same as ever, and the house as full of books as yours is, and the cypresses having been growing now stand like dark candles about the hills.

All love and thanks for such good days.

FREYA

Spetsai
14 September 1979

JOHN GREY MURRAY

Dearest Jock,

I would like to linger with you about these islands and tell you that I swam 350 strokes today in their sea – but here is sterner stuff and Mrs. Izzard wanting to write a biography. Now surely eight volumes of Letters and *Traveller's Prelude* etc., etc. are enough? But, as you will see by the enclosed, I would agree to a story (a very short booklet) to explain the Brothers of Freedom, because I think they were a benefit to the art of

[214] Friends in Athens.

308

Persuasion and might do good to publish? Will you get John to consult (as you and I are getting on) and let me know what you think?

Dear love,

FREYA

SIR MICHAEL STEWART

Asolo

19 September 1979

Dearest Michael,

I am just back, quite renovated by Greek islands and Paddy Leigh Fermor's conversation and the *sparkling* quality in even the simplest sort of activity. On the island of Spetsai (full of retired diplomat friends of yours) the circulation is still done by the little pony-traps of my youth – and the sea was perfect and I managed to swim 500 (very gentle) strokes. I found Shan in Athens, nearly making me lose an aeroplane by plunging into politics at 7.30 a.m. – I came back rather soon because I got a poisoned finger, now nearly cured.

A long letter from Dick about the Nepal journey but no word about you! Is it yet decided? I do long to hear. We are to be leaving about mid-December from London.

All love to you both and the children,

FREYA

MR. MAGYAR[215]

Asolo

21 September 1979

Dear Mr. Magyar,

I have just come back from a holiday in Greece and find your kind letter on my desk. I have not much time to answer all, but am much touched by your kind words. I must tell you that I am eighty-six years old, and have now stopped writing, and am enjoying these last years by reading. When I look back I see that my real and deep interest in travel was not so much geographic as human: what I have been and still am interested in is the development of the human creature and one can watch this through the centuries and look with deep interest at its geographic varieties which are yet so deeply the same. I have not alas! seen more than a little of the coast of Yugoslavia.

215 Yet apparently Yugoslav.

As you can imagine, my interest being *human*, I like to travel where I can speak the language, and have learned enough to get about in ten of them, but that of course is not nearly enough.

I still hope to manage a short visit to your *beautiful* country, which seems to me to have just the right mixture of cultivated landscapes and wild.

I thank you again for writing so kindly.

Yours sincerely,

FREYA STARK

HON. CLAUD PHILLIMORE Asolo

11 October 1979

My dear Claud,

People keep on asking me *why* I like to travel. When truly expert, one could just sit at home and *think*, but it is still pleasant to be a moving object in the landscape and look at people sitting in their homes; and perhaps one may eventually come to see why the Almighty made this strangely varied world and to see the thread that ties us to animals, and plants and stones, rolling through so much ruin, *whereto?*

Do not omit Asolo dear Claud on your next visit. It was such a short glimpse this time.

All love,

FREYA

SYBIL, LADY CHOLMONDELEY Asolo

15 November 1979

Dearest Sybil,

Was this our hotel garden in Shiraz? or the school in Isfahan? I have collected these old pictures for Xmas wishes and send you this so full of happy memories and love.

Also the news that I hope for a glimpse of you. Mr. Parkinson has committed me to a television interview about a week before I leave for Himalaya.[216] Will all this turn out well? I have no idea, but am, like you, unwilling to let old age interfere too much: after all we have had the capital of life in our hands and if it ceases giving interest, there is no call to grumble. But I am hoping for the good of a tiny glimpse of you between 17th and

[216] F.S. appeared as a television guest of Michael Parkinson.

22nd in London? Hope to stay with Angela Nevill and fly to Katmandu on 23rd.

Love always,

FREYA

NURI BIRGI   Asolo
                                                                  2 April 1980

My dear Nuri,

I found your letter of 3 January when I landed here all among my Xmas letters. I was: 1) televisirg; 2) riding for three weeks round about Anna-purna – the base not the top! – in Nepal; 3) relaxing among the Melanesian islands; 4) undoing the relaxation in London; 5) finally two days ago reaching Asolo.

I have a hope of Istanbul and your great view in autumn and your letter gives me a second one of seeing you in Asolo, but that must be in the very first days of June as I have to go to London for Royal Geographical celebra-tions from 5th on.

I share your pessimism and surprised a friend (who goes by way of being a Christian) who asked me why I seem to worry so little about our next world? 'Because,' I said, 'I think it is going to be better than this one.' She seemed to think I was talking nonsense.

It is very good to think of you in Asolo.

Affectionately,
FREYA

SHAN SEDGWICK   Asolo
                                                                  2 April 1980

Darling Shan,

Your letter has been waiting an age here on my table, and I ought to have written but I was travelling, riding on a pony at the feet of the Himalayas and ending with the spice islands with their lovely names – Bali, Java, Sumatra, and home by way of Delhi and London, and back here only two days ago. And here I have found all my Xmas mail waiting and unanswered, and you are among my very first, so you must not complain! The adventure has been long delayed (because so expensive), but it worked out with no mishap except that most *shoes* seem to have been stolen from my luggage. Nothing mattered when one was back in the mountains, their dazzling teeth edges in the sun. We followed one river up and another down to the base of

Annapurna, the tallest after Everest and shrouded in snowfall till the last morning when she shone like sculpture in the sunshine. My little pony galloped along the even, grassy ledges with waterfalls and great perpendicular spaces dropping below to where the turbulent rivers were threading their gorges and filling them with roaring. The immense walls looked like architecture, though not for men. The Sherpas looked after us and we spent three weeks (I riding), seven or eight hours' exercise a day (so that I now weigh ten kilos less than before). In every little gully where the great mountain shoulders begin to think of rivers, the stones were tumbled down to the water and up the other side, so that Pony had to climb and I must lift myself between my knees from the saddle to ease the weight for him; so one slept easily in a tent when the day was over.

Darling Shan, this lovely life was quite unsuitable for letters, but I sent you a loving thought at times. You would have loved the greatness of those hills. I am now settling till autumn here and will let you know later plans.

Love,

FREYA

E. HODGKIN   Asolo

3 April 1980

My dear Teddy,

I am just back from my very happy voyage. I stopped a few days in Delhi on my way and found those hopeless people apparently concentrating on their dislike of *Pakistan* – when I imagine their backdoor is relatively safe only because that little country exists. There is a 'twilight of the Gods' feeling about in the world isn't there? I can't tell you what a joy it was to reach the great bastions like the outworks of some immense fortification and see the shining edges like swords in the sun. We got as far as the pine-woods of Annapurna, riding and walking through them, but the pass over to the north side was blocked – two days in a room kindly lent in the last village (W.C. down nineteen steps smoothly sheeted in ice). I was offered an icy little room to myself but preferred a warm corner with Dick Waller and the ten Sherpas; and on the third morning, when we were already packed, the clouds went off like a group of Valkyrie and there was the great mountain, a ridge of spikes like lances in the sun, a loveliness unforgettable.

I wish you could both come out here again.

Love to you all dear Teddy,

FREYA

                                                                22 April 1980
My dear Peter,

I have just been reading your letter very carefully for the second time, and have twice come to the conclusion that you and I feel exactly the same on this army matter. In my faraway childhood Ramsay MacDonald refused to fight in the South African war because he thought it a bad cause (at least this is what I seem to remember): this is, I believe, the true and admirable British attitude of which we are fundamentally, but not superficially, aware. It is the basis of that 'Mandate' policy, which is the factual modern imperial version of English thought – 'to give independence when the capacity for independence as been reached'. This is what the army cooperates in, stepping (during my lifetime) into one war for the guaranteed liberty of Belgium and another for that of Poland, both guaranteed by us. Apart from South Africa where we climbed down soon after the war was over, I don't believe we have fought a war of conquest for a very long time (the garrison in Lucknow were more than half Indian). The fact remains however that the army itself probably is unaware of how pacific it is and the London School of Economics continues to draw a picture of it that seems to me startlingly untrue. What a worker for peace has to consider (it seems to me) is whether he can work better *inside* or *outside* the army; but the objective is the same. But you must think of what work you enjoy doing for itself and surely that requires one of your languages and the wideness of the world?

    With lots of wishes and love,

                                       FREYA

MISS MARLOW   Asolo
                                                                23 April 1980
Dear Miss Marlow,

I am always interested to hear from someone who wishes to find out more about this strange world we live in, and you seem to me to have discovered the sort of way to set about it. You are a little younger than I was when I first took to Arabic and spent a winter in the Lebanon hills, and so got more and more drawn to the surrounding lands. I don't think you need worry about safety: the Arab feeling for women's propriety is so strong that you need only be careful to *show* that you are a modest creature by covering up to the neck, down more or less to ankles and wrists, and the hair (I used to

[217] A grandson of Lord Killearn, Ambassador in Cairo during the Second World War.

wear woollen stockings – to protect myself against the sun); a skirt *over* my riding breeches; long sleeves and riding shirt buttoned to the neck – and got no suggestions other than quite numerous proposals of marriage, which I countered by explaining that my mother would not like me to settle so far away. This careful dressing, and the fact that one was genuinely interested in Learning, was quite enough for Arab or Persian: one should be a little older in Turkey, but even there the secret is clothes. I used to cover up my hair with a kerchief and only let it loose across mountain passes in Persia where (in a revolution very like the present) there was a probability of robbers in ambush who might shoot believing one to be a man.

As for funds, that is a general, and lasting, difficulty. I came at last to realise that, so long as one does not really mind about being comfortable, one can live on as little abroad as at home. This has seen me through many situations.

I would add one thing you may or may not find useful, but I think of as important: that one should have a quest of one's own – history, literature, photography, anything like a pursuit to give an added reason and interest for travel.

I do wish you all good luck and as much interest in it all as I have enjoyed.

Yours sincerely,

FREYA STARK

Index

Index

323